New Castle County Delaware

LAND RECORDS

1728–1731 and 1734–1738

Carol J. Garrett

HERITAGE BOOKS
2020

HERITAGE BOOKS

AN IMPRINT OF HERITAGE BOOKS, INC.

Books, CDs, and more—Worldwide

For our listing of thousands of titles see our website
at
www.HeritageBooks.com

Published 2020 by
HERITAGE BOOKS, INC.
Publishing Division
5810 Ruatan Street
Berwyn Heights, Md. 20740

Heritage Books by the author:

New Castle County, Delaware Land Records, 1728–1731 and 1734–1738
New Castle County, Delaware Land Records, 1738–1743
New Castle County, Delaware Land Records, 1762–1765
New Castle County, Delaware Land Records, 1764–1769
New Castle County, Delaware Land Records, 1777–1785
New Castle County, Delaware Land Records, 1785–1789

International Standard Book Number
Paperbound: 978-1-68034-492-9

CONTENTS

iii

INTRODUCTION

Few records of the Swedish Colony (1638-16550 have survived. From 1655 to 1664 and from 1673 to 1674, the Dutch West India Company and the city of Amsterdam were proprietors of the land which became Delaware (ignoring claims by the Calverts of Maryland). the surviving records are held by the Archives of New York at Albany. For an excellent treatment of many of the Swedish families, see Peter Stebbins Craig, *The 1693 Census of the Swedes on the Delaware*. For a list of the Swedes who took the oath of allegiance in 1683 to the new English government in 1683 under William Penn, see *History of Delaware, 1609-1888*, by J. Thomas Scharf, p. 612.

The Duke of York was proprietor from 1664 to 1673 and from 1674 to 1682. These land records are held at Albany. *Original Land Titles in Delaware, commonly known as the Duke of York Record, 1646-1679*, was printed by order of the General Assembly of the State of Delaware (1899), reprinted by Family Line Publications in 1989.

The patent which granted William Penn territory, soon to be called Pennsylvania, was signed by King Charles in 1681. Delaware, as a part of Pennsylvania was referred to as the Lower Three Counties upon Delaware.

The Hall of Records at Dover holds copies of the deeds of New Castle County beginning in 1673. There are a number of gaps in these deeds. Published to date are the following volumes: 1673-1710; 1715-1728 (except for 1719-1722 which is missing); 1749-1752; 1755-1762; 1762-1765. This volume covers the period 1728-1738 except for 1731-1734 which pages are missing.

F. Edward Wright
Lewes, Delaware
2001

Deed I Vol 1

1. Deed. 10 Aug 1699. Andrew Friend of Newcastle Co. in Territories of Pennsylvania, in consideration of a valuable price, sold unto Jacobus VanderCulen of Co. of Chester in same Province, a parcel of land containing 200 acres, lying in Newcastle Co. It begins at the head of Mill Creek running into Christiana Creek and bounds the land of Matthias Defoss and Springers Run. Signed: Andrew Friend. Wit: Ralph Whitton, John Grantum. Ack: 15 Aug 1699. James Claypool. (I1-1)

2. Notice. Newcastle 23/1728. 'The unhappy differences that hath arisen between you & your Parishoners hath given us Verey great Concern not only for that you have declined (for some time past) giving that accordance at our Church there to discharge your duty according to your Appointment but Especially because those misunderstandings between Ministers of the Church of England ane their Parrishoners tend Greatly to the Reproach of our most Holy Religion, and to bring us into Contempt, And foras much as you have thought fit to Vindicate your Reputation by a Prosecution at Law and have Recovered Damages for the words Spoken of you, we Request you as a Minister of the Church of England, and a Christian to lay aside your Resentments and Return to the Care of your parish where you Shall not fail to meet with all the Respect and Good usage due to a Minister of the Gospell and a Good man while you Continue to Live as Shuch amongst us, we are in Behalf of our Selves and the Parishoners of Appoquinamink.' Signed: your most Humb. Serv.: Andw. Peterson, John Gooding, Eam. Garitson, Rd. Cantwell, Jacob Gooding. (I1-2)

3. Deed. 12 Aug 1728. Jonas Stalcop, otherwise called Jonas John Stallcop of Christiana Ferry in Co. of Newcastle upon Delaware being one of the Counties annexed to the Prov. of Penn., yeoman, and Eleanor his wife, for the sum of 200 pounds, sold unto Ellis Lewis of the Township of Kent in Co. of Chester in sd Prov., yeoman, two messuages situate on the north side of Christiana Creek in sd Co. Also several pieces of land and marsh. One of them sits by Kings Road and Ferry Road and contains 38 acres. Another, called the 'home land' sits by Christiana and contains 101-1/2 acres of fast land and 21 acres of marsh below the rocks, and 7 acres above the rocks. Together with all edifices. This is whereas sd Stalcop by a conveyance became jointly seized with his eldest brother Jszael Stallcop of several messuages, lands tenements & hereitements in fee simple situate in a neck of land between the two creeks of Brandywine & Christiana in sd Co. Then sd Jonas and Jszael made equal division of sd premises. Jonas' share was two messuages & parcels of land and marsh. On 13 Nov 1722, sd Jszael by his deed poll did grant this. Signed: Jonas John Stallcop, Eleaner Stallcop. Wit: Jacob Vandever (mark), Richd Hoe. Ack: 20 Aug 1728.

Certifyed by Robertson. (I1-3)

4. Deed. 28 April 1728. Jonathan Howston of Co. of Newcastle, farmer, for the sum of 50 pounds and lawful interest, sold unto Cornelius Garrettson of sd Co., carpenter, one equal undivided half tract of that Island of land and marsh situate at Christiana Creek, commonly called 'Swart Rutten Island', alias 'Switzers Island'. This together with one equal undivided half part of an outhleth (?) called 'Beshy let', together with all singular on it. Signed: Jonathan Houstown. Wit: Robt Gordon, David French. Ack: 12 Aug 1728. Certifyed by Robertson. (I1-5)

5. Deed. 21 Aug 1728. Thomas Reiland of Cecil Co. in Province of Maryland, planter, and Mary his wife, for the sum of 55 pounds, sold unto Joseph Road of Redlyon Hun. in Co. of Newcastle, blacksmith, a parcel of land and marsh. It is situate in Newcastle Hun. on the south side of Maryland Road opposite to John Reinolds plantation. It begins by sd road and is bounded by land of Jacobus Williams and Peter Anderson. Sd land contains 101 acres. The marsh goes by the River Delaware and bounds marsh of Peter Alrichs and Jacobus Alrichs and contains 16 acres. Signed: Thomas Reiland. Wit: Jasper Yeates (other unreadable). Ack: 20 Aug 1728. Certifyed by Robertson (I1-7)

6. Deed. 24 Aug 1728. William Battel of Newcastle Co., Gent., and Parnella his wife, for the sum of 120 pounds, sold unto James James Jun. of sd Co., merchant, a parcel of land situate near Christiana Bridge in sd Co. It begins by the road to White Clay Creek to stable of John Ogles and contains 10 acres 15 perches, together with all singular. Signed: W. Battell, Pernallah Battell. Wit: Wm Read, Robertson. Ack: 20 Aug 1728. Certifyed by Robertson. (I1-8)

7. Notice. 7 Aug 1728. 'Know all men that I, Thomas Noxon (late of the Island of Jamacia but now of Co. of Newcastle in North America) merchant, for good causes, me thereunto moving and more especially for consideration of several Negroes to me this day assigned and set over of a Hogshead of Rum and a Hogshead of Sugar by Thomas Simson, late of sd Island but now of the City of Philadelphia, gent.... I assign to sd Simsom a judgement obtained in 1724 against the Estate of Thomas Cardiff, late of sd Island, Esq., decd., now on record in the Court of Spanish Town in sd Island for the sum of 182 pounds..' Signed: Thomas Noxon. Wit: Cantwell Garetson, Mary Willson. Affidavit by Andrew Petterson, one of His Majesties Justices, that on 8 Aug 1728, Thomas Noxon personally appeared before him and swore voluntary act to Deed. (I1-9)

8. Deed. 20 July 1727. Charles Read and Henery Hodges, both of the City of Philadelphia in Prov. of Penn., merchants, and Jehu Curtis of Newastle Co., Gent., Execs. of the Last Will and Testament of Ann Wood, late of Newcastle,

Widdow, dec'd., for the sum of 220 pounds, sold unto William Read of the Town of Newcastle, merchant, a tract of land with appurtenances, situate in Swanwich in sd Co. It begins at the Dyke that runs up the marsh up Delaware and bounds land of Peter Jacquett and contains 320 acres. This is land that Joseph Wood, late of sd Co., Gent., dec'd, by virtue of sundry conveyances was seized of. By sd Wood's Last Will dated 12 Dec 1721 he did bequeath sd land with appurtenances unto his wife, Anne Wood. Then sd Anne on 7 Oct 1723 did make her Last Will in which she appointed afsd Charles Read, afsd Henery Hodges and Jehu Curtis as Executors. Signed: Cha. Read, Henery Hodges, Jehu Curtis. Wit: David French, John Gooding. Ack: Nov 1728. (I1-10)

9. Deed. 27 April 1728. Thomas Sharp of Duck Creek Hun. in Co. of Kent on Del., Gent., and Rachel his wife, for the sum of 12 pounds, sold unto Thomas Jackson of Appoquinimink Hun. in Co. of Newcastle, yeoman, a parcel of land situate, in Newcastle. It begins on the north side of a branch of Blackbirds Creek where John Cowgils tanyard standeth, being also the most southern bounds of the land sd Jackson now dwelleth on. It bounds land of Job Bunting and contains 80 acres. This is part of 1,000 acres that was conveyed from afsd John Cowgil unto sd Sharp. Signed: Thomas Sharp, Rachel Sharp. Wit: Isac Whelldon (mark), Mary French. Afsd Sharp appointed David French to be their Attorney on 19 Aug 1728. Ack: 20 Aug 1728. Certifyed by Robertson. (I1-12)

10. Deed. 30 July 1728. John Stephenson of White Clay Creek in Co. of Newcastle, wever, for the sum of 47 pounds 4 shilling sold unto Francis Land of Christiana Creek, yeoman, his Plantation tract of land containing 152 acres with improvements, situate on the north side of Christiana Creek. Signed: John Stephenson, Grace Stephenson (mark). Wit: John Harris, Rose Hill (mark), Susanah Hill (mark). Ack: 20 Aug 1728. Certified by Robertson. (I1-14)

11. Deed. 25 July 1727. William Read of Town and Co. of Newcastle, merchant, for the sum of 270 pounds, sold unto Jehu Curtis of Swanwick in sd Co., Gent., a tract of land situate in sd Swanwick in sd Co. It begins at the Dyke that runs up the marsh up Delaware and bounds land of Peter Jacquett and contains 320 acres. Signed: William Read. Wit: David French, John Gooding. Ack: 3 Nov 1728. David French, pro. (I1-15)

12. Deed. 4 Sept 1728. Henry Metcalf of Christeen Creek in Co. of Newcastle on Del., farmer, Joseph Metcalf of the same place, farmer and Mary his wife, for the sum of 50 pounds, sold unto William Parsons of M Creek Hun in sd Co., yeoman, a parcel of land situate on the East side of Christeen Creek. It bounds the land of Giles Barrett and contains 200 acres. This land was granted by Warrent from Commissioners of Property and laid out by order of the Chief

Surveyor on 19th day first month 1680 unto John Dunn. Whereas sd Dunn by deed dated 12 Oct 1691 granted sd land unto Anthony Sharp and William Sharp. Before sd Anthony's death he made his share unto sd William by his Last Will. Then sd William Sharp by deed dated 24 March 1696 granted sd 200 acres unto Thomas Metcalf, father of afsd Henry and Joseph Metcalf. Then in 1708 by the Last Will of sd Thomas, sd land was bequeathed unto his wife Martha, during her life or widdowhood and (then) to his four sons, Thomas, Henry, Joseph and William. Signed: Henry Metcalf (mark), Joseph Metcalf (mark), Mary Metcalf (mark). Wit: James James Jun., So Evans, Elston Wallis, Mary Simmans, John Braselton. Ack: 19 Nov 1728. David French, pro. (I1-16)

13. Deed. 16 Nov 1728. Alexander Adams of St. Georges Hun. in Co. of New Castle on Del., farmer, for the sum of 162 pounds 18 shillings, sold unto Owen Carthy of same place, marriner, a tract of land and premises containing 210 acres, situate in sd Co. called 'Philips Point' on the NW side of Snowdens Branch. This together with 10 acres of marsh situate in Lugh hook marsh adjoining the plantation of Garret Dushane. Signed: Alexander Adams. Wit: Garret Dushane, Abrm Goulden. Ack: 19 Nov 1728. David French, pro. (I1-18)

14. Deed. 22 Nov 1728. Charles Stout of St. Georges Hun. in Co. of New Castle on Del., farmer, for the sum of 150 pounds, sold unto John Goforth of sd Co., farmer, a parcel of land containing 140 acres, situate upon Maryland road that goes to Bohemia. This is land that Benjamin Stout of sd Hun. and Co. was seized of, and then by his Deed of Gift dated 6 Sept 1721 did grant same unto afsd Charles Stout. Signed: Charles Stout. Wit: Jeremiah Bell, Robertson. Ack: 19 Nov 1728. David French, pro. (I1-20)

15. Deed. 18 Nov 1728. John Justis of and Bridget his wife of Christiana Hun. in Co. of New Castle, farmer, for the sum of 100 pounds, sold unto Jonas Wallraven of same place, wever, a messuage or tenement tract of land plantation containing 105 acres, situate in sd Co. This is whereas sd John Justis by Warrent from the Court in 1677 (became seized of) a tract of land containing 390 acres situate on the east side of Red Clay Creek in sd Co. It begins by land of Peter Stalcop. And whereas John Anderson of same creek by his deed dated 13 day 1st month 1688/9 did sell over sd 390 acres unto afsd Stalcop. Then sd Stalcop in 1704 surveyed and divided sd land unto his son-in-law John Justis, laid out for 100 acres, by Deed of Conveyance dated 20 day 6th month (commonly called August) 1707. And also by virtue of the Last Will of sd Stalcops dated 3 Sept 1709 in which he gives sd Justis 4 or 5 more acres of land left out of a tract lately surveyed to Jonathan Evans. Signed: John Justis, Bridget Justis (mark). Wit: John Philips, Jno Richardson. Ack: 19 Nov 1728. David French, pro. (I1-21)

16. Appointment. 1 Jan 1728/9. Patrick Gordon, Esq., Leut. Gov. of Co. of New Castle, Kent and Sussex upon Delaware and Province of Pennsylvania. TO: William Shaw of New Castle sends Greeting.. and granting him power, authority in afsd Courts, to Go Have Hold and Enjoy the Office of his Majesties Attorney General for afsd Counties. Signed: P. Gordon. (I1-22)

17. Notice. 'This may certifye that Thomas Dakeyne, upon his request & application obtained an Entrey made in the proprietors Land Office for a parcel of vacant land near his other land at the Redlyon branch in New Castle Co. Application made before Evan James from sd Office Philadelphia 26 day 5th mo 1727.' Signed: James Steel. (I1-23)

18. Deed. 18 Nov 1728. Owen Carthy of Georges Hun. in Co. of New Castle, marriner, for the sum of 63 pounds 17 shillings, sold unto Francis Land of Christeen Creek in sd Co., yeoman, his Plantation and tract of land containing 210 acres, situate in sd Hun. and Co. It begins by Snowden's Branch to line of land formerly belonging to William Philips, known by the name 'Philips Point'. Also 10 acres of marsh situate in High Hooke marsh adjoyning the land of Garret Dushane. Signed: Owen Carthy. Wit: John Daneil Tonay, Jno Lefever. Ack: 19 Nov 1728. David French, pro. (I1-23)

19. Deed. 20th day 6th mo. (Aug) 1706/7. 'To all shall come Peter Stalcop of Red Clay Creek in Co. of New Castle upon Delaware River in ye parts of America, yeoman, Sendeth Greeting.' Whereas there was a tract of land containing 390 acres situate on the east side of sd Creek by the land belonging to John Stalcop. This land was granted by Warrant in 1677. Whereas John Anderson of sd Creek by deed dated 13 day 1st month 1688/9 sold sd 390 acres unto Peter Stalcop. Whereas sd Stalcop surveyed and divided land unto his son-in-law John Justis containing 100 acres. 'Now Know Yee that for 20 pounds paid by sd John Justis I confirm sd 100 acres unto him'. Signed: Peter Stalcop (mark). Wit. Thos Pierson, Richd Empson, Edw Robinson (mark). Ack: 19 Nov 1728. David French, pro. (I1 24)

20. Deed. 16 Nov 1728. Conrad Constantine of Christeen Hun. in Co. of New Castle, yeoman, for the sum of 23 pounds 5 shillings, sold unto Francis Land of Christeen Creek in sd Co., yeoman, his plantation tract of land situate on the north side of sd creek in sd Co. It bounds land formerly belonging to sd Constantine and contains 300 acres (except 60 acres of rough land formerly sold to John Richardson) Together with buildings and improvements. Signed: Conrad Constantine (mark). Wit: John Daniell Toney, John Sefever. Ack: 19 Nov 1728. David French, pro. (I1-25)

6

21. Deed. 25 Oct 1728. Benjamin Burleigh of Christeen Creek in Co. of New Castle, turner, for the sum of 20 pounds 1 shilling 3 pence, sold unto Frances Land of same place, yeoman, a parcel of land premises containing 6 acres, situate on the north side of sd Creek in sd Co. This is part of a larger tract of 75 acres near Christeen Bridge, formerly belonging to John Ogle, dec'd., but now in possession of Doctor Rees Jones. Signed: Benjamin Buraleigh. Wit: Isiah Lewden, Joseph Lewden. Ack: 19 Nov 1728. David French, pro. (I1-26)

22. Deed. 4 Nov 1728. 'To all Christian people shall come Adam Short of Co. of New Castle, yeoman, and Martha his wife, Relict and Executrix of Thomas Metcalf, yeoman, of sd Co., dec'd., Send Greetings.' Know ye that for the sum of 16 pounds from the hand of William Parsons of White Clay Creek in sd Co., yeoman, and also other good causes them therunto moving, sd Adam and Martha Short discharge unto sd Parsons their Right Title to any Dowry in a parcel of land containing 200 acres, situate on the east side of Christiana Creek. This land was granted by the Proprietors in 1689 unto John Dunn, who in 1691 granted same unto Anthony Sharp. Sd Sharp in his Last Will granted sd land unto his brother, William Sharp, who by his deed dated 24 March 1696 did grant sd land unto afsd Thomas Metcalf. In sd Metcalf's Will written 1708, he bequeathed land to sd Martha during her widdowhood, and to his four sons, Thomas (since dec'd) Henry, Joseph and William. Signed: Adam Short, Martha Short. Wit: Conn Evan, William Metcalf. Ack: 19 Nov 1728. David French, pro. (I1-27)

23. Deed. 7 Nov 1728. Owen Carthy of St. Georges Hun. in Co. of New Castle, marriner, for the sum of 120 pounds, sold unto Garret Dushane of same place, yeoman, a parcell of land situate in sd Co. on the western side of Appoquinaminck road. It bounds the land of Peter King and contains 60 acres. This land was sold by Cornelius King unto Samuell Mahoe by Deed dated 19 Aug 1723; then by sd Mahoe's Deed to Peter Saroux dated 20 May 1724. Then by sd Saroux's Deed to afsd Owen Carthy dated 1 Nov 1727. Signed: Owen Carthy. Wit: John Ashton, Abraham Gooding. Ack: 19 Nov. (I1-28)

24. Deed. 14 Nov 1728. 'To all Christian People shall come John Ashton of Georges Hun. in Co. of New Castle, yeoman, Sendeth Greeting.' Know that sd Ashton for the sum of 70 pounds from Alexander Adams of sd Co., yeoman; and also for good causes and considerations him thereunto moving, sd Ashton releases unto sd Adams a Plantation tract of land situate in sd Co. It begins at Snowden's branch to land belonging to William Philips, and contains 210 acres of land known as Philips Pointe, together with buildings etc. Signed: John Ashton. Wit: Cha Robinson, Fr. Land. Ack: 19 Nov 1728. David French, pro. (I1-29)

25. Deed. 12 Oct 1672. 'Know all men by these presents that Wee the Heirs Sucessors of Seneca Brewer, dec'd, for the sum of 930 Gilders, have sold unto Justin Anderson his certain inhabited plantation lying in Appoquinaminck. Now I, Justin Anderson for consideration of another parcell of land lying on Ches & Bread (Island) have changed with Thomas Snelling. Know Wee the Heirs of Seneca Brewer and Justin Anderson doe transport unto sd Snelling that plantation.' Signed: Thomas Jacobson (mark), Woole Poalson (mark), Henrihas Jackson, Brewer Seneke, Andrew Senike (mark). Robert Gullert (mark), Brewer Senneck. (I1-29)

26. Deed. 1 March 1679/80. 'To all Xptian People shall come Robberd Tallent and Ellen his wife, the late widdow of John Hartop, dec'd, Sendeth Greetings'. Whereas sd Hartop before his decease did sell unto John Ogle of Christeen Creek in this River of Delaware, a quantity of 150 acres of land, lying in the neck between Blackbird and Appoquiniminck Creeks, next to the land formerly belonging unto Sinxon Brewer. This was part of a greater quantity of 1,000 acres granted by pattent from Gov. Frances Lovelance unto sd John Hartop and his son, Henery Hartop on 19 June 1671. Know ye herefore that Wee sd Robberd Tallent and Ellen, Exec. of sd Hartop have granted unto afsd John Ogle the afsd 150 acres of land. Signed: Robert Tallent (mark), Ellen Tallent (mark). Wit: E. Cantwell, Jeret Otto. (I1-30)

27. Deed. 14 day of 11th month Valgurly called January in the year according to English amount 1683. Thomas Snelling of Black Birds Creek in Co. of New Castle, planter, for the sum of tenn thousand pounds of tobacco in hand paid by Edmund Cantwell of the Town of New Castle, Gent., sell unto sd Cantwell a tract of land situate in sd Co., it being the first firm land on the south side of Appoquinaminck Creek. It begins by Blackbirds Creek by Gravely Runn and bounds land of John Henery Hartups to creek called beaver dam or Dumaseus Creek or Cantwells Creek to land formerly belonging to Senche Brewer. This land sd Cantwell has for some years been in possession with premises. (Terms of sale spelled out) Signed: Thomas Snelling. Wit: William Chute, Jan Juraince, Je. Haes. (I1-30)

28. Patent. 25 March 1676. 'Edmund Andros, Esq. Gov. under his Royal Highness James Duke of York, Sendeth Greetings. Whereas there is a tract of land called the Chops on the west side of Delaware Bay at the head of Hangmans Creek, which by virtue of a warrent was set out for John Streit. It bounds land of Robert Tallerts and contains 200 acres. Now Know Yee by authority given me I grant unto John Streit afsd land and premises.' Signed: E. Andros. Examined by Mathias Nicholls. Entered in Office of Records. (I1-32)

29. Patent. 25 March 1692. 'Know all men that John Mackarty, Administrator of Robert Talent for a valuable consideration to him in hand paid by Richard Hollywell, assigns to sd Hollywell a written pattent for a parcell of land and premises. Signed: John Macharty (mark). Wit: John Walker (mark), John Watts (mark). Ack: 25 March 1692. Ja. Claypooll. (I1-32)

30. Patent. 20 March 1698. 'Know all men that Richard Hollywell for a valuable consideration to him in hand paid by Richard Cantwell, assigns to sd Cantwell his title to the within pattent tract of land. Signed: Richard Halliwell. Wit: Jos. Wood, Jno Smith. Ack: 25 March 1698. Ja. Claypooll. (I1-32)

31. Patent. 17 Jan 1678/9. 'Know all men that I, John Street of Appoquinaminck in Co. of Delaware, planter, doe assign over all my right title, and my wife Joanes of this within mentioned patten unto Robert Morton of sd river. Signed: John Streete, Joanes Streete (mark). Teste: Thomas Moore, Andrew Cornelyon (mark). (I1-32)

32. Patent. 25 March 1676. 'Edmund Andros, Esq. Gov. under his Royal Highness James Duke of York, Sendeth Greetings. Whereas there is a parcell of land called Poplar Hill lying on the west side of Delaware Bay on the north side of Hangmans Creek, which by virtue of a warrent hath been set out for Robert Tallent. It bounds land of Robert Morton and contains 200 acres of land. Now Know Ye by authority given me I have granted sd land and premises to afsd Robert Tallant, he making improvement on sd land according to law and continueing in obedence by conforming himself to the laws of this government and yeilding two bushels of good winter wheat as quit rent. Signed: E. Andros. Examined by Mathias Nicholls. (I1-33)

33. Patent. 30 Jan 1676. 'Know all men that I, Robert Tallant have assigned and set over unto Robert Morton of Appoquinaminck in Province of Delaware all my whole title claim to this Pattent for a valuable consideration. Signed: Robert Tallant. Wit: Walter Wharton, Albert Blook. (I1-33)

34. Bill of Sale. 24 Sept 1728. 'Know all men that I, Arthur Tough of New Castle on Delaware, merchant, for divers good causes and considerations me hereunto moving, but more for sundry goods and wares and merchandizes which I have received from James Stevenson, merchant, of the City of Dublin, I have acknowledged and delivered unto Thomas Hendrey of the Towne of New Castle, marriner, all Bills, Bonds, books, debts, accts, all debts owing to me, and all title of houses, lands, plantations together with their loadings of furniture and apparel whatever, lying or being in Philadelphia, Prov. of Penn., New York, East or West Jersy's of Counties of New Castle, Kent and Sussex, Etc. Signed:

Arthur Tough. Wit: William Shaw, Jacobus Williams. (I1-33)

35. Deed. 15 Jan 1683. Helen Moreton, widdow and Administrator of Robert Moreton, late of Appoquinaminck, planter, dec'd., for the sum of 60,500 pounds of tobacco in hand paid, sold unto Edward Cantwell of New Castle, Gent., a parcel of land lately devided between sd Cantwell and William Grant containing 261 acres. This is part of 500 acres granted to afsd Robert Moreton by Frances Lovelace by his pattent dated 16 June 1671, situate on the west side of Delaware River between Blackbirds Creek and Appoquinaminck. It bounds the land of John Hartop, Henery Hartop and Seneca Brewer, call Hangman's Hooke. Signed: Helena Moreton (mark). Wit: William Welsh, D. Burch. Ack: 16 April 1684. John White, clerke. (I1-34)

36. Deed. 16 May 1683. Justa Anderson of the Town of New Castle in Prov. of Penn., innholder, for a valuable consideration sold unto William Price of Elk River in Prov. of Maryland, planter, a tract of land called Popler Hill, lying on the west side of Delaware bay and on the north side of a creek called Hangman's Creek. It bounds land formerly belonging to Robert Moreton and contains 200 acres. Signed: Justa Anderson. Wit: Alattia Winfry. Ack: 11 March 1683/4. John White, clerk. (I1-35)

37. Patent. 9 day 6th mo 1684. William Penn, Proprietor etc... Sendeth Greetings. Whereas there is a tract of land in Co. of New Castle called Wedgebarry, situate on the west side of Delaware River on a branch of Christiana Creek, called White Clays Creek, to a branch known as Millan about two miles back from Bread and Cheese Island. It goes by land of Arent Johnson, to a branch of Red Clay Creek. It contains 700 acres of land, 538 acres thereof being the land by William Guest bought of Charles Ramsey, and the remainder being new land taken up a grant from the Justices of New Castle, (no date) surveyed by Ephram Harman on 28 of 8th month 1682 unto sd Guest who requested me to confirm same by Patent. Now Know Ye I give, grant this land unto afsd William Guest, thc sd 700 acres with its appurtenances. Signed: Wm Penn. (I1-35)

38. Assignment. 17 day 4th mo 1691. 'Know all men that William Guest do clerly assign and make over all my Right Title to within patin unto Anne Robinson of the Co. of New Castle in Prov. of Penn., hei hcirs forovor, excepting 200 acres formerly sold to Richard Mankin, lying next or joyning to William Josop, Bryant Mc Donaldson.' Signed: William Guest. Wit: Jno Donaldson, Henery Hollingsworth. Ack: 15 Sept 1691. Ja. Claypool. (I1-36)

39. Assign. Feb 1693/4. 'Know all men that I, Anne Robinson, do clearly make

over all my right and title to within pattent unto Benjamin Gill of Co. of New Castle in Prov. of Penn., excepting 200 acres formerly sold to Richard Mankin joining to William Jesopo and Bryant McDonalds land, upon consideration of marriage and of paying to my 3 youngest children. To wit: John, Ann and Joseph 30 pounds of money at day of marriage or as they come to age.' Signed: Ann Robinson (mark). Wit: Thomas, William Guest. (I1-36)

40. Deed. 15 day 7th mo 1691. 'To all Christian People shall come we, William Guest of Co. of New Castle and John Donaldson of same Co., merchant, Sendeth Greetings.' Know ye that for the sum of 115 pounds 10 shillings paid by Ann Robinson, widdow of George Robinson, dec'd., of sd Co., we sold unto her a tract of land being the plantation whereon sd William Guest lived upon, called Wedgbarry, situate on the west side of Delaware River and by White Clay Creek to Red Clay Creek. This land was granted by patent unto sd Guest in 1684 and was mortgaged by him unto Alexander Creeker, now dec'd., to afsd John Donaldson. (Mortgage dated 20 Dec 1688 Liber B, pp 10/11). Signed: William Guest, John Donaldson. Wit: Henry Hollingsworth, Thomas Johnes (mark). Ack: 15 Sept 1691. Ja. Clapooll. (I1-37)

41. Appointment. 27 Nov 1728. Patrick Gordon, Esq., Lieut. Gov. of Co. of New Castle, Kent and Sussex upon Delaware and Province of Pennsylvania. TO: Robert Gordon of sd New Castle Esq., Greeting. I have ordained and constitute sd Robert Gordon to be Register of the Probate of Wills and granting letters of Administration for sd County. (duties etc). Signed: P. Gordon. (I1-38)

42. Appointment. 6 Nov 1728. Patrick Gordon, Esq., Lieut. Gov. of Co. of New Castle, Kent and Sussex upon Delaware. TO: David French Esq., of Co. of New Castle, Greetings. I have ordained and constituted sd David French to be Clark of the Peace and Prothonatary of the Court of Common Pleas of New Castle. Signed: P. Gordon. (I1-38)

43. Appointment. 4 Oct 1728. George the Second by the Grace of God... TO: William Read of the Co. of New Castle within our Gov., Greetings. We nominate sd William Read to be Sheriff of sd Co. (duties etc). Signed: P. Gordon. (I1-39)

44. Confirmation. 4 Oct 1728. George the Second.. King of Great Britain etc... To all Judges, Justices, Magistrates and other officers Freemen within the Co. of New Castle, Greetings. We have granted unto William Read the office of Sheriff of sd Co. Witness: Patrick Gordon Esq. by virtue of a Commission for Springer Penn, Esq., grandson and heir at law of William Penn, Esq. late proprietor. Signed: P. Gordon. (I1-39)

45. Deed. 27 Sept 1728. Jacob Rogers of White Clay Creek Hun. in Co. of New Castle, yeoman, and Johana his wife, for the sum of 71 pounds 10 shillings, sold unto Francis Land of Christiana Creek in sd Co., yeoman, all their plantation and tract of land situate on the south side of White Clay Creek in sd Hun. and Co. It bounds the land late of John Brewster, land of Hugh Marshland and land late of James Claypoole. It contains 200 acres called 'Greenland' together with all buildings etc. Signed: Jacob Rogers, Johana Rogers (mark). Wit: Charles Springer, Picffer Blanson (mark). Ack: 28 Feb 1728. David French, pro. (I1-40)

46. Deed. 14 Feb 1728. Isaack Cannon of Co. of Newcastle and Eleanor his wife, for the sum of 47 pounds, sold unto Peter Lawson of same place, yeoman, a tract of land containing 110 acres, situate near Dragon Swamp in sd Co. This is land that Rowland Fitzgerald, high sheriff of sd Co., by his Deed dated 16 Oct 1719 did convey unto Samuel Grifith of sd Co., cordwainer. It formerly belonged to Henery Hanson. Then sd Griffith by his Deed in 1724 did grant same unto afsd Isaak Cannon. Signed: Isaac Cannon (mark), Elinor Cannon (mark). Wit: John Stout, Abraham Gooding. Ack: 28 Feb 1728. David French, pro. (I1-42)

47. Deed. 1 Oct 1728. Col (?) John French of Newcastle in sd Co., for the sum of 50 pounds, and also for love and affection, sold unto his son-in-law Robert Robertson of the same place, Gent., an equal half or moiety of a lott of land. This is whereas Anthony Houston, late of sd Co., Administrator of the Will of William Houston, late of sd Co., dec'd., was lately in Court of Common Pleas (to recover against) Elizabeth Bikerstaff, Execrix of Last Will of Phebe Miller, dec'd, who was Execrix of the Last Will of James Miller, of same place, dec'd., for a debt of 45 pounds 17 shilling 2 pence and damages. Whereas Richard Clark Esq., High Sheriff of sd Co., by Writ of Exponas dated 2 Nov 1713 was commanded that the lands and houses of sd James Miller be taken in execution to pay debt. Sd sheriff did convey unto Robert Ellis of Philadelphia, merchant all that messuage house and lott of land situate in Town of Newcastle. It bounds the River Delaware, the market place, and lott of Thomas Tresse. Whereas sd Ellis by his Deed dated 5 Nov 1713 did sell same unto afsd Anthony Houston Then whereas sd Houston by his Last Will dated 29 June 1724 did bequeath unto Jonathan Houston, his son, afsd property. Then sd Jonathan Houston by his Deed dated 18 Feb 1725/6 did sell same unto afsd Col (?) John French; who was seized of another lott in sd town formerly belonging to George Lamb, bounding the lott called the Quaker's Meeting House Lott, and lott of John Richardson. Signed: John French. Wit: John McDowal, James Glon, Thomas Smith. (I1-44)

48. Deed. 28 Jan 1728. Edward Blake of Newcastle in sd Co., cordwainer, and Anna his wife, for the sum of 13 pounds, 10 shilling, sold unto Richard Enos of

sd Co., yeoman, a certain part of marsh, situate in sd Co. It adjoyns the south side of the outlet of Blak Wallnutt Island, and contains 10 acres. Signed: Edward Blake, Anna Blake (mark). Wit: John Reynolds, John Rite. Ack: 28 Feb 1728. David French. (I1-46)

49. Deed. 17 Feb 1728. William Baffell, Exec. of Last Will of John French, late of Newcastle Co., dec'd., for the sum of 92 pounds, sold unto Andrew Miller of sd Co., yeoman, a parcel of land situate in sd Co. It bounds land late of Doctor Sprire and John White and contains 300 acres. This is land that sd French in his lifetime was seized of, and in his Last Will empowered his Exec. to sell same. Signed: W. Baffoll. Wit: Benj Burleigh, Christine Warlone (mark). Proved: Feb 1728. David French, pro. (I1-49)

50. Deed. 10 Jan 1728. William Rees of Cecill Co.in Prov. of Maryland, blacksmith, and Mary his wife, for the sum of 38 pounds, sold unto William Williams of Penkader Hun. in Co. of Newcastle upon Del., yeoman, a parcel of land situate in Pencader Hun., containing 232 acres, together with houses etc. This is land that William David and David Evans by their Deed dated 28 Dec 1721 did grant unto Rees Evans of Red lion Hun. in Newcastle Co. It bounded land of John Rowland and William Lewis. Sd Evans by another grant became seized of another parcell of land, and by his deed did grant part of sd land unto afsd William Rees. Wit: Joseph Moore (mark), Rees Evan. Appointed attorney was Roger William of Penkader Hun. in sd Co., cooper. Signed: William Rees (mark), Mary Rees (mark). Ack: 28 Feb 1728. (I1-52)

51. Deed. 1 Feb 1728. James Anderson of St. Georges in Redlion Hun. in Co. of Newcastle, yeoman, for the sum of 64 pounds, sold unto John Richardson of the sd Co. and Christiana Hun., merchant, a tenement and tract of land containing 275 acres plantation, situate in Redlion Hun. in sd Co. It begins on King's Road, by Dragon and then down George Creek. This is property that sd Anderson by virtue of a release from his brother, Peter Anderson, as eldest son to his father, James, dec'd.; by virtue of Deed from Henery Evertson to his father; and from Hendrick Vanderburgh by another Deed from Robert Soams; came to be seized of. Signed: James Anderson. Wit: Bwr. Sinnixon, Mathias Peterson. Ack: 28 Feb 1728. David French pro. (I1-53)

52. Deed. 1 May 1729. George Robinson of Miln Creek Hun. in Co. of Newcastle upon Del., yeoman, for the sum of 98 pounds, sold unto Duncan Drumond of the same place, merchant, 110 acres (minus 10 acres) situate in sd Co. It bounds the land of John Cann. This is land that William Penn by pattent under the hand of James Claypoole and Robert Turner did grant unto Aaron Johnson Vandenburgh, situate near Runn Creek, now called Miln Creek in sd

Co., containing 110 acres. This pattent dated 12 July 1685. Then sd Vandenburg made his Last Will and Testament, dated 20 Nov 1701, and devised unto his wife, Barbara James Johnson Vandenburg all his estate (including sd land and premises), and reversion part of sd residue to the Reverend Ericus Biork of Christiana Hun. in sd Co., (part unto the Swedish Church). By virtue of sd Will, sd Biork and sd Barbara Vandenburg did grant unto James Robinson, late of sd Co., Gent., dec'd., (father of afsd George Robinson) the afsd 110 acres and appurtenances by deed dated 9 June 1714. Then sd Robinson by Deed of Gift did grant unto the Honorable London Protesant Society for Propagating the Gospel, 10 acres of sd land in 1726. Then sd Robinson by his Last Will did bequeath unto his son, afsd George, part of the land 'adjoyning to my now dwelling plantation' which he had improved, along with a feather bed and furniture. Signed: George Robinson. Wit: Saml. Kirk, W. Conne. Ack: 2 June 1729. (I1-55)

53. Deed. 23 May 1729. Andrew Hamilton of City of Philadelphia, Esq., for the sum of 95 pounds, sold unto Andrew Peterson of Newcastle Co., Gent., 400 acres of land, buildings and improvements, situate near Appoquinimink Co. in sd Co. This is land that Daniel Lindsey of sd Co. by his Deed Poll dated 1 Feb 1676 did sell unto John Moll* of sd Co. Terms were that that sd Lindsey should pay him 1,847 pounds of tobacco at some convenient place on the Delaware River on 20 Dec (deed date) or Deed would be void. In case of nonpayment, sd Moll* would take possession of land and premises. Then sd Lindsey did not pay sd tobaco or any part of it. Then sd Moll by assignment upon the Deed of sd Lindsey dated 18 June 1684 did grant 400 acres unto Robert Purkinson of sd Co., farmer. Then sd Purkinson by Deed Poll dated 9 Aug 1705, for a Judgment for 58 pounds 5 shilling 5 pence recovered against him by Benjamin Chambers in behalf of the Free Society of Traders in Penn., did sell sd 400 acres unto Chambers. Then sd Chambers died and Admin. of his Estate was granted unto Elizabeth, the wife of Stephen Foukson of the City of Phila., merchant, heir to sd Chambers. Then sd Foukson and wife did recover against John Moll* the goods and chattles of sd Daniel Lindsey and the sum of 2,500 pounds of tobaco for damages in Court of Common Pleas. Same court ordered sd Moll, as Administrator, to sell land and tenements of sd Lindsey to pay damages. Sd 400 acres sold to afsd Andrew Hamilton. Signed: A. Hamilton. Wit: John Richardson, William Read. Ack: 2 June 1728 (9?). (* name could be Moll, Wroll or Pore). (I1-59)

54. Deed. 22 May 1728. Francis Bradley of Miln Creek Hun. in Co. of New Castle, yeoman, and Rebecca his wife, for the sum of 85 pounds, sold unto Robert Boe of same place, blacksmith, a parcel of land, half of 200 acres. It bounds the lands of Thos. Bracken, John Read, William Emmit and John

14

Bracken, and contains 114 acres with improvements. This is part of the land that Joshua Morgan, late of NE in Province of Maryland, cordwainer, did grant and convey unto afsd Francis Bradley on 17 Feb 1706. It was called Amliston, situate in afsd Co. on the north side of White Clay Creek back in the woods, and contained 200 acres. Signed: Francis Bradley, Rebecka Bradley (mark). Wit: Evan Rice, Joseph Hadly, Robt. Robertson. Ack: 2 June 1729. (I1-62)

55. Deed. 23 May 1729. William Williams of Pencadder Hun. in Co. of New Castle on Del., yeoman, and Jane his wife, for the sum of 190 pounds, sold unto James Crawford of same place, two parcels of land containing 201-1/2 acres, known by the name 'half way house land'. This is whereas William Markham, Esq., on a warrant under his hand dated 15 Feb 1691 did order surveyed for Chas. Gorsuch, 400 acres in sd Co. by Henry Hollingsworth, Chief Surveyor. Then John Gorsuch, his son and heir, by deed dated 5 Nov 1721 did grant 200 acres of sd land unto afsd Williams. It bounded land now in tenure of James Sykes. Then James Logan, Richard Hik and Isaac Noris by their warrant dated 1 Jan 1722 did grant unto sd Williams 200 acres of land. Whereas John Edward by indenture dated 20 Jan 1717 did grant unto sd Williams a piece of land bounding land of sd Edwards. Signed: William Williams, Jane Williams. Wit: Alexander Parker, Jacobus Williams, Jonathan Houston, Edward Blake. Ack: 6 June 1729. (I1-64)

56. Deed. 17 March 1728/9. Joseph Horsey of Co. of New Castle, taylor, and Sarah his wife, for the sum of 40 pounds, sold unto George Gregg, farmer of sd Co., three parcels of land. One is commonly called the Island. It bounds line of Erick Anderson, Johanes Defoss and sd Horsey's plantation, and contains 48 acres. Another bounds line of sd Gregg, John Deno, and sd Johanes Defoss' house, and contains 77 acres 42 perches, excepted 37 acres 23 perches of clear land left by Mathias Defoss to his son, Johanes, (the remaining part is 42 acres 19 perches). The third bounds line of sd Deno and Jonas Scoggins, and contains 13 acres 95 perches. This is whereas afsd Mathias Defoss, dec'd., in his lifetime was seized of sundry tracts of land situate on the west side of Brandywine Creek. Sd Defoss made his Will dated 17 May 1705 and bequeathed unto his son, Hance Defoss a tract containing 100 acres of land and meadow. Then sd Hance Defoss made his Will dated 25 Jan 1707 and did bequeath unto his daughter, Sarah, wife of afsd Joseph Horsey, then being an infant. Signed: Joseph Horsey, Sarah Horsey (mark). Wit: John Hore, Geo. Gregg. David French, Esq., appoint Attny. Examined by Thomas Janvier. Ack: 6 June 1729. (I1-66)

57. Deed. 22 May 1729. John Potts of New Castle Co. and Sarah his wife, niece of Thomas Halliwell, late of Bale Beare Hamlet in Parish of Clasoop in Co. of

Darby in Kingdom of Great Britain, yeoman, (only son and heir of Thomas Halliwell, late of same place, dec'd., who was the brother of Richard Halliwell, late of New Castle Co., merchant, also dec'd.), for the sum of 30 pounds, sold unto Richard Grafton of same Co., merchant, a Bank lott, situate in sd Co. It begins on Front Street and house and lott now in tenure of John Finney, Gent. with moiety of piece of land lately sold to Joseph Saile, wheelright. This is whereas William Penn by his pattent dated 12 June 1707, did grant unto afsd Richard Halliwell a Bank or Water lott. It was in breadth 60 feet and extending into the River 600 feet. Then afsd Thomas Halliwell by Deed did grant unto afsd Sarah (then by name of Sarah Needham), the messuages and lotts of land. Signed: John Potts (mark), Sarah Potts. Wit: Robert Gordon, William Read. Ack: 3 June 1729. David French, pro. (I1-69)

58. Deed. 7 May 1729. Thomas VnDyke of East Jersey in Co. of Summerset, weaver, son of Isaac VnDyke, in pursuance of an agreement by his father and the sum of 225 pounds, grant unto Ann Brank of St. Georges Hun. in Co. of New Castle, widdow, a parcel of land situate in sd Hun. and Co. containing 205 acres. It bounds the land of Andrew Anderson and sd Brank along Augustine Creek. This is whereas afsd Isaac VnDyke, in his lifetime, for the sum of 300 pounds to be paid to Peter Brank, husband of afsd Anne., (since dec'd.), did agree to convey to him sd parcel of land. Sd Isaac Vandyke died before legal conveyance of same. Signed: Thomas Vandyck. Wit: William Gordon, John Hore. Ack: 3 June 1729. (I1-71)

59. Deed. 10 March 1728. Julyne Campbell, widdow and Exec. of Last Will of John Campbell, late of New Castle Co., farmer, dec'd., for the sum of 22 pounds, grants unto Charles Campbell, yeoman, a tract of land containing 100 acres. This is whereas afsd John Campbell in his lifetime by an instrument dated 25 Dec 1719, for the sum of 50 pounds granted unto afsd Charles Campbell 100 acres of land (part of a greater tract). Sd John died before conveyance could be made so his widow appealed to Court to impower her to convey same. Signed: Julyne Campbell (mark). Wit: Samuel Johnson, William McMechen (mark), James McMechen, James Armitage. Appoint Attny: Simon Hadley, James James jun. and Benjamin Gibbs. Ack: 8 June 1729. (I1-73)

60. Deed. 21 May 1729. William McMechen of Miln Creek Hun. in Co. of New Castle, yeoman, and Jennet his wite, tor the sum ot 80 pounds, sold unto William Emmitt of same place, yeoman, a parcel of land containing 115 acres, situate in sd Hun. and Co. It bounds the lands of Robert Boe, William Bracken, sd Emmitt and Josiah Ramage. This is part of a larger tract that William Aubrey, late of City of London in Kingdom of Great Brittain, merchant, and Letitia his wife, by their attorneys James Logan, late of Co. of Phila., gent., by an indenture

dated 2 June 1702 did grant unto afsd William McMechen containing 961-3/4 acres in three parcels. Signed: William McMechen (mark), Jannet McMechen. Wit: James McMechen, J. Gonne. Ack: 6 June 1729. (I1-75)

61. Deed. 15 May 1729. Anne Brank of St. Georges Hun. in Co. of New Castle, widdow and relict of Peter Brank, dec'd., for the sum of 160 pounds, sold unto Robert Mauay of same place, farmer, a plantation parcel of land situate in sd Hun. and Co. This is whereas by sd Peter Brank's Last Will dated 15 Feb 1728, he appointed his loving wife whole and sole Exectrix, and impowered her to sell the plantation she now dwell to pay his just debts and funeral charges. And whereas Thomas VnDyke of East Jersey in Co. of Summerset, weaver, son of Isaac Vandyke, late of sd Hun., dec'd., by an indenture dated 7 May 1729 did grant unto afsd Anne Brank a parcel of land whereon sd Brank's did live. Signed: Anne Brank (mark). Wit: Andrew Vandyke, John Horse. Ack: 6 June 1729. (I1-77)

62. Deed. 3 March 1728. Andrew Wooten of Town of New Castle, blacksmith, for the sum of 21 pounds, sold unto Thomas Smith of sd Town, merchant, a lott of ground and premises, situate in sd town. It bounds Beaver Street in front, Otter Street in back, Hart Street to the north, with John Powell and Richard Reynold to the other side. It contains 250 feet in length and 62 feet in breadth. William Shaw, Esq. appointed Attorney. Signed: Andrew Wootten. Wit: Robert Robertson, Alexander David (mark). Memo: 'On 27 Feb 1728, quiet peacable lawful possession livery seizen with contained premises was given made and delivered by Tuft and Twig by Robert Wooten and Andrew Wooten to Thomas Smith in presence of us: Herm Alricks, John Powell (mark).' Ack: 21 May 1729. (I1-79)

63. Deed. 21 May 1729. Francis Bradley of Miln Creek Hun. in Co. of New Castle, yeoman, and Rebeca his wife, for the sum of 103 pounds, sold unto John Read of sd Hun. and Co., merchant, a parcel of land, half of 200 acres herein described. It bounds the land of Thomas Bracken, John Champion, Josiah Ramage and Robert Boe and contains 114 acres. This is whereas Joshua Morgan, late of NE in Province of Maryland, cordwainer, did by Deed dated 17 Feb 1706, convey unto afsd Bradley a parcel of land called Amliston, situate in sd Co. on the north side of White Clay Creek back in the woods, containing 200 acres. Signed: Daneil Bradley, Rebecca Bradley (mark). Wit: Robt. Ertson, Jo. Hadley, Evan Rice. Ack 21 May 1729. (I1-81)

64. Deed. 1 May 1729. Samuel Kirk of Christiana Hun. in Co. of New Castle, gentleman, and Alice his wife, for the sum of 180 pounds, sold unto John Richardson of sd Hun. and Co., merchant, a tenement and tract of land, two grist

mills and two boalting mills, mill house and new dwelling house and all out
houses and all other premises thereunto belonging, situate at Brandywine Creek
in sd Co., containing 20-1/2 acres. This is property that became sd Kirks by
virtue of a Deed from Timothy Stedham, who derived his right of heirship being
eldest son of Lillefe Stedham, dec'd.. This Deed dated 12 Nov 1727 from sd
Stedham and Elizabeth his wife. Signed: Samuel Kirk, Alice Kirk. Wit: Chas.
Springer, Jos. Parker. Ack: 21 May 1729. (I1-83)

65. Deed. 5 April 1729. John Gorsuch of Baltimore Co. in Prov. of Maryland,
planter, for the sum of 30 pounds, sold unto Adam Short of New Castle Hun.
and Co., yeoman, a tract of land situate in sd Hun. and Co. upon Elk River
Road. It bounds the land late of John Dunn to Christine Creek to land late of
Giles Barrefo, and contains 300 acres. This sd land became sd Gorsuch's by
right, by virtue of an order from William Markham, one of the Commissioners
of Property, dated 15 day 12th mo 1631/2. It was surveyed 17th day same
month unto Charles Gorsuch, father of afsd John. Signed: John Gorsuch. Wit:
Fr. Land, John Land. Ack: 21 May 1729. (I1-85)

66. Deed. 21 May 1729. William MitCalfe of Christeen Creek in Co. of New
Castle, farmer, for the sum of 25 pounds, sold unto William Parsons of Miln
Creek Hun. in sd Co., yeoman, all his right title, interest or property claim on a
parcel of land situate on the east side of Christeen Creek, containing 200 acres.
This land was granted by Warrant and layed out on the 19th day of 1st Mo 1689
unto John Dunn. Then sd Dunn by Deed dated 12 Oct 1691 granted same unto
Anthony Sharp and William Sharp. Then sd Anthony by his Last Will divided
his share of the 200 acres unto his brother, William. Then sd William by his
Deed dated 24 March 1696 granted sd land to Thomas MitCalfe, father of afsd
William MitCalfe. Then sd father Thomas by his Will in 1708 did bequeath sd
land unto his wife Martha during her widdowhood and to his four sons, Thomas,
Henery, Joseph and afsd William. Signed: William Mitcalf (mark). Wit: Benj.
Gibbs, Robert Courtney. Ack: 21 May 1729. (I1-86)

67. Deed. 10/12 May 1729. Thomas Evans of Appoquinamink in Co. of New
Castle, blacksmith, and Elizabeth his wife, daughter and sole survivor heir of
Thomas Snowden, late of sd Co., yeoman, dec'd., for the sum of 40 pounds, sold
unto Trustram Shoreland of same place, yeoman, a parcel of land containing
125 acres, situate in St. Georges Hun. in sd Co. It begins by Drawyer's Creek
and is part of a greater tract that contained 235 acres. Signed: Thomas Evans,
Elizabeth Evans (mark). Wit: Andw. Peterson, Elston Wallis. Ack: 21 May
1729. (I1-88)

68. Deed. 23 April 1729. Hugh Shennan of Co. of New Castle, yeoman, and

Anne his wife, for the sum of 28 pounds, 5 shillings, sold unto Francis Land of sd Co., yeoman, their plantation and tract of land situate lying in Redlyon Hun. in sd Co. It bounds the lands of George Dakeyn and Obediah Holto by Maryland Road, and contains 200 acres together with buildings and improvements. Signed: Hugh Shennen, Ann Shennen. Wit: Francis James, James James jun. Appointed Atty: William Read, Esq. Ack: 21 May 1729. (I1-90)

69. Quit Claim Deed. 26 Feb 1728/9. 'To All Christian People Greetings'. Know that Robert Wooten of Kent Co., carpenter, for divers good causes him thereunto moving, hath released and quit claimed unto Andrew Wooten a certain lott situate lying in the Town of New Castle. It bounds Beaver Street, Otter Street, Hart Street and lotts of John Powell and Richard Reynolds. Signed: Robert Wooten (mark). James Foster, Robert Robertson and John Land witnessed executing sd deed and sd Andrew paying 14 pounds to sd Robert, being the consideration money agreed upon by this sd deed to his brother. Ack: 21 May 1729. (I1-91)

70. Deed. 18 April 1729. Robert Eyre of Town and Co. of New Castle, carpenter, and Elizabeth his wife, for the sum of 28 pounds 11 shillings 4 pence, sold unto Francis Land of Christeen Creek in sd Co., yeoman, two lotts of land situate in sd Town and Co., near the Town Marsh, together with all buildings and improvements. One lott bounds Front Street to land late of Coll. French. The other is bounded by the River Delaware, afsd marsh and lott formerly belonging to James Merrewether. Signed: Robert Eyre, Elizabeth Eyre (mark). Wit: Thomas Janvier, John Chambley (mark). Appointed Attorney was trusted friend, William Read, Esq. Ack: 21 May 1729. (I1-92)

71. Power of Attorney. 20 Aug 1728. 'Know All Men that I, Isaac Phipps, at present of PenCathrines in Co. of New Castle, yeoman, have constituted by trusty loving wife, Eleanor Phipps, my true Lawful Attorney for me in my name, to demand or sue or receive sums of money of accounts, dues, debts and demands whatsoever.... to sell convey every parcel of land I am invested with in Co. of New Castle as in the Province of Maryland...' Signed: Isaak Phipps (mark). Wit: Thomas Hayes (mark), Thos. Currey. Witnesses Thomas Hayes and Thos. Currey came before Henery Hays, Justice of Peace, on 30 Aug 1728 and upon their solemn affirmation declared afsd Power of Attorney. (I1-94)

72. Deed/Mortgage. 22 May 1729. Andrew Hamilton of City of Philadelphia, Esq., for the sum of 5 shillings, grant unto Andrew Peterson of New Castle Co., gentleman, a tract of land situate near Appoquinimink Creek in sd Co., containing 400 acres together with all singular. It bounds sd creek, sd Peterson's

land and land of Roloef Dehaes. Signed: A. Hamilton. Wit: John Richardson, William Read. Ack: 21 May 1729. (I1-94)

73. Deed/Mortgage. 16 June 1729. Thomas Janvier of Town and Co. of New Castle, gent., for the sum of 5 shillings, sold unto Jacob Gooding of sd Co., farmer, seven tracts of land and marsh situate near Reeden Island in sd Co. The first bounds land of Isaac Gooding and contains 17-1/4 acres. The second bounds lands of John Hanson jun., and John Hanson sen., Peter Stryker and contains 35 acres. The third bounds Augustine Creek and lands of sd Hanson, William Pattison and sd Gooding, and contains 150 acres. The fourth bounds marsh of John Berge and sd John Hanson, and contains 8 acres of marsh. The fifth bounds marsh of sd Berge and sd Hanson and contains 8 acres of marsh. The sixth being the uppermost contains 8 acres. The seventh bounds woodland of John Goodings and contains 20 acres. All seven lotts contain in the whole 245-1/4 acres. Signed: Thomas Janvier. Wit: David French, William Graham. Ack: 21 May 1729. (I1-95)

74. Deed/Mortgage. 17 June 1729. Jacob Gooding of Co. of New Castle, farmer, for the sum of 200 pounds, sold unto Thomas Janvier of Town of New Castle in sd Co., merchant, seven tracts of land and marsh situate near Reeden Island in sd Co. The first bounds land of Isaac Gooding and contains 17-1/4 acres. The second bounds lands of John Hanson jun., and John Hanson sen., Peter Stryker and contains 35 acres. The third bounds Augustine Creek and lands of sd Hanson, William Pattison and sd Gooding, and contains 150 acres. The fourth bounds marsh of John Berge and sd John Hanson, and contains 8 acres of marsh. The fifth bounds marsh of sd Berge and sd Hanson and contains 8 acres of marsh. The sixth being the uppermost contains 8 acres. The seventh bounds woodland of John Goodings and contains 20 acres. All seven lotts contain in the whole 245-1/4 acres. Sd 200 pounds at 6% interest, full sum due 1 April 1735. Signed: Jacob Gooding. Wit: David French, Wm. Graham. Ack: 21 May 1729. (I1-97)

75. Deed. 30 June 1729. Johannes VanEecklen of Co. of Kent on Delaware, farmer and son and heir of Johannes Vanekeler, for the sum of 5 pounds, sold unto Thomas Janvier of Town and Co. of New Castle, Gent., one equal eighth part of all marsh belonging to a tract of land in Co. of New Castle, commonly called Reeden Island, situate on the west side of Delaware River. It is bounded by Creek of Appoquinamink, a branch called Silver Runn, also by land formerly belonging to Edward Green by Kings Road, and contains 2,809 acres. This was purchased of Casparus Herman, late of Bohemia River in Province of Maryland, merchant, by John Hanson sen. (3/8th parts of whole), Isaac Gooding (1/8th part), John Hanson jun. (1/8th part), Johannes Vanekeler (father of afsd) (1/8th

part), Barnett Jooster (1/8th part), Johannes Seking (1/8th part). Signed:
Johannes VanEecklen. Wit: John Burmingham, Isaac Janvier. Ack: 21 May
1729. (I1-100)

76. Deed. 10 June 1729. Samuel James of Peckader Hun. in Co. of New Castle,
gent., for the sum of 400 pounds, sold unto John White and Abraham Taylor,
both of the City of Philadelphia in Prov. of Penn., merchants, a tract of land
containing 200 acres 126 perches, situate in sd Hun. and Co., with the
messuages and plantation and forge thereon, almost finished, for the forging of
iron barro out of the grosser metal. It bounds lands of Thomas Watts, Elijhia
Thomas, James James jun., James James sen., Thomas James, Thomas John,
Hugh Morris, the Anabapists Meeting House and Phillip James. Terms of
mortgage principal and interest spelled out. Signed: Samuel James. Wit: Reid
Grafton, Thomas Crowder, J. Hores jun. Ack: 21 May 1729. (I1-102)

77. Deed. 26 Dec 1728. Elioner Phipps of Hun. of Pencader in Co. of New
Castle, the wife of Isaia Phipps (lately Absconded) and lawful Power of
Attorney under him ordained 12 Aug last, and testified by evidence before
Henery Hages, Esq., justice of peace for Co. of Chester in Prov of Penn., for
consideration and conditions set here, sold unto David Mirick of same Hun. and
Co., yeoman, a tract of land laying in sd Co. containing 327 acres. It bounds the
lands of David Price and Samuel James. This is part of a larger tract taken up by
William Davies and David Evans by virtue of a warrant dated 18 Oct 1701. It
was afterwards sold by them unto Thomas John, lately dec'd. Sd John in his
lifetime sold same unto Izaiah Phipps. The Deed from sd Davies and sd Evans
to sd John, and the Deed from sd John to sd Phipps, were in sd Phipps
possession and were accidently destroyed by fire. New Deeds were requested.
Signed: Elioner Phipps (mark). Wit: Thomas Evans, Thos. James, William
Davies. Memorandum: Three acres out of sd parcel bordering upon Batchelor's
Hope is in debate and surveyed by both Pennsylvania and Maryland. Ack: 21
May 1729. (I1-104)

78. Judgement. 16 June 1729. 'William Read, Sherrif of Co. of NewCastle
Sendeth Greetings.' Whereas James James jun. and Henery Snicker were lately
in Court of Common Pleas before Justices and recovered against William James
of sd Co., yeoman, the sum of 8 pounds 16 shillings 8 pence and damages.
Whereas by Writ by John Gooding, Esq., late High Sheriff, commanded to seize
lands and chattles of sd James. Taken in execution was one messuage and
tenement parcel of land with appurtenances, containing 150 acres, situate in sd
Co. It begins on White Clay Creek road by the bridge and bounds the lands of
Evan Morgan, Morgan Morgan, William Wooleston, William Cann, John Lewis
and John Hanzey. Appraised by William Wooleston and John Lewis, and sold

to William Parsons of sd Co., as the highest bidder for 84 pounds. Signed: William Read. Wit: Andrew Peterson, David French. Ack: 21 May 1729. (I1-106)

79. Deed. Aug 1729. Isaac Janvier of New Castle in same Co., joyner, for the sum of 20(?) pounds, sold unto Francis Janvier of same place, a piece of a parcel of land situate in sd place. This is whereas Ann Allet, Joshua Storie and John Silsby, Exec. of the Last Will of Thomas Allet, late of same place, innholder, dec'd., by an indenture did grant unto Joseph Hill of sd place, wheelwright, and afsd Isaac Janvier, a lott of land situate in sd place. Then sd Hill and Mary his wife by an indenture dated 27 Feb 1724, did grant unto sd Janvier a piece of the lott. It is bounded by the lott late of Josiah Rolfe and marsh of Nicholas Meer and land of sd Hill. (No signatures, states parties not compelled to travel more than 10 miles from their place of abode.) Wit: Jane Read, J. Gonne. Ack: 23 Aug 1729. (I1-107)

80. Mortgage/Deed. 21 Aug 1729. Edward Blake of New Castle in same Co., cordwainer, and Ann his wife, for the sum of 130 pounds, sold unto John Lewden Sen., of sd Town and Co., one equal half of a tract of land called Swarton N? Island, containing 300 acres in the whole, and premises now in his actual possession. Also one half of the land adjoyning called Beshye, containing in the whole 100 acres, and being the lower half of sd Island and outlet situate upon Christiana Creek in sd Co. This by virtue of an indenture for one whole year starting the day before this date. Signed: Edward Blake, Anna Blake (mark). Wit: John Harris, Robert Robertson. Memorandum: On 16 Aug sd Lewden gave sd Blake 12 pounds for Articles of Agreement for sd sale. Signed: Robert Robertson. Wit: Stephen Lewis, Jacobus Hains. Ack: 23 Aug 1729. (I1-110)

81. Judgement. 22 Aug 1729. 'To all Christian People shall come William Read, Esq. high Sheriff of Co. of Newcastle, send greetings'. Whereas John Richardson and Joseph England, surviving trustees of Gen. Loan Office were at Court of Common Pleas for judgement to recover against Aveo Sprenth and William Battell, Exec. of the Last Will of John French, late of sd Co., gent., dec'd., for the sum of 100 pounds and damages. Afsd Sheriff ordered to seize in execution two lotts of ground and one tenement, situate lying the the Town of New Castle which was mortaged by sd John French in his lifetime to afsd trustees. One of the lotts fronts River Delaware and bounds lott late of Thomas Trese, now in the tenure of John Vengezelle. The other lott is a bank lott opposite the first extending into sd river. Sd property appraised and notice of sale and sold unto David French as the highest bidder for 47 pounds 5 shilling. Signed: William Read. Wit: William Shaw, John Rice. Ack: 23 Aug 1729. (I1-

112)

82. Mortgage/Deed. 22 Aug 1729. William Battell of Co. of New Castle, gent., for the sum of 40 pounds, grants unto Andrew Hamilton of the City of Philadelphia in Prov. of Penn., Esq., a tract of ground, in his actual possession now by virtue of an indenture by sd Battell for consideration of 5 shillings for the term of one year. It is situate in Town of New Castle, bounded on the E with Front St., on the S with street leading to the Church, on the W with the house lott lately in possession of Mathias Vnderkeyden, and on the N with lott formerly belonging to Capt. Cantwell. Signed: William Battell. Wit: Gilb Falconer, Gideon Griffith. Ack: 23 Aug 1729. David French pro. (I1-113)

83. Deed. 20 Aug 1729. Mary Vance of Mill Creek Hun. in Co. of New Castle, widdow and Exec of the Last Will of John Vance, late of sd Co., yeoman, dec'd., for the sum of 83 pounds, sold unto Nathan Hussey of New Castle Hun. in sd Co., yeoman, a messuage and tract of land, situate in Letitia Penn's Mannor in sd Co., containing 100 acres 6 perches. This is property whereas sd Hussey by an indenture dated 18 Aug 1727, did convey unto afsd John Vance. (Liber H, pp 213). Then thus seized, sd Vance died. Then by Petition by sd Mary Vance to the Court of Common Pleas stating sundry debts were still due from the estate and permission to sell land to cover debts. Afsd land and premises offered at Publick Vendue and sold unto afsd Hussey as the highest bidder. Signed: Mary Vance (mark). Wit: Simon Hadly, John Rice. Ack: 23 Aug 1729. (I1-115)

84. Mortagage/Deed. 22 Nov 1728. William Battell of Co. of New Castle, merchant, for the sum of 211 pounds, grant unto Hugh Graham of the City of Philadelphia, practioner in Chirurgery and physick, a parcel of ground situate in sd Co. It begins by Christeen Creek and contains 200 acres, together with several tenements thereon erected. Together also with all houses, out houses, mills, lands tenements, meadows (etc). Terms that sd Battell shall pay unto sd Graham the full sum of 211 pounds 16 shilling 8 pence on or before 23 Nov 1730 with lawful interest. Terms of default given. Signed: W. Battell. Wit: Ralph Ashton, John Herbert. William Shaw appointed Attny. Wit: Robert Gordon, Thomas Janvier. Ack: 23 Aug 1729. (I1-117)

85. Deed. 30 July 1729. Samuel Pound of Appoquinamink Hun. in Co. of New Castle, marriner, for the sum of 70 pounds, sold unto Edward Dwoof of sd Co., yeoman, a parcel of land and premises containing 146 acres, situate by Black Bird Creek in sd Co. It bounds the line of Richard Hale and Daniel Large. This is land that sd Hale sold unto sd Pound by an indenture dated 15 Feb 1724. Wit: John Cowley, Thomas Noxon. Signed: Samuel Pound. Ack: 23 Aug 1729. (I1-118)

86. Deed. 22 Aug 1729. William Battell of White Clay Creek Hun. in Co. of New Castle, gent., for the sum of 62 pounds, sold unto Robert Mears of sd Co., yeoman, a parcel of land containing 116 acres 38 perches, bounding the So. side of the Welsh road in sd Co. Signed: William Battell. Wit: Jacobus Williams, John Russell. Ack: 23 Aug 1729. (I1-120)

87. Deed. 18 Aug 1729. Henery Snitgar of Christiana Hun. in Co. of New Castle, farmer, and Cathrine his wife, for the sum of 105 pounds, sold unto William Dixon of Mill Creek Hun. in sd Co., farmer, a parcel of land situate in Christiana Hun. in sd Co. containing 221 acres. It bounds the lands of Paul Roses, John Wayland, Herman Hinky and Henery Gaests. Signed: Henery Snicker, Cathrine Snicker (mark). Wit: Edward Robinson (mark), John Hore. Ack: 23 Aug 1729. (I1-122)

88. Deed. 21 Aug 1729. John David Rees of New Castle Co., mill wright, for the sum of 30 pounds, sold unto Griffith John of sd Co., farmer, a parcel of land containing 50 acres, situate in sd Co. This is land that Samuel Griffith, late of sd Co., was seized of in his lifetime. He then sold same unto afsd Rees and afterwards dyed. His widdow, Mary Griffith appealed to Orphans Court in 1728 that her husband did sell sd land and wished to be enabled to convey sd land unto sd Rees, which she did. This land bounded land of Thomas Griffith and land Thomas John now liveth and where as John David Rees by an Article of Agreement did warrant sd land unto Griffith John. Signed: John David Rees (mark), Mary David Rees (mark). Wit: James James jun., Robert Robertson. Ack: 23 Aug 1729. David French pro. (I1-123)

89. Deed. 21 Aug 1729. William Parsons of White Clay Creek in Co. of New Castle, yeoman, for the sum of 120 pounds, and also more especially (his) moving, sold unto Garret Garretson of same place, yeoman, his Right Title and Interest in a parcel of land containing 150 acres, situate in sd Co. It begins by a small bridge on sd Creek and bounds line of John Henzey, Evan Morgan, Morgan Morgan's island, William Woleaston's ford, William Cann's house plantation and John Lewis' ford. This land was formerly the possession of William James, late of sd Co., yeoman, but now in Possession of sd Parsons by virtue of a Deed under the hand of William Read, Esq. High Sheriff of sd Co., dated 17 June above written, together with appurtenances. Signed: William Parsons. Wit: John Henzey, Valentine Dempey. Ack: 23 Aug 1729. (I1-125)

90. Deed. 20 Aug 1729. Edward Blake of New Castle Co., cordwainer, and Anna his wife, for the sum of 130 pounds, sold unto John Lewden Sen., of sd Co., farmer, a moiety of a parcel of land called Swarton Nuleen Island, situate upon Christiana Creek, containing 300 acres in the whole, and appurtenances

24

belonging to half the island. And also one equal half of land adjoyning called
Beshye containing 100 acres and appurtenances belonging to the lower half of
sd island. Signed: Edward Blake, Anna Blake (mark). Wit: John Harris, Robert
Robertson. Memorandum: 16 Aug 1729 sd Lewden rendered unto sd Blake the
sum of 12 pounds as first payment mentioned in Article of Agreement, together
with interest due 'and at the same time required him to sign the lease for one
year which he absolutely refused to do..' Signed: Stephen Lewis, Jacobus Harris,
Robert Robertson. Ack: 23 Aug 1729. (I1-127)

91. Deed. 24 June 1729. John Cox of Georges Creek in Co. of New Castle,
yeoman, for the sum of 59 pounds, sold unto Francis Land of Christeen in sd
Co., yeoman, his plantation and tract of land situate on the north side of Georges
Creek in sd Co. It bounds the land of Charles Cox and Augustine Cox, and
contains 234 acres together with all buildings and improvements. Signed: John
Cox. Wit: Richard Grafton, Daniel Goulden. Ack: 23 Aug 1729. (I1-128)

92. Deed. 16 June 1729. Adam Short of New Castle Hun. and Co., yeoman, and
Martha his wife, for the sum of 26 pounds, sold unto Francis Land of Christeen
Creek in sd Co., yeoman, his plantation and tract of land situate in sd Hun. and
Co. It begins by Elk River Road to sd creek and bounds land late of Giles
Barret, and containg 300 acres, together with buildings and improvements. (no
signiture). Wit: James James jun., Francis James. Ack: 23 Aug 1729. David
French pro. (I1-129)

93. Appointment. 6 Oct 1729. 'George the Second by the Grace of God of Great
Brittain, France & Ireland King Defender..etc.. TO William Read of Co. of New
Castle within our Gov.. Greetings'. Sd Read appointed to be Sheriff of sd Co.
and his duties spelled out, by virtue of a Commission from Springett Penn, Esq.,
Grandson and heir at Law of William Penn.. Signed: P. Gordon. (I1-130)

94. Verification. 6 Oct 1729. 'George the Second by the Grace of God of Great
Brittain, France & Ireland King Defender..etc.. To all Judges, Justices,
Magestrates and other Officers, Freemen within Co. of New Castle, Greeting'
(Notifying them that William Read has been appointed Office Of Sheriff).
Signed: P. Gordon. (I1-131)

95. Deed. 19 Nov 1729. John Lewden Sen., of Hun. and Co. of New Castle,
yeoman, and Margaret his wife, for the sum of 70 pounds, sold unto Joseph
Parker of same place, brickmaker, the herein described lott of ground, situate in
sd Hun. and Co. This is land that James Hog, late of sd Co., yeoman, and
Johanna his wife, and George Gregg of sd Co., yeoman, and Sarah his wife
conveyed unto afsd John Lewden by an indenture dated 17 Feb 1724. This

granted unto him a half lott of ground which had on the NE the house in the tenure of Thomas Janvier, Esq.; on the NW with piece of lott in the possession of sd George Hog; on the West with the dwelling house and lott of Ann Hog and John Hog; on the SE the street. Signed: John Lewden, Margaret Lewden (mark). Wit: Edward Blake, Robt. Martin, John Rice. Ack: 23 Nov 1729. (I1-131)

96. Deed/Mortgage. 17 June 1729. Thomas Janvier of Town and Co. of New Castle, Gent., for the sum of 200 pounds, and further sum of 5 shillings confirms unto Jacob Gooding of sd Co., farmer, (in his possession) seven parcels of land situate near Reeden Island. One bounds land of Isaac Gooding and contains 17-1/4 acres of land. Also to be released land bounding line of John Hanson Jun., John Hanson Sen. and Peter Stryker, containing 34 acres. Also a parcel beginning by Augustine's Cripple at corner of sd Hanson and William Pattison, containing 150 acres. Also a parcel of land bounding John Berges marsh containing 8 acres of marsh. Also two other 8 acre parcels of marsh bounding sd Bergeo and sd Hanson's. Terms of mortgage defined. Signed: Thomas Janvier. Wit: David French, William Gordon. Ack: 23 Nov 1729. (I1-133)

97. Deed. 22 Aug 1729. Andrew Miller of White Clay Creek Hun. in Co. of New Castle, carpenter, for the sum of 123 pounds, sold unto John Allin, late of Ireland now of same place, fuller, a tract of land commonly called Northampton, situate in sd Co. containing 200 acres. It is bounded on the West by Delaware River and the north side of most southern branch of Christiana Creek toward the head. Signed: Andrew Miller. Wit: Philip James, John Deniox. Ack: 23 Nov 1729. David French pro. (I1-136)

98. Deed/Mortgage. 21 Nov 1729. Jacob Gooding of Co. of New Castle, gent., in consideration of the sum of 200 pounds, grants unto Thomas Janvier of sd Co., merchant, (in his actual possession, by virtue of an indenture of Bargain & Sale dated the day before the day herein made by sd Gooding, in consideration of 5 shillings paid by sd Janvier, for the term of one year), transferring into possession seven tracts of land and marsh lying near Reeden Island in sd Co. They contain in the whole 201-1/4 acres of land and 44 acres of marsh. Signed: Jacoab Gooding. Wit: David French, William Gordon. Ack: 23 Nov 1729. (I1-137)

99. Deed/Mortgage. 21 Nov 1729. Thomas Janvier of the Town and Co. of New Castle, gent., of one part and Jacob Gooding of sd Co., farmer, of the other part. This is whereas sd Gooding by his Indenture of Bargain & Sale bearing even date for the sum of 200 pounds did grant unto sd Janvier seven parcels of land and marsh near Reeden Island; also one third of the great swamp near the Hans

Hanson's dwelling house; also one eighth undivided marsh by sd island, together with all rights. Now sd Gooding shall pay unto sd Janvier the full sum of 200 pounds with interest on the 1st of April 1735 at the Court House in sd Town. Signed: Thomas Janvier. Wit: David French, William Gordon. Ack: 23 Nov 1729. (I1-139)

100. Deed. 19 Nov 1729. Elizabeth Waters of Co. of New Castle, widow, Admin. of James Waters, late of sd Co., weaver, dec'd., for the sum of 55 pounds, sold unto William Patterson of White Clay Creek Hun. in sd Co., yeoman, a parcel of land situate in Sd Hun. near Christana Creek containing 143 acres. It begins by an old line formerly claimed by Abraham Bickly, but now found to be vacant land and runs between lands of sd Waters and Jeremiah Shennan to Paul Garretson's old house and Still up the run, a corner of land late of Colonel John French, containing 100 acres 68 perches within pattent and without the Pattent the vacant land is 43 acres. This is land that once belonged to Christopher Sheagle, late of sd Co., yeoman, who on 2 Nov 1724 did convey same land unto afsd James Waters. Then sd Waters died and sd deed remained unpaid. Sd widow petitioned to Orphans Court to impower her to sell land and premises to pay off sd Deed which they did. Signed: Elizabeth Waters. Wit: James James Jun., John Garretson Jun. Ack: 23 Nov 1729. (I1-140)

101. Deed. 20 Nov 1729. Alexander Adams of Drawyers Creek in Co. of New Castle, yeoman, for the sum of 300 pounds, sold unto John Vance of the same place, yeoman, a tract of land lying on the north side of sd creek, called Rowles Sepulchen, containing 250 acres. This land was granted by Warrant dated 26 day 10th month 1677, and surveyed the 25 day of 1st month 1678 unto Walter Rowles, and confirmed by Patent from James Claypoole and Robt. Turner, Comm. under William Penn in 1684. Then sd land and premises was sold by deed dated 23 May 1717 from Abm. Bickley of Philadelphia, merchant unto Alexander Adams, late of sd Co., dec'd., and confirmed to afsd Adams by a release from Thomas Evans and his wife Elizabeth dated 13 Aug 1717; and by sd Adam's Last Will and Testament dated 17 April 1703, was left unto James Adams, late of sd Co.; and by sd James Adams Last Will dated 3 Dec 1706 was left unto above named Alexander Adams. Signed: Alexander Adams. Wit: John Gooding, David Stuart, Fras. Taylor. Ack: Nov 1729. (I1-142)

102. Deed. 18 Sept 1729. Jonathan Houston of Co. of New Castle, carpenter, for the sum of 30 pounds, sold unto John Lewden Sen., of sd Co., farmer, one equal half of a tract of land called Swarten Nutten? Island, situate upon Christiana Creek, containing in the whole 300 acres. Also an equal half of the land adjoyning called Beshye of Out-Lott? containing in the whole 100 acres. Signed: Johnathan Houston. Wit: Jacobus H..?, Corne. Garretson. Ack: Nov

1729. (I1-144)

103. Judgement. 4 Aug 1729. 'To all People shall come William Read, Sheriff of Co. of New Castle, Send Greetings'. Whereas John French, late of sd Co., gentleman, was seized of a parcel of land containing 300 acres, situate in sd Co. Sd French by an instrument of Mortgage, dated 3 Feb 1723, did grant unto James Richardson and Joseph England, Trustees of the General Loan Office for 6,000 pounds in Bills of Credit with sd land assigned to sd Trustees. Then sd Richardson and England were lately in Court of Common Pleas for default of payment of 10 pounds 10 shillings, part of money due on 3 Feb 1728, as per indenture. By Writ of Execution sd land was seized to pay debt of 140 pounds and damages. Sd land and premises were sold to Andrew Miller of White Clay Creek Hun. in sd Co., yeoman, for 81 pounds as the highest bidder. It bounds the land late of Doctor Spries and of John White. Signed: W. Read. Wit: H. ?onne, John Rice. Ack: Nov 1729. (I1-145)

104. Deed. 3 Oct 1729. Hugh Rainy of Co. of New Castle in Prov. of Penn., and Agnes his wife, for the sum of 170 pounds, sold unto John Parkinson of Red Lyon Hun. in Co. of New Castle, a tract of land containing 200 acres, that sd Parkinson now liveth upon in sd Hun., commonly called Grubby Neck. This is part of a larger tract of 1,100 acres of land and marsh that was granted unto George Dakenye by a Patent from William Penn, dated 28 Oct 1701, under the hands of Edward Shippen, James Logan, Griffith Owen and Thomas Story (then Proprietary Deputies). Then sd Dakeyne and his wife (no name) by Deed dated 17 Sept 1724, did grant 200 acres of sd land unto afsd Hugh Rainy. Signed: Hugh Rainey, Agnes Rainey (mark). Wit: Jos. England, Andw., Peterson, Wm. Roddye. Ack: Nov 1729. (I1-146)

105. Deed. 12 Nov 1729. Richard Reynolds of Cecil Co. in Prov. of Maryland, cordwainer, (son of Richard Reynolds late of Co. of New Castle, gent., dec'd.), William Kellum of Brandywine Hun. in sd Co., yeoman, and Mary his wife (daughter of sd dec'd.), for the sum of 16 pounds, sold unto William Cocks of New Castle Co., a piece of ground situate in New Castle on Bear St. It lays between the lott now in possession of John Jewel, and the house and lott late in the possession of Peter Johnson, dec'd. Signed: Richard Reynolds, William Kellan (mark), Mary Kellum. Wit: Arthur Ingrum, John Rice. Ack: Nov 1729. (I1-149)

106. Deed. 3 Nov 1729. Stephen Cornelius of the Co. of Chester in Prov. of Penn., husbandman, for the sum of 85 pounds, sold unto Israel Springer of Co. of New Castle in Christiana Hun., a tract of land containing 100 acres, situate in Co. of New Castle where sd Stephen formerly did dwell. It lies upon Red Clay

Creek and includes plantation house, outhouses, barns, stable, cleared land, (etc). Signed: Stephen Cornelius (mark), Willemein Cornelius (mark). Wit: Duncan Drummond, Charles Springer. Ack: Nov 1729. (I1-149)

107. Deed. 9 Nov 1729. Jacobus Cullen of Salem Co. of West Jersy, husbandman, for 18 pounds, sold unto Charles Springer, of Co. of New Castle in Christiana Hun., a tract of land containing 200 acres, whereon sd Springer now liveth, which sd Cullen bought from Andrew Friend (son and heir of Nealslarson Friend). In the year 1684 sd land was granted by Commissioners unto sd Neals, and sd Andrew conveyed same 200 acres unto afsd Jacobus ` Cullen. Then sd Cullen sold same unto his brother Reyner Cullen, who again sold the sd tract unto Charles Springer sen., but was not transferred. Sd land bounds land of Matthias Defoss. Signed: Jacobus Cullen (mark). Wit: John Hendrickson sen. (mark), John Hendrickson jun. (mark), Gregorius Cullen (mark). Ack: Nov 1729. (I1-150)

108. Deed. 15 Nov 1729. Jonas Anderson of Georges Creek in Co. of New Castle, yeoman, for the sum of 20 pounds, sold unto Derick Seebing of same place, yeoman, a parcel of land containing 193 acres situate on Georges Creek. It begins at the land of Johnen Cools. Signed: Jonas Anderson (mark). Wit: Henry Newton, Fra. Land, John Anderson (mark). Ack: Nov 1729. (I1-152)

109. Deed. 17 Nov 1729. Garret Garretson of White Clay Creek in Co. of New Castle, yeoman, for the sum of 62 pounds, sold unto Francis Land of Christeen Creek in sd Co., yeoman, his plantation and tract of land containing 150 acres, situate in White Clay Creek. It begins on the south side of the bridge and bounds lines of John Henry, Evan Morgan, Morgan Morgan, William Canns house and plantation and John Lewis' ford. Signed: Garet Garetson (mark), Esther Garetson (mark). Wit: James James Jun., William Parsons. Ack: Nov 1729. (I1-153)

110. Deed. 3 Jan 1726. Col. John French of Co. of New Castle, and Aves his wife, for the sum of 650 pounds, sold unto Captain William Battele of White Clay Creek Hun. in sd Co., a tract of land called Langshaw, containing 200 acres, situate in sd Co. It begins by Christiana Creek and bounds land of Gilles Barrett. This land was granted Thomas Langshaw by pattent, and was sold by him to Neil Cook; and by assignment of sd Deed conveyed to John Latham; and by Aaron Latham (son and heir of sd John) sold to afsd Col. John French. Signed: John French, Aves French. Wit: Will. Roddye, George Houston. Ack: Nov 1729. (I1-154)

111. Deed. 11 Feb 1729. Edward Philpot and William Nichols, both of Co. of

New Castle, yeomen, for the sum of 130 pounds, sold unto Charles Campbell of sd Co., farmer, a parcel of land and plantation (in his actual possession now by virtue of a bargain of sale bearing date before date here, for the term of one year, under the rent of a peppercorn if demanded.) This is property that sd Philpot and sd Nichols lately dwelled. It is situate in Hun. of Mill Creek in sd Co. and contains 200 acres. This is part of a larger tract of 400 acres, bounding the line of Charles Hedges. David French was empowered as Attorney. Signed: Edw. Phillpot, William Nicholls (mark). Wit: (unreadable). Ack: Feb 1729. (I1-155)

112. Deed. 18 Feb 1729. Nicholas Meers of the Town and Co. of new Castle, farmer, Exec. of the Last Will and Testament of Jane Davis, late of same place, widow, dec'd., for the sum of 51 pounds 10 shillings, sold unto Sigfredus Allricks of sd Co., yeoman, a tenement and lott of ground, situate in sd Town and Co. This is property that sd Jane Davis was seized of by virtue of sundry conveyances, and by her Will dated 5 Oct 1726, did empower sd Meers to dispose of sd property. Signed: Nicholas Meers. Wit: William Little, Isebal Duglas (mark). Ack: Feb 1729. (I1-157)

113. Deed. 27 Jan 1729/30. William Patterson of St. Georges Hun. in Co. of New Castle, farmer, and Mary his wife, for the sum of 100 pounds, sold unto Moses McKinly of same place, farmer, a parcel of land in sd Hun. and Co. containing 74 acres. This is part of a larger tract of 100 acres that sd Moses Mackinly and Elizabeth his wife, daughter to William Patterson, late of sd Co., yeoman, widdow of John Greenwater, likewise late of sd Co., dec'd., by an indenture dated 23 Aug 1722, sold unto Elias Naudin. It began by Augustine Creek and contained 100 acres with appurtenances. Then by an indenture dated 20 May 1724, sd Naudin sold same unto Samuel Mohoe. Then by an indenture dated 19 May 1727, sd Mohoe sold part of sd 100 acres, containing 74 acres, unto afsd William Patterson. Signed: William Patterson (mark), Mary Paterson (mark). Wit: Hans Hanson, Philip Guyon. Ack: Feb 1729. (I1-158)

114. Deed. 3 Feb 1729. Daniel Moore of the Town and Co. of New Castle, gent., for the sum of 31 pounds, sold unto William Shaw of same place, Esq., a lott of ground situate in sd town and Co., (now in his actual possession by virtue of an indenture dated one day before this date, for the term of one year, under the rent of a Pepper Corn if demanded). Sd lott begins on Mary's Street at lott in tenure of Joseph Hill, to Beaver Street. Signed: Dan Moore. Wit: Jno Finny, David French. Ack: Feb 1729. (I1-160)

115. Indenture. 10 Feb 1729. Edward Philpot and William Nicholls, both of Co. of New Castle, yeomen, for the sum of 5 shillings paid by Charles Campbell of

sd Co., farmer, have bargained and sold unto sd Campbell a parcel of land and plantation situate in Mill Creek Hun. in sd Co. It bounds the land of Charles Hedges along Red Clay Creek and contains 400 acres (except 200 acres of sd tract formerly conveyed to Griffith Lewis), together with all improvements. Terms from this date to the end of one whole year, paying to sd Philpot and sd Nicholls one Pepper Corn if demanded. Signed: Edward Philpot, William Nicholls (mark). Wit: Be. Campbell, David Lewis. Ack: Feb 1729. (I1-162)

116. Deed. 14 Feb 1729. Eliacum Husey of the Co. of New Castle, cooper, for the sum of 100 pounds, sold unto John Stoop of sd Co., cordwainer, a tract of land situate on the west side of the River Delaware, and south side of Christiana Creek. It bounds the land of Josiah Hussey and contains 75 acres. Together with one equal half of the marsh and cripple adjoyning containing 50 acres in the whole. Signed: Eliakim Husey. Wit: Roam Short, John Hore. Ack: Feb 1729. (I1-163)

117. Deed. 16 Feb 1729/30. Cha. Robinson of St. Georges in Co. of New Castle, cordwainer, for the sum of 67 pounds, sold unto James Briggs of same place, carpenter, a moiety of a parcel of land situate in sd Co. on the south side of Scots Run. It bounds land of James Turner and contains 30 acres. Sd land was granted by Warrant from James Bradshaw bearing date March 15 1686 to Amos Nicholls; and by sd Nicholls by deed dated 22 July 1686 was sold to Edmund Parkins; and by sd Parkins by deed dated 20 April (?) was sold to John James; and by sd James by deed dated 4 June 1697 was sold to Edward Gibbs; and by sd Gibbs by deed dated 15 Aug 1699 was sold to Matthias Errickson; and by sd Errickson by deed dated ? Jan 1700 was sold to Phillip Vepel; and by a deed from John French, Sheriff of sd Co., dated 1707, did sell same unto John Greenwater; and by sd Greenwater by deed dated 15 May 1725 did sell same unto afsd Charles Robinson. Signed: Cha. Robinson, Mary Robinson (mark). Wit: John Courtony, Mary Jack (mark). Ack: Feb 1729. (I1-164)

118. Deed. 18 Nov 1729. Griffith Thomas of Hun. of St. George in Co. of New Castle, farmer, for the sum of 51 pounds 10 shillings, sold unto Howell William of Hun. of Pencader in sd Co., farmer, two parcels of land joyned together containing 100 acres lying in sd Hun. of Pencader. The first with premises etc bounds the land of Wm Darby and John James by Georges Creek, and contains 42 acres. This was formerly surveyed and laid out for Thomas Lloyd. Sd Lloyd improved land and sold it to Evan David and confirmed the same to him by a Deed from Wm Davies and David Evans, undertakers of the tract called Pencader. Another tract contained 62 acres which was surveyed for sd Evan David on 16 July 1716 and joyned together with the first. Signed: Griffyth Thomas. Wit: John David, Thos. Evans. Ack: Feb 1729. (I1-165)

119. Deed. (no date) Daniel Barker of Christiana Hun. in Co. of New Castle, farmer, and Elizabeth his wife, for the sum of 158 pounds, sold unto Archibald Stuart of Milln Creek Hun. in sd Co., farmer, a tract of land containing 200 acres, situate in sd Co. It begins at a heap of stone on the line of William Cleany's, and bounds land of Mary Nichols and William Kirkpatrick. This is part of a larger tract containing 350 acres deprived for not improving the same according to Law that was on 13 Feb 1691, granted by Wm Markham to (unreadable) and John Goodson unto Thomas Sawyer; afterwards by sd Sawyer conveyed to Edward Mathews, and by him by deed dated 17 Nov 1702 did convey same 350 acres unto Herman Kincky of Cecil Co. Then afterwards sd Kinchy and Margery his wife conveyed same unto John Beard of Christiana Hun.; and by sd Beard conveyed unto afsd Daniel Barker. Signed: Daniel Barker, Elizabeth Barker. Wit: W. Battell, Robertson. Ack: Aug 1729. (I1-166)

120. Deed. 7 Jan 1729. Benjamin Burleigh of Co. of New Castle, tanner, for the sum of 75 pounds, sold unto James James Jun., merchant of sd Co., a parcel of land containing 6 acres, situate lying near Christiana Bridge in sd Co., beginning at sd creek. Together with tenement thereon erected and improvements etc. Signed: Benjamin Burleigh. Wit: John Welsh, Owen Meridith. Ack: Feb 1729. (I1-168)

121. Deed. 13 Sept 1729. Robert Box of Miln Creek Hun. in Co. of New Castle, blacksmith, and Phillis his wife, for the sum of 85 pounds sold unto John Champion and Archibald McDonald, both of sd Co., farmers, one messuage or tract of land situate in sd Hun. and Co., containing 114 acres 30 perches. It begins on the north side of Thomas Brackin's land, being also a corner of John Reed's land, and runs to land of Joseph Ramage and land of William Emmit. Signed: Robert Box, Phillis Box (mark). Wit: John Read, James Jordan (mark). Ack: Feb 1729. (I1-169)

122. Deed. 17 Feb 1729. George Williams of Appoquinimink Hun. in Co. of New Castle, blacksmith, and Sarah his wife, for the sum of 85 pounds, sold unto Patrick Brooks of St. Georges Hun. in sd Co., tayler, a parcel of land containing 200 acres, together with appurtenances, situate in Appoquinimink Hun. in sd Co. It lies near the head of Duck Creek on Kings Road and bounds the land of Humphrey Best. This land was granted sd Williams by an indenture dated 19 Aug 1726 from Isaac Griffith, yeoman, of sd Co. Signed: George Williams, Sarah Williams (mark). Wit: Gill Alconat, John Chusgany, Andw. Peterson. Ack: Feb 1729. (I1-171)

123. Deed. 17 Feb 1729/30. John Day and Rebecca his wife of Brandywine Creek in Co. of New Castle, yeoman, for the sum of 220 pounds, sold unto

Nathun Husey of sd Co. and New Castle Hun., weaver, a tract of land containing 110 acres, situate near sd Creek in sd Co. It bounds the lands of Mathias Defoss, William Griggs, Edward Mathers, Johanes Defoss and John Weyland. This is part of a greater tract of 400 acres that was granted by Patent under the hand of William Penn dated 5th day 6th month 1684, unto Matthew Defoss. Then sd Defoss by Deed dated 23 July 1701, granted unto his daughter, Elinor, 50 acres of sd land. Then sd Defoss made his Last Will dated 7 May 1705 in words "I give unto my youngest son Johanes, my now dwelling plantation after mine and my wifes decease..". Then sd Elinor and her husband Howard Mathews and sd Johanes Defoss by Deed dated 25 April 1709 did grant sd 50 acres of land unto afsd John Day. Then sd Johanes and Hannah his wife by another Deed dated 13 May 1714 did make over 60 acres of sd land unto afsd Day. Signed: John Day, Rebecca Day (mark). Wit: Cornelis Garetson, Henry Ewing. Ack: Feb 1729. (I1-173)

124. Deed. 3 Feb 1729. Jacob Rogers of White Clay Creek Hun. in Co. of New Castle, yeoman, for the sum of 150 pounds, sold unto Peter Clauson of New Castle Hun. in sd Co., yeoman, his plantation and tract of land containing 185 acres, situate in sd Hun. and Co. It bounds other land of sd Rogers, formerly James Claypool's, to Francis Land's land, formerly John Brewsters, to land late of Hugh Marston, standing by the side of a thick swamp. This is part of a greater tract of 200 acres granted to Edward Green by virtue of a Warrent dated 27 day 5th month 1685; then sd 185 acres conveyed by sd Green to Jacob Rogers (father of afsd), by Deed dated 17 Nov 1696. (There was a mortgage of sd Francis Land dated 27 Dec 1728 and title dispute). Signed: Jacob Rogers, Johana Rogers (mark). Wit: Cornelius Jaquet (mark), Fr. Land, Andw. Elder. Ack: Feb 1729. (I1-174)

125. Deed. 23 Dec 1729. Thomas Elliot and Benjamin Gibbs, Exec., of the Estate of Andrew Elliot of Co. of New Castle, yeoman, lately dec'd., for the consideration of 50 pounds (12 pounds pd to sd Andrew in his lifetime), grant unto John Elliot of sd Co., yeoman, 100 acres of land, situate in White Clay Creek Hun. in sd Co., upon Christiana Creek. It bounds land late of John Ogle, and land late of William Semples. This is land that afsd Andrew Elliot was seized of and which he granted to his brother John Elliot by agreement. Then sd Andrew died before agreement effected, and in his Last Will and Testament he appointed his brother, afsd Thomas, and afsd Benjamin Gibbs to be his Exec. They complete transfer of property by order of Orphan's Court. Signed: Thomas Elliot, Benj. Gibbs. Wit: Thomas Willing, Gilbt. Falconat. Ack: Feb 1729. (I1-176)

126. Deed. 6 Jan 1729. Phillip James of Pencader Hun. in Co. of New Castle,

yeoman, for the sum of 78 pounds, sold unto Francis Land of Christiana Creek in sd Co., yeoman, the eastward half of two tracts of land situate on sd Creek in sd Co., containing 200 acres. One tract bounds the land of Thomas Wattson on the north, on the south is sd creek, on the east by land of Howel James, and on the west by land of James James. The other tract begins at the fence of David Thomas to the fence of sd James James. Each tract contains 200 acres. Signed: Philip James, Anne James. Wit: James James jun., Francis James. Ack: Feb 1729. (I1-177)

127. Deed. 10 Nov 1729. William Davies of the Township of Cadnor in Co. of Chester in Prov. of Penn., gentleman, and David Evans of Pencader Hun. in Co. of New Castle, yeoman, for consideration herein mentioned, grants unto Thomas John of sd Hun. and Co., yeoman, 1,156 acres of land situate in New Castle Co. It bounds lands of Henry David and Jno. Morgan. This is part of a tract of land granted sd Davies and Evans by William Penn by an agreement dated 15 Oct 1701. The condition is that sd Thomas John is to pay all money due with interest on sd land (terms). Signed: Wm Davis, Da. Evans. Wit: Thos. Evans, William Williams, Daniel James, John Lewis. Ack: Feb 1729. (I1-179)

128. Deed. 4 Feb 1729. Robert Street of Co. New Castle, plaisterer, and Elizabeth his wife, Admin. of All which were of John Kent, late of sd Co., cordwainer at the time of his death, for the sum of 75 pounds, sold unto John Land of sd Co., bricklayer, a lott of ground and improvements, situate in sd Co. It bounds land late of Edward Blake along the street to the Court House, to the lott late of Josep Hed, to lott late of Wessell Alricks. This is property that sd Kent was seized of by virtue of an indenture dated 12 June 1723 under the hand of sd Blake, late of same place. Sd Kent then dyed intestate, and Administration for his estate granted to sd Elizabeth by John French, Esq., then Register for the Probate of Wills (etc). At Orphans Court on 17 June last, sd Elizabeth (then married to sd Robert Street) was ordered to sell sd lott and improvements at publick vendue unto afsd John Land for the sum of 75 pounds, as the highest bidder. Signed: Robert Street, Elizabeth Street. Wit: Wm. Read, Bourn. Ack: Feb 1729. (I1-180)

129. Deed. 18 Dec 1729. George Holt of Red Lyon Hun. in Co. of New Castle, bricklayer, for the sum of 25 pounds, and for other divers good causes and considerations, him thereunto moving, sold unto Cornelius Truex, of sd Hun. and Co, yeoman, a parcel of land situate in sd Hun. and Co., containing 39 acres. This is part or one third of a tract which was purchased from Darby Caffy by Charles Miles, containing 118 acres. Then sd Miles by his Last Will did bequeath sd land to be equally divided between his three sons, Zacharius Miles, Azarius Miles and Caleb Miles. Then sd Zacharius by deed dated 6 Jan 1725 did

convey his part of sd land unto Peter Hanson, yeoman, of sd Co., lately dec'd., who by his Last Will dated 5 April 1729 did bequeath same unto his son-in-law, afsd George Holt. Signed: George Hoult. Wit: John Willson, Fra. Land. Ack: Feb 1729. (I1-181)

130. Deed. 17 Nov 1729. Peter Watkins of Pencader Hun. in Co. of New Castle, taylor, for the sum of 40 pounds herein have granted unto Evans Evans of New Castle Hun. in sd Co., husbandman, all his right and title and claim unto 202 acres of land situate in Pencader Hun., together with all singular. This is part of a tract formerly granted by Wm Penn unto David Evans by Article of Agreement dated 15 Oct 1701. Land surveyed and transferred over by Deed from William Davies and David Evans unto Edward Thomas. Then by Deed from sd Thomas unto William Williams; and from sd Williams by Deed dated 4th day of this Inst. unto afsd Peter Watkins. Signed: Peter Watkins. Wit: Wm Williams, Jane Williams. Ack: Feb 1729. (I1-183)

131. Deed. 10 Feb 1729/30. John Willson of Co. of New Castle, yeoman, for the sum of 20 pounds, grant unto Edward Edwards of sd Co., a tenement or tract of land containing 48 acres, 144 perches, situate in the Welsh Tract. This is part of a great tract taken up by William David's Company by virtue of a warrant from the Proprietors. It bounds the land of Thomas Griffith, Henry Davis, Thomas Johns and sd Wilson and called the land whereon sd Thomas Johns now dwelleth. Signed: John Willson. Wit: Edmund Shaw, Isaac Willson, Josiah Willy. Ack: Feb 1729. (I1-184)

132. Deed. 29 Jan 1729. John Beard, late of Chester Co. in Prov. of Penn, blacksmith, and Rebecca his wife, for the sum of 242 pounds, sold unto Daniel Barker of Christiana Hun. in Co. of New Castle, yeoman, a tract of land containing 350 acres, situate in sd Hun. and Co., near Red Clay Creek. This sd land was surveyed and laid out by Thomas Pierson unto William Stockdale, but sd Stockdale was deprived of it for not improving it according to regulations, and was afterwards granted by Wm Markam, Robert Turner and John Goodson, Commissioners, unto Thomas Sawyer on 13 Feb 1691. Then afterwards by sd Sawyer conveyed unto Edward Mathews; sd Mathews by Deed did confirm same unto Harman Kencky on 17 Nov 1702 (confirmed under the hand of William Tonge, then Clerk of Court). Then from sd Kencky granted to afsd John Beard by Deed in 1725. Signed: John Biard. Wit: N. Battell, Robertson. Ack: Feb 1729. (I1-185)

133. Deed. 10 Sept 1729. William Cooper of Co. of Chester, Prov. of Penn., yeoman, eldest son and heir of Oliver Cooper, late of Co. of New Castle, yeoman, dec'd., and Mary his wife, John Cooper of the Township of Bradford in

Co. of Chester, yeoman, the other son of sd dec'd., and Charity his wife, Hugh Blackwell of sd Co. of New Castle and Elizabeth his wife, the daughter of sd dec'd., for the sum of 140 pounds, sold unto Adam Buckley of Co. of New Castle, yeoman, a messuage tenement and 160 acres of land, situate in Co. of New Castle. This is part of two contiguous parcels of land that Samuel Carpenter, William Markham and Robert Turner, former Commissioners of Wm Penn by a Patent dated 15 Feb 1792 (1692?) did convey unto sd Oliver Cooper containing 130 acres in the whole, for the yearly Quit Rent of one English silver penny for each acre. Then by Warrent in 1692, sd Cooper was also granted 200 acres; and by his Last Will dated 26 May 1697, he did devide one half of his land to his children to be equally divided between them (the eldest to have a double share), the other half to his wife, Rebecca, during her widowhood and after to go to children equally. Sd Rebecca has since dec'd and her land and premises was vested in afsd William, John and Elizabeth. And whereas Edward Slippen, Thomas Story and James Logan (under direction of heirs) directed Isaac Taylor to survey and divided. Sd William got 175 acres. One part began at Naaman's Creek and bounded land of John Buckly, Jeremiah Cloud, John Drew and contained 160 acres. Signed: William Cooper, Mary Cooper (mark), John Cooper, Charity Cooper (mark), Hugh Blackwell, Elizabeth Blackwell. Wit: Thomas Babb, Edward Whiteaker. Ack: Feb 1729. (I1-187)

134. Deed. 17 March 1729. John Land of New Castle Co., bricklayer, and Rebecca his wife, for the sum of 75 pounds 15 shillings, grant unto Robert Street of sd Co., plaisterer, and Elizabeth his wife, a house and lott of ground situate in Newcastle. It bounds the lott late of Edward Blake on the street towards the Court House, and the lott late of Joseph Hill and lott late of Wessell Alricks. This is the same property that sd Street's by an indenture dated 4 Feb last, did grant unto afsd John Land. Signed: John Land, Rebeccah Land. Wit: Wm Read, Bourn. Ack: Feb 1729. (I1-189)

135. Deed. 8 April 1729. Abigal Aldricks of Co. of New Castle, spinster, for the sum of 330 pounds, sold unto Peter Aldricks of sd Co., farmer, (in his actual possession now by virtue of a Bargain dated day next before the day of this, for the term of one year), one moiety of a piece of land called Greoningen, lying on the NE side of Augustines Creek. This is land that Edmond Andros by his Deed dated 25 March 1676 did grant unto Peter Aldricks, late of sd Co., dec'd., gentleman, grandfather to afsd Abigail. Sd Peter made his Last Will dated 23 June 1697, and bequeathed sd land to his son, Hermanus Aldricks; who dyed intestate leaving afsd Abigal, Peter and Mary (since dec'd) equal shares. The land bounds land of Ann Walts on sd Creek and contains 280 acres. Signed: Abigal Aldricks (mark). Wit: Henry Goodien, Fra. Taylor. Ack: Feb 1729. (I1-190)

136. Deed. 22 Jan 1729. "To all Xtian People, greetings", John Vangezell of New Castle in sd Co., ta?ler, for the sum of 115 pounds, sold unto Richd Grafton of sd town and Co., a piece of marsh situate on the north end of sd town. It bounds marsh's of Thomas Eliats, John Sylbee and Daniel Mercie, and contains 3-3/4 acres 20 perches. And also two lotts of ground situate in sd town. One lott lies between the dwelling house of sd Vangezell and dwelling house of the late George Hogg, containing 35 foot breadth in the front, 35 feet in the back and 308 feet in lenth. The other lott lies on the bank of the Delaware River. It bounds sd Hogg's bank lott and James Millers bank lott. Both together with houses etc. Signed: Jno Vngezell. Wit: W. Battell, Margaret Bitler. Ack: Feb 1729. (I1-192)

137. Deed. 17 March 1729/30. William McMechen of Co. of New Castle, farmer, for the sum of 149 pounds, grants unto Thomas Craighead of sd Co., gentleman, a tract of land and premises, so mortgaged to him by sd McMechen. This is whereas sd Creaghead by his indenture of release dated 21 Feb 1729, for consideration, did sell unto sd McMechen a parcel of land and premises, situate in sd Co., containing 402 acres, beginning at Pock Creek, a branch of White Clay Creek. This with a condition that if sd Creaghead should pay unto sd McMechen the full sum of 133 pounds together with interest before 21 Feb 1732. Signed: William McMechen. Wit: David French, John Legate. Ack: Feb 1729. (I1-193)

138. Deed. 17 March 1729/30. Thomas Creaghead sen., of Co. of New Castle, gentleman, for consideration of natural love and affection which he beareth, and also in consideration of the sum of 60 pounds, grant unto Thomas Creaghead jun., son of afsd, of sd Co., yeoman, a parcel of land situate in sd Co. containing 150 acres. This is part of a larger tract of land whereon sd Creaghead Sen. now dwelleth. This is part of a larger tract containing 402 acres, that is bounded by Pock Creek, a branch of White Clay Creek. Signed: Thom. Creaghead. Wit: David French, John Legate. Ack: Feb 1729. (I1-194)

139. Deed. 17 March 1729. John Chambers of White Clay Creek Hun. in Co. of New Castle, yeoman, and Deborah his wife, for consideration of the natural love and affection which they bear unto Richard Chambers, their son of same place, and also for the sum of 5 shillings, grant unto him land now in his actual possession. It begins by sd creek and bounds the land of William Chambers and contains 130 acres. These are actually two tracts of land. One on the tracts contain 90 acres and is situate on the SW side of sd Creek, opposite of the land commonly called 'Hopyard Land'. It was purchased by afsd John Chambers from John Richardson, late of Christiana Hun. in sd Co., Esq., by an instrument of release dated 24 Feb 1717, and acknowledged in Court August term 1726.

The second tract contains 50 acres and is adjacent to the first. It was purchased by sd Chambers from James Couts, late of sd Co., merchant, by his Attorney Robt Reynold, by an indenture dated 14 June 1720. Signed: John Chambers (mark), Deborah Chambers. Wit: James James Jun., Joseph Thomas, ? Bourn, H. Gonne. Ack: Feb 1729. (I1-196)

140. Deed. 17 March 1729. John Chambers of White Clay Creek Hun. in Co. of New Castle, yeoman, and Deborah his wife, for consideration of the natural love and affection which they bear unto William Chambers their son of same place, and also for the sum of 5 shillings, grant unto him land now in his actual possession, containing 130 acres. (Same land as described in Record 139). Signed: John Chambers (mark), Deborah Chambers. Wit: James James Jun., Joseph Thomas, H. Honne, ? Bourn. Ack: Feb 1729. (I1-198)

141. Deed/Mortgage. 18 Sept 1729. Johnathan Houston of New Castle in same Co., carpenter, for the sum of 130 pounds, sold unto John Lewden Sen., of sd Co., farmer, land in his actual possession by virtue of a bargain & sale for one whole year by indenture dated the day before the day next. This land is a moiety of a tract of land commonly called Swarten Nullen Island containing 300 acres in the whole; and also a moiety of land adjoyning called Beshye containing 100 acres in the whole, situate upon Christiana Creek. Signed: Johnathan Houston. Wit: Corne. Garretson, Jacobus Hains. Ack: Nov 1729. (I1-200)

142. Deed. 10 March 1729/30. John Garretson of Christiana Hun. in Co. of New Castle, farmer, and Jane his wife, in consideration of the Natural Love and Affection which they beareth toward their daughter, Mary, wife of William Patterson of sd Co., mariner, and for the sum of 143 pounds, grant unto them a parcel of land containing 143 acres situate in sd Co., part of a larger tract. It bounds the lands of Thos McDuff, William Parson, Catherine Garretson, land formerly of Thos Daykne but now of John Reynold, and land of Arthur Faris. Signed: John Garretson (mark), Jean Garitson. Wit: Jeremiah Prat, Petr Dollawn. Ack: Feb 1729. (I1-202)

143. Deed reward. 5 Jan 1667. Richard Nicholls Esq., Prin. Comm. from His Maj. New England Gov. Gen. under His Royal Highness James Duke of York.. etc. to all Sendeth Greeting: Whereas there is a parcel of meadow valley or marsh ground situate in Delaware River near the fort containing 150 acres, not long since in the tenure of Alexander D'Hinosa, bounded by the land of Gerret VanSworing, the plantation commonly called Landery, and by the land lately belonging to John Webber. Now it being sufficiently known that sd D'Hinosa then Govr. was in Hostility agst his Majesty for which reason all his Estate stands confiscated. Know ye that by authority to me given and for consideration

of good service performed by Capt. John Carr in storming and reducing the fort at Delaware, I do confirm and grant unto sd Carr the afsd piece of land and all singular the appurts. Signed: Richard Nicholls. Examined by me Matthias Nicholls. (I1-204)

144. Deed. 7 April 1729/30. Rebecca Dyre, Admin. of all that was of James Dyre, late of New Castle Co., Gent., dec'd., and Bridget Garretson of sd Co., single woman, for an unnamed amount, grant unto Elizabeth Garretson of sd Co., widow, a tract of land and premises called the Home Plantation. This is property that sd Elizabeth Garretson by an indenture of Release dated 1 Feb 1723 did grant to afsd James Dyre. It joined upon the publick landing at Apoquiniminck and contained 200 acres together with houses etc. Condition was payment to sd Dyre the sum of 50 pounds for the use of sd Bridget and Halliwell Garretson. Signed: Rebecca Dyre, Bridget Garretson. Wit: David French, John Rice. Ack: Feb Term. (I1-204)

145. Deed. 10 Feb 1729. Sigfridus Alrichs of Co. of New Castle, yeoman, and Jacobus Alrichs of Town of New Castle in sd Co., yeoman, for the sum of 20 pounds, grant unto Peter Alrichs of sd Co., farmer, a parcel of land situate in sd Co. It bounds the lands of sd Sigfridus and Jacobus Alrichs and contains 220 acres of land. Also a parcel of marsh containing 32-1/2 acres. Together with tenements thereon erected. Signed: Jacobus Alrichs, Sigfridus Alrichs. Wit: David French, John Legate. Ack: Feb Term 1729. (I1-205)

146. Deed. 7 April 1730. David Miller of Co. of New Castle, gent., for the sum of 40 pounds, sold unto William Roddey of sd Co., farmer, the plantation whereon the sd Roddey now liveth, situate in sd Co. This is part of a larger tract of land called Poplar Neck. It bounds the lands of Peter Anderson, sd Miller, John Garretson and John Reynolds, and contains 150 acres. Signed: David Miller. Wit: David French, Thomas Creaghead. Ack: Feb Term 1729. (I1-207)

147. Deed. 10 March 1729/30. John Garretson of Christina Hun. in Co. of New Castle, farmer, and Jane his wife, in consideration of the natural love and affection which they beareth their daughter, Dorrety, wife of Arthur Ferais of sd Co., blacksmith, and for the sum of 100 pounds, grant unto them a tract of land situate in sd Co. It bounds the lands of John Renolds, Peter Anderson, Henry Land and Catherine Garretson, and contains 143 acres. Signed: John Garretson (mark), Jean Garson (sp). Wit: Jeremiah Pratt, Peter Dollan. Ack: Feb 1729. (I1-208)

148. Deed. 21 March 1729/30. William Battell, Admin. of all which were of Nicholas Callender of New Castle, dec'd., who dyed interstate, for the sum of 18

pounds, sold unto Peter Dollan of same Co., yeoman, a parcel of ground situate on the south side of Christiana Bridge in sd Co. It begins at a stake some distance from the door of John Lewden sen.'s dwelling house, down line to sd Lewden's then house, and contains 1-1/4 acres 25 perches. Together with buildings etc. This is whereas sd Callender at the time of his death was indebted to sd Wm Battell and to divers others in sundry sums of money -- more than all the personal Estate of sd Callender which came into custody of sd Battell. Whereas by virtue of an order of the Court of Common Pleas in Feb Term 1724, sd Battell was empowered to sell real estate of sd Callender to satisfy debts. Signed: W. Battell, admin. Wit: Jeremiah Pratt, Arthur Faries, Wm Paterson. Ack: Feb Term 1729. (I1-210)

149. Land sale. (no date) Francis Land of Christiana Creek in Co. of New Castle, for the sum of 30 pounds paid by James Merewether of the Town & sd Co., currier, do release unto sd Merewether, in his possession, all interest in a lott of land and premises. Signed: Fr. Land. Wit: Saml. Land, Christian Land. (I1-211)

150. Deed. 10 Feb 1729. Peter Alrichs, farmer, and Sigfredus Alrichs, yeoman of New Castle Co., for the sum of 20 pounds, sold unto Jacobus Alrichs of the town of New Castle in sd Co., yeoman, a parcel of land situate in sd Co. It begins on the east side of King's Road and bounds land of sd Peter and contains 110 acres of land and 16 acres of marsh, together with all messuages etc. Signed: Peter Alrichs, Sigfredus Alrichs. Wit: David French, John Legate. Ack: Feb Term 1729. (I1-212)

151. Deed. 10 Feb 1729. Peter Alrichs of Town & Co. of New Castle, yeoman, and Jacobus Alrichs, for the sum of 20 pounds, sold unto Sigfredous Alrichs, yeoman, a parcel of land containing 126 acres, situate in sd Co. It begins at King's road at a corner of the land late of the Widow Alrichs to land of sd Peter Alrichs. Signed: Peter Alrichs, Jacobus Alrichs. Wit: David French, John Legate. Ack: Feb term 1729. (I1-213)

152. Deed 28 March 1730. Elizabeth Gerritson of Co. of New Castle, widow and Admin. of all that were of Henery Gerritson, late of sd Co. dec'd, (one of the daughters of Edmund Cantrell, late of sd Co., gent., dec'd.), for the sum of five pounds, sold unto Edmund Garretson of sd Co. yeoman, two tracts of land in sd Co. This is whereas sd Edmund Cantrell in his lifetime, before 1679, came into possession of a tract of land situate in sd Co. on the west side of Delaware River and SE side of Blackbird Creek, containing 837 acres, and called by the name of Shrewbarry. Also another tract of land in sd Co. called the Cliff, bounded north on Apoquinaminck Creek, west by branch of Sasafras Creek, containing about

1,500 acres. Then sd Cantrell erected several messuages and plantations on sd land. In his last Will dated 28 Oct 1679, "he ordered three plantations on Apoquinaminck Creek be kept going forward & furnished both with stock and hands. The lower plantation bought of Thomas Snelling and Mr Lars shall be for the wife of my son Richard & his heirs; the midlen plantation shall be for the use of my daughter, Johannah & her heirs; the uppermost plantation on Sasafras Creek to be kept for the use of my daughter, afsd Elizabeth & her heirs. But if any die without heirs then the land belongs to survivors. Whereas sd Johannah died without heirs, her share went to sd Elizabeth. Signed: Elizabeth Gerritson. Wit: Jacobus Williams, George Monroe. Ack: Feb term 1729. (I1-215)

153. Deed. 9 Feb 1676/7. John Lars of New York, merchant, sold unto Justa Andries of New Castle, innholder, all his right on two lotts of ground containing about 11 acres, with a dwelling house thereupon, also some pieces of timber for building, situate in the town of New Castle on the strand of the river. They are bounded on the west by lott of Hendrick Janvier, on the east by lott of Catherine Hanry. Sd Lars bought sd house & lotts of sd Justa in two half deeds. It contained 131 acres, part of the land granted by a Patent 16 June 1671 for 500. Half of this Thomas Snelling hath, the other 250 includes the above 131 acres. Signed: John Lars, Justa Anders?. Wit: Thos. Williston, Eph. Herman Clark. "Know all men that I, John Lars make over unto Capt. Edmond Cantwell.. all right in this Bill of Sale this 17 Feb 1678/9" Wit: John Tyes, Thos Iplry. (I1-217)

154. Deed. 1729/30. John Ball of White Clay Creek in Co. of New Castle in Territory of Pensylvania, blacksmith, Sendeth Greeting. Whereas there is a tract of land, part of a tract of 400 acres called New Design, situate on the west side of Delaware River & west side of branch of White Clay creek, commonly called Mill Creek. It bounds the lands of sd Ball, Joseph Cook and John Smith. Sd John Ball sell this land to James Bell, husbandman, of the same place. Signed: John Ball. Wit: James James Jun., Sa. Evans. Ack: Feb term 1729. (I1-218)

155. Deed. 1 April 1730. Paul Jaquat of New Castle Co, farmer, for the sum of five shillings, grant unto Peter Jaquat, yeoman, and Anthony Jaquat, blacksmith, both of sd Co., two parcels of land and marsh situate on Christiana Creek in sd Co., containing about 192 acres. This is part of a tract bounding land late of Jacob Clawson to land of late called Jaquats Creek containing 290 acres. Signed: Paul Jaquat (mark). Wit: Cornelius Jaquat (mark), John Rice. Ack: Feb Term 1729. (I1-219)

156. Deed. 10 March 1729/30. John Garretson of Christiana Hun. in New Castle Co., farmer, and Jean his wife, in consideration of the natural love & affection

they beareth toward their daughter, and for the sum of 100 pounds, grant unto Catherine Garretson, seamstress, a tract of land situate in sd place. It is part of a larger tract bounding land formerly of Henery but now of John Nenotol, land of Arthur Fairis, land formerly of Thos. Daykne but now of John Renolds, land of William Patterson, land formerly of Thos. Midciff but now of William Parsons, containing 153 acres. Signed: John Garretson (mark), Jean Garretson. Wit: Jeremiah Pratt, Pettr. Dollar. Ack: Feb term 1729. (I1-221)

157. Deed. 17 March 1729. George Yeates of New Castle Co., Gent., and Mary his wife, of the one part, and Henery Usher, yeoman, of sd Co., of the other part. Whereas William Penn, Esq., by Patent did grant unto John Harminson, late of sd Co., carpenter, a tract of land called Knottenburgh, situate on the west side of Delaware River, back in the woods towards the upper part of Red Lyon Hun.... (end of document, no signatures). (I1-223)

158. 'Know all men that I, Henry Peirce of Chester Co., Exec. & Admin of Francis Smith, late of Cecil Co. in the Province of Maryland am held and firmly bound unto Robert Eyre of ye sd Co. in ye full just sum of 200 pounds to be paid to sd Eyre. Sealed with my Seal & dated 16 Feb 1721-1/2. Condition is that sd Peirce and sd Eyre agree that that sd Eyre shall have all that part of a tract of land on Elk river called Krowlewood, formerly belonging to Francis Smith. It begins by ye Shallop Cove.' Signed: Henry Peirce. Sealed with their mark: John & Elizabeth Walis. (I1-223)

159. 'Know all men that I, Robert Eyre of New Castle, carpenter for the sum of 5 shillings paid by Thomas Calvill of Cecil Co. in ye Province of Maryland, merchant, have assigned to sd Calvill all my right title & demand of ye within Bond. Witness this 23 March 1729-30'. Signed: Robt Eyre. Wit: William Shaw, John Rice. 'Recd this 7th day of July 1730 from Henry Peirce, Exec. of Francis Smith & Sarah his wife & Henry Pierce jun., as Deed of conveyance for 200 acres.' Signed: Tho. Colvill. Wit: W. Battell. (I1-224)

160. Deed. 17 March 1729. John Garretson Sen., of New Castle Hun. in ye Co., farmer, & Jean his wife, for the sum of 100 pounds, sold unto Jeremiah Pratt of ye town of New Castle, cordwainer, and his heirs begotton upon ye body of Elizabeth his wife, formerly Elizabeth Garretson, a lott of ground situate in sd Town where sd Pratt now liveth. It bounds Market St. This lott formerly belonged to Thomas Spry, dec'd, who by his Last Will left and bequeathed (same) unto Anneky Egbert and Abiah Egbert, daughters of Barnet Egbert. Sd Abiah Egbert intermarried with afsd John Garretson Sen., party to this being survivor by ye sd Will of sd Spry. Signed: John Garretson (mark), Jean Garretson. Ack: Feb term 1729. Witness: David French. (I1-224)

161. Deed. 17 March 1729. George Yeats of New Castle Co., gent., and Mary his wife, for the sum of 60 pounds, sold unto William Read of sd Co., merchant, half of a tract of land, containing 285 acres herein described. This is whereas William Markham, late of Philadelphia, gent., by an indenture dated 4 Feb 1694, did grant unto Jasper Yeats, late of Chester in Prov. of Penn., merchant, a tract of land and marsh then known by the name of Markham's Hope, situate on the west side of Delaware River just below the town of New Castle in sd Co., containing about 1,078 acres. Sd Deed was certified by James Claypoole, then Clerk. And whereas Richard Carr, son & heir to John Carr, late of sd Co., dec'd gent., and George Otdfield then intermarry'd with Febronella, the late widow of sd dec'd, did endorse on the back of sd Deed forever quit claim unto sd Jasper Yeats. (Release dated 18 May 1697). Then sd Yeats at the time of his death, sd land granted to his sons George Yeates and Jasper Yeates, then vested & settled in William Trent, Joshua Carpenter, Andrew Hamilton of Philadelphia, gent. Then sd Trent, Carpenter and Hamilton in 1724 did convey unto Robert Gordon, Gent., part of sd land. It bounded the land of Thomas Fenton and Mill Creek and contained 570 acres. Then sd Gordon conveyed same unto afsd George Yeates on 23 Aug 1728. Signed: Geo Yeates, Mary Yeates. Wit: James James Jun., Charles Killgore. Ack: Feb 1729. (I1-227)

162. Deed. 17 March 1729. Alexander White of Co. of Chester, Gent., for the sum of 104 pounds 10 shillings, sold unto William Patterson of Co. of New Castle, yeoman, a piece of land situate on the north side of Christiana Creek upon a point called Eagle Mill. It bounds the marsh of John Lewden and contains 3-1/2 acres containing messuage, land and improvements. Signed: Alex White. Wit: David French, John Legate. Ack: Feb 1729. (I1-231)

163. Deed. 17 March 1729. William Patterson, one of the Exec. of the Last Will of Samuel Patterson, Mariner, dec'd., of Co. of New Castle, for the sum of 104 pounds 10 shillings, sold unto Alexander White of Co. of Chester, farmer, a piece of land situate on the north side of Christiana Creek containing 3-1/2 acres. This is whereas sd Samuel Patterson by his Last Will dated 20 April 1729 did appoint his wife, Jane Patterson together with William as Exec. Whereas sd Samuel at the time of his decease was indebted to several persons in sundry sums & sd William did pay debts of 29 pounds 6 shillings 4 pence over the Estate. Court ordered land sold to pay debt. Signed: Wm Patterson. Wit: David French, John Legate. Ack: Feb Term 1729. (I1-232)

164. Deed. 17 April 1730. Francis Land of Christiana Creek in New Castle Co., yeoman, for the sum of eighty pounds paid by David Miller of same place, do sell unto him a tract of land containing 300 acres with improvements. Signed: F. Land. Wit: David French, Thomas Clayhead. (I1-233)

165. Deed. 21 March 1730. George Ross of Town & Co. of New Castle, gent., and Catharine his wife, and John VnGezel of same place, sadler, and Mary his wife, for the sum of 20 pounds, confirm unto Gertrude VnGezel of sd town, widow, of all that messuage, tenement and lott of ground situate in sd town. It is bounded by Front Street on the bank of the River Delaware and contains in breadth 25 feet, in length 70 feet. Signed: Geo Ross, Jn VnGezell, Ann Catharine Ross, Mary Vangezell. Wit: W. Battell, Wm Becks. Ack: Feb Term 1729. (I1-234)

166. Deed. 27 Dec 1729. John Elliot of Georges Creek in Co. of New Castle, yeoman, for the sum of 55 pounds, sold unto James Stewart of Christiana Creek in same Co., yeoman, a certain Plantation or parcel of land situate in White Clay Creek Hun. in sd Co. It begins on the north side of Christiana Creek, thence by the line of the land of late John Ogle to land of late William Semples, thence down sd creek to the mouth of Giles Barrch run, also a corner of John Stephenson's land, thence up sd run to beginning, containing 100 acres. Signed: John Elliot (mark), Mary Elliot (mark). Wit: W. Battell, Fr. Land. Ack: Feb Term 1729. (I1-235)

167. Deed. 5 April 1730. William Patterson of New Castle Co., mariner, and Mary his wife, for the sum of 130 pounds, sold unto William Parsons of sd Co., farmer, a parcel of land containing 143 acres. It bounds the lands of Thomas Midriffs, (now William Parsons), Catharine Garretsons, Thomas Dakeyns (now John Renolds) and Arthur Fairis. This is whereas John Garretson of sd Co., yeoman, by virtue of sundry conveyances was seized of a tract of land containing 400 acres. Then sd Garretson and Jane his wife by deed dated 10 March 1729/30 for consideration, did sell 143 acres of sd land to afsd William Patterson. Signed: W. Patterson, Mary Patterson. Wit: James James, Jun., George Hillhous. Ack: Feb Term 1729. (I1-236)

168. Deed. 18 May 1730. John Vanlewenigh and Henry Vanlewenigh, both of St. Georges Hun. in New Castle Co., yeomen, for the sum of 60 pounds, sold unto Thomas Noxon of same place, planker, a tract of land situate on the north side of Appoquinamink Creek. This is land that sd Vanlewenigh's purchased from Koelef Dehaus, late of sd Co. It bounds the land of afsd Noxon and Richard Hambley, and contains 200 acres. This tract commonly called 'Black Walnut Landing'. Signed: John VanLeuvenigh (mark), Henry VanLeuvenigh (mark). Wit: Joseph Fisher, Hannah Hynson. (I1-238)

169. Deed. 27 April 1730. Abigal Alrich of Co. of New Castle, Super Delaware Semstress, for the sum of 20 pounds, sold unto Edward Blake of Town & Co afsd., a lott of ground situate on the SW side of sd town. It is bounded on the

east with Front St., on the west with lott now in the tenure of Joseph Hill, on the NE with Eliaum Hussey's lott, on the SW with lott of Fredrick Alrich. It contains 40 feet front, 300 foot Amsterdam wood measure. Lott with premises and improvements. Signed: Abigal Alrich (mark). Wit: Jn VnGezel, John Hore. Ack: Feb Term 1729. (I1-238)

170. Deed. 21 April 1730. Francis Land of Christiana Creek in Co. of New Castle, yeoman, for the sum of 60 pounds, sold unto William Derickson, a tract of land and premises now in his possession. Signed: Fr. Land. Wit: Jacob Bebber, John Land. (I1-241)

171. Gift Deed. 10 March 1729/30. "Henry Bevan of Pencadder Hun. in Co. of New Castle, farmer, send greetings. For the paternal Love good will & Affection which I have & do bear unto my Son, David Bevan of same place, Batcherlour, do grant unto him 150 acres of the land whereon I now live. After my decease wholey to him - the Stock Grain and Household & Implemts of Husbandrye of all my Goods.." Signed: Henry Bevan (mark). Wit: Thos Evans, Simon James, Tom Williams. Memorandum: Land delivered by Turf & Twig, as also a horse, a Calf in behalf of the rest of the living creatures, a Chair in behalf of the household stuff, etc. (I1-242)

172. Deed. 17 Dec 17--. Robert Hutchinson of Co. of New Castle, Planter, for a valuable sum, do grant unto John Hussey a certain tract of land lying in sd Co., containing 196 acres. It is bounded by the road of Christiana Bridge, land of John Lewden and land of sd Hutchinson. Signed: Robt Hutchinson. Wit: Thos Homan, Benja. Swett. (I1-242)

173. Deed. 17 June --. John Hussey for the sum of 30 pounds, sold unto John Wilson, the above mentioned (#172) tract of land and premises. Signed: John Hussey. Wit: Richard Halliwell, Jno Donaldson. (I1-243)

174. Deed. 30 Dec 1729. James Stewart of Christeen Hun. in Co. of New Castle, yeoman, for the sum of 30 pounds, and for other considerations him there unto especially moving, sold unto John Elliot of George Hun. in sd Co., yeoman, a tract of land situate on the north side of Christeen Creek in sd Co. It bounds the land late of John Ogles, to the mouth of Giles Barrets Run, being a corner of John Stephensons land to beginning, containing 100 acres. Terms are 30 pounds with interest from the 20th day of February next ensueing at or upon the 30th day of December 1732. Signed: James Stewart, Mary Stewart. Wit: W. Battell, Fran. Land. Ack: Feb Term 1729. (On side: New Castle 10 May 1749 Thomas Quant who intermarried with Mary the widow of sd John Elliot ack. to have received full satisfaction of within mortgage. Signed: Rich. William, rec.) (I1-

243)

175. Deed. 22 Dec 1729. William Battell, Adm. of all which were of Edward Williams, late of New Castle Co., carpenter, for the sum of 16 pounds, sold unto Jacob VanBebber of same place, merchant, a lott of ground and premises, late of sd Williams, situate at St. Georges in sd Co. It bounds the lott of Philip Truax. Signed: W. Battell. Wit: Mor. Morgan, Jno VnGezel. (I1-245)

176. Deed. 20 April 1730. Edward Blake of the Town of New Castle, cordwainer, for the sum of 37 pounds, sold unto John Richardson of Christiana Hun., merchant, a messuage lott of land. This is whereas sd Blake by virtue of release from Samuel James and Sarah his wife, dated 11th day of May 1723, and as son heir of Edward Blake his father, dec'd., by deed from Robt Turner and Susanna his wife dated 4 June 1687, became seized of the tenement house & lott with I now dwell in. It is bounded by lotts of sd Richardson, Fredase Alreck, Robart Diger, Nichlas Mars and Alicam Husey, and contains in length 92 feet. Signed: Edward Blake. Wit: Gisberd Walleven (mark), Robt. Richardson. Ack: Feb Term 1729. (I1-246)

177. Deed. 8 May 1730. Jonas Anderson of St. Geroges in Co. of New Castle, yeoman, for the sum of 3 pounds, grant unto John Daniel Toney of Red Lyon Hun. in sd Co., miller, all his right to a piece of land situate in St. Georges. It bounds the land of John Priestly to the Mill Damm and contains 56 acres. Signed: Jonas Anderson. Wit: Owen Carthy, Jacob Bebber. Ack: Feb term 1729. (I1-247)

178. Deed. 21 May 1730. William Parker of Philadelphia City, merchant, for the sum of 80 pounds, sold unto Jacob VanBebber Jun., of Red Lyon Hun. in New Castle Co., inholder, a piece of land situate being near to Georges Mill. It begins at a corner stake to the end of John Gills house by the street to the end of the house built by Thomas Griffith, cooper or his shop, to fence of sd Gills, containing one lott of land. Signed: William Parker. Wit: Valentin Dushene, Robertson. Ack: Feb Term 1729. (I1-248)

179. Deed. 2 April 1730. John Hill of New Castle Hun. & Co., yeoman, for the sum of 47 pounds, sold unto Francis Land of Christian Creek in sd Co., yeoman, his plantation & tract of land called Putney, and premises situate on the south side of Christian Creek. It bounds land of sd Land and land late of Giles Barrett, and contains 185 acres. Signed: John Hill, Rose Hill (mark). Wit: James James Jun., Daniel James. Ack: Feb Term 1729. (I1-249)

180. Deed. 20 May 1729. Benjamin Shurmer of Co. of Kent on Delaware, gent.,

for the sum of 20 pounds paid by Thomas Jackson of ye Co. of New Castle, yeoman, as for other good causes me hereunto moving, release unto sd Jackson in his full & peaceable possession that piece of land situate on the north side of the road of Black Birds Creek in New Castle Co. It bounds the lands late of John Cowgill called Springfield, the lands now in possession of sd Jackson, and land belonging to Sapiens Russell, containing 100 acres. Also that other piece of land situate on the NW side of the sd Jackson, binding with lands of sd Cowgill on the present road that now passes over a bridge on sd Creek a little below sd Cowgills Tan house to sd Russell, containing 50 acres. This land was laid out to sd Shurmer by Warrant from the Commissioners of Property. Signed: Benjamin Shurmer. Wit: Jno Rees, John Sunt, Dall Rees. Ack: Feb Term 1729. (I1-251)

181. Deed. 18 May. Jonas Anderson of St. Georges in New Castle Co., yeoman, for the sum of 150 pounds, sold unto Hendrick Booram, yeoman, of same place, a parcel of land situate in sd Co. containing 193 acres and premises, situate on the west side of Scott's Run. This land, part of 582 acres, was granted by Court of sd Co in 1681, in favour of Derrick & Mandrick Robertson and surveyed unto Jn Wright, conveyed to Justa Anderson, and by the heirs of sd Justa conveyed to John French by Deed dated April 20 1708. It was resurveyed and confirmed unto sd French by a Patent under the Great Seal of this Gov. dated 8 Sept 1709; and by the sd John French's Deed dated 30 Jan 1710 was confirmed to Urian Anderson, father to sd Jonas Anderson by his Last Will & Testament. 193 acres of land was left to sd Jonas together with equal share of marsh lying on St. Georges Creek near sd Urian's home Plantation. This marsh now in actual possession of sd Henry Booram, together with houses etc. Signed: Jonas Anderson. Wit: Owen Carthy, Jacob VBebber. Ack: Feb Term 1729. (I1-252)

182. Deed. 12 April 1730. John Vance of Drawyers Creek in Co. of New Castle, yeoman, for the sum of 141 pounds, sold unto Francis Land of Christana Creek in sd Co., yeoman, a plantation & tract of land called Rowles Squaliker, situate in sd Co. on the north side of Drawyers Creek, containing 250 acres. And also another 140 acres of land, part of a tract called Lackford Hall, situate on the north side of sd creek. This tract contained 620 acres, and bounded as 'exprest' in a Patent from Gov. Penn dated 26 March 1684. Signed: John Vance, Hanah Vance (mark). Wit: James James Jun., John Britten. Ack: Feb Term 1729. (I1-254)

183. Deed. 4 May 1730. Jeroone Dushene of Georges Hun. in Co. of New Castle, yeoman, for the sum of 124 pounds, sold unto Francis Land of Christiana Creek in sd Co., yeoman, his plantation & tract of land, situate in Georges Hun. It bounds the land late of Mouns Anderson, Kings Road and land of John Prieshy, and contains 223 acres, together with all buildings and

improvements. Signed: Jeroon Dushene, Mary Dushene (mark). Wit: James James Jun., Henry Hughes. Ack: Feb Term 1729. (I1-255)

184. Deed. 28 April 1730. Moses McKenley of Georges Hun. in Co. of New Castle, yeoman, and Mary his wife, for the sum of 41 pounds 6 shillings, sold unto Francis Land of Christiana Creek in sd Co., yeoman, their plantation & tract of land situate in Georges Hun. It bounds the lands of Samuel Mohoes and William Paterson, to Augusteen Creek, and contains 100 acres of land, and 18 pches. Signed: Moses Muknly, Mary Muknly (mark). Wit: James James Jun., Henry Hughes. Ack: Feb Term 1729. (I1-257)

185. Deed. 9 April 1730. William Parsons of Mill Creek Hun. in Co. of New Castle, yeoman, for the sum of 137 pounds 12 shilling 8 pence, sold unto Francis Land of Christiana Creek in sd Co., yeoman, two tracts of land. One is a plantation & tract of land situate on the east side of Christiana Creek. It bounds land of Gilles Barret and contains 200 acres of land. The other tract begins at stake of Thomas Mitcalfs, now William Parsons line, also a corner stake of Catherine Garretsons land, thence to corner stake in Thomas Dayeyne's, now John Reynolds line, to stake of sd Garretson's and Arthur Fairises, and contains 143 acres of land. Signed: William Parsons, Margaret Parsons (mark). Wit: James James Jun., Owen Meredith. Ack: Feb Term 1729. (I1-258)

186. Deed. 30 May 1719. Wessell Alricks of Salem in Province of West New Jersey, jeweler, for the sum of 125 pounds, sold unto John Bryan of New Castle Co., farmer, a tract of land situate near the River Delaware adjoining to the land of Jasper Yeates Esq. It begins by the Maryland Road, being a corner of Major Donaldson's land and runs along King's Road, to land of Widow Torneur alias Alrick's land to sd river, and contains 257 acres of land and marsh. Signed: Wessell Alricks. Wit: Jasper Yeates, Richard Halliwell, Joshua ?orce. Ack: 18 Aug 1719. Signed: Tho. Duncon. Memorandum Witnessed by Wm Guest, Nicholas Callender, ?old FitzGerald. (I1-260)

187. Deed. 20 May 1730. Edward Blake of New Castle Co., cordwainer, and Anna his wife, for the sum of 14 pounds, grant unto Eliankim Hussey of sd Co., cooper, in his actual possession by virtue of an indenture dated the day next before this day, for the term of one year, under the rent of one peppercorn, a certain piece of ground in sd Co. It bounds the land of Edward Frost, Robert Street, Henry Williams, and contains in length 58 feet, and in breadth 31-1/2 feet. These premises are part of a larger lott of land formerly belonging to Robert Turner & Susanna his wife of Philadelphia, gent. Sd Turner's conveyed same to Edward Blake, late of New Castle, father of afsd Edward Blake, by indenture dated 24 June 1687. Sd Blake died seized of premises leaving issue

only one son and one daughter, to wit, afsd Edward and Sarah Blake, who has since intermarried with Thomas James of Philadelphia, marriner. Sd James and Sarah his wife did release their right to premises by instrument dated 11 May 1723. Signed: Edward Blake, Anna Blake (mark). Wit: Henry Williams, Bourn. Ack: May Term 1730. (I1-262)

188. Deed. 10 April 1730. John Gregg of Christiana Hun. in Co. of New Castle, yeoman, and Elizabeth his wife, as well for the natural Love and Affection which they bear to their son, William Gregg of same place, yeoman, and for five shillings, grant unto him a parcel of land and premises containing 200 acres, situate in sd Co. This is land that Edward Pennington, by his Deed Poll dated 17 Aug 1702, did in the name of Latitia Penn, grant unto afsd John Gregg, under the yearly quit rent of two shilling beginning the first day of March forever. (Recorded Book B: page 319). Signed: John Gregg, Elizabeth Gregg (mark). Wit: Simon Hadly, Joseph Robinson, John Hogg. Ack: May Term 1730. (I1-264)

189. Deed. 28 May 1729. Edward Blake of New Castle Hun. in sd Co., cordwainer, and Anna his wife, for the sum of 20 pounds, sold unto Henry Williams of sd Co., sadler, a piece of property, which is one fifth of herein described lott. It bounds the house and lott of Abraham Jessop, the house now or late of Abigal Alrichs and the lott of Eliacum Hussey. It contains in breadth 40 feet, in length 58 feet. This is whereas Robert Turner, late of Philadelphia, merchant, and Susanna his wife did by indenture dated 24 June 1687, grant Edward Blake, late of sd Co., father of afsd, a house and lott of ground situate in the Town of New Castle. It contained in length 187 feet and in breadth 58 feet. Then sd Blake Sen. made his Last Will dated 15 Nov 1695 and bequeathed property to afsd Edward Jr. Signed: Edward Blake, Anna Blake (mark). Wit: Eliakim Hussey, Wm Read. Ack: May Term 1730. (I1-265)

190. Deed. 10 May 1730. Isaac See of St. Georges Hun. in Co. of New Castle (son and heir of Isaac See, dec'd, of same place), farmer, and Ann his wife, for the sum of 110 pounds, sold unto Isaac See, son to Peter See of same place, farmer, a tract of land containing 130 acres, situate in sd Co. This being part of a larger tract containing 173 acres 108 perches that Jonas See by virtue of sundry good conveyances became seized of. So seized, sd Jonas dyed intestate leaving issue one son, two daughters. Court ordered sd Isaac is entitled to two-fourths of sd tract. And whereas Randal Mullin hath intermarried with Ester See (one of the daughters), they did convey unto sd Isaac one-fourth of sd tract, (dated 29 July 1728). Signed: Isaac See (mark), Anne See (mark). Wit: Cha. Robinson, John Hore. Ack: May term 1730. (I1-267)

191. Deed. 16 Nov 1729. John Goforth of Georges Hun. in Co. of New Castle, tanner, for the sum of 35 pounds, sold unto Jacob Vanbebber of sd Hun. & Co., merchant, a messuage or tenent and lott of ground situate near Georges Creek in sd Co. Also two water lotts, bounding Miln Dam. Also one orchard Lott, beginning at the lott now or late of John Gill containing one quarter of an acre. Together with all singular. Signed: John Goforth. Wit: William Anderson, Mary Vandike. Ack: May Term 1730. (I1-270)

192. Appointment. 3 Oct 1730. George the Second by the Grace of God of Great Britain.. TO William Read of Co. of New Castle, Greetings. Know as reposing special Trust in your Loyalty (etc) we have appointed you to be Sheriff of sd Co... we authorize and command you to perform all acts... according to the Constitution of our Gov. Witness: Patrick
Gordon, Esq. by virtue of Commission from Springet Penn, Esq., Grandson and Heir at Law of William Penn, Esq. Signed: P. Gordon. Wit: Robt. Gordon, David French. (I1-272)

193. George the Second by the Grace of God of Great Britain... To all Judges, Justices, Magistrates and other Officers Freemen within Co. of New Castle, Greetings. Where we have appointed William Read.... so long he shall well behave himself... we therefore command you that sd Read be aiding and assisting in all things that the Office of Sherif do or may do... Witness: Patrick Gordon. (I1-272)

194. Power of Attorney. 13 July 1725. "Know all men that I, Richard Edwards of Philadelphia, do ordain in my place by trusty Friend Martha Edwards of ye same place my true and lawful Attorney granting full power in my name." Signed: Richard Edwards. (I1-273)

195. Deed. 18 May 1730. Johannes Defoss of Co. of New Castle, yeoman, and Hannah his wife, for the sum of 55 pounds, sold unto Nathan Maddox of sd Co., taylor, a plantation and tract of land situate in sd Co. It bounds the lands of John Day and George Gregg, and contains 45 acres. This is part of a larger tract of 400 acres that Mathias Defoss, the late father of sd Johannes, in his lifetime was seized of. He made his Last Will dated 7 May 1705 and in these words: "I do give unto my youngest Son Johannes my now dwelling Plantation that is after my wife's decease the plantation with the housing etc and half the wood land." Signed: Johannes Defoss (mark), Hannah Defoss. Wit: David French, William Whillet. Ack: May Term 1730. (I1-273)

196. Deed. 12 May 1730. Cornelius Peterson of Swanhook in Co. of New Castle, yeoman, and George Peterson of Georges Hun. in sd Co., yeoman, sons

of George Peterson, late of Swanhook, yeoman, dec'd, for the sum of 160 pounds, sold unto William Derrickson of Brandywine Hun. in sd Co., yeoman, in his actual possession now by virtue of indenture for the Term on one whole year, a plantation piece of land situate on the north side of Georges Creek in sd Co., containing 210 acres. Also a point of marsh running into sd plantation. Also 14 acres of mowable marsh lying in the marsh lately belonging to Cox's dwelling plantation. This land was granted to sd Peterson Sr. from Charles Cox, John Cox and Augustine Cox by indenture dated 2 July 1719, and in his Last Will dated 8 June 1725 did bequeath the same to his two sons, afsd Cornelius and George. Sd sons on 11 May 1727 (Lib H pp 198/9) did grant same unto Francis Land. Sd Land by another release 28 April 1730 did release same unto afsd Derrickson. Signed: Cornelius Peterson (mark), George Peterson. Wit: H. Gonne. John Rice. Ack: May Term 1730. (I1-275)

197. Deed. 8 April 1730. Cornelius Williams of Appoquinamink Hun. in Co. of New Castle, yeoman, and Mary his wife, for the sum of 200 pounds, sold unto Henry Pecker of Red Lyon Hun. in sd Co., yeoman, a tract of land and premises containing 300 acres, situate on the NW side of a branch of Appoquinimink Creek, commonly called Sasafraas Creek. This is land that William Check late of sd Co. was granted from the Proprietor by Warrent dated 25 Sept 1684. Thomas Pearson, surveyed and laid out the sd 300 acres. Then sd Check, conveyed same to Isaac Wheeldon of Blackbird Creek. Then Joseph Wheeldon, son & heir of sd Isaac, granted the same to afsd Cornelius Williams by Deed dated 19 Sept 1711. Signed: Cornelius Williams (mark), Mary Williams (mark). Wit: Andrew Peterson, Wm Peterson. Ack: May term 1730. (I1-278)

198. Judgement. 21 May 1730. William Read, Sheriff of Co. of New Castle send Greetings. Whereas Robert Box, late of Miln Creek Hun. in sd Co., blacksmith, was seized of a tract of land in sd place containing 114 acres 30 perches and premises by Deed, and sd Box did grant same unto Joseph England and John Richardson, gent., surviving trustees of the Gen. Loan Office by mortgage dated 5 June 1729. Sd England & Richardson were before the Justices to collect 25 pounds for sd mortgage due 10 April this year, as well 50 pounds 10 shillings. Sheriff commanded to seize property & at Publick Vendue did sell sd land & premises to Josiah Ramage of Miln Creek as the highest bidder for the sum of 80 pounds 15 shilling. It bounds the land of Thomas Bracking, also a corner of the late John Read, other land of sd Ramage, land late of William Emmit and land late of Thomas Brackin. Signed: Wm Read Sheriff. Wit: David French, John Gooding. Ack: May Term 1730. (I1-280)

199. Deed. 22 April 1730. Jasper Yeates of Co. of Kent in Prov. of Maryland, sadler, for the sum of 12 pounds, sold unto John Potts of the Town & Co. of

New Castle, (farmer?/turner?), a lott of ground situate in sd Town & Co. It
bounds the shop of Philip Janvier on Land Street. This is whereas Richard
Halliwell of sd Town & Co, gent., who by sundry conveyances was seized of
land in sd place, and in his Last Will dated 4 Dec 1716 did bequeath unto his
four God Children (viz) Jasper Yeates Jun., William Bedford, John Ross and
Prizcilla Robinson, to each of them a Lott of ground. Signed: Jasper Yeates.
Wit: Edward Died?, John Lef?ver, ?arth ?dmarsh. Ack: May Term 1730. (I1-
282)

200. Deed. 30 April 1730. John Mannce of St. Georges Hun. in Co. of New
Castle, and Anne his wife, for the sum of 28 pounds, sold unto Henry Hook of
sd Co., gent., a tract of land containing 43 acres 67 perches, situate in sd Co. It
bounds the lands of Owen McCarty, Peter See and Isaac See. This is part of the
land that Isaac See was seized of by sundry conveyences, containing 173 acres
108 perches. Then sd See died Intestate leaving issue one son and two
daughters. Whereas afsd John Mannce hath intermarried with afsd Anne, one of
sd See's daughters. Signed: John Mannce, Anne Mannce (mark). Wit: John
Mance, Ann Mannce (mark), John Thomas (mark), John Cross, Moses Mikinly.
Ack: May Term 1730. (I1-283)

201. Judgement. 19 May 1730. William Read, Sheriff of Co. of New Castle,
send Greetings. Whereas Isaac Miranda was lately in the Court before Justices
did recover against Jerome Dushane of St. Georges Hun. and Mary his wife,
Admin. of the Goods & Chattles which were of Samuel Griffith, late of sd Co.,
merchand, dec'd., at the time of his death the sum of 139 pounds 13 shillings 9
pence which sd Griffith was adjudged as damages. Now by writ of firi facias
dated 22 Nov 1729, sheriff demands property of sd Griffith to pay debt. Seized
and taken was a piece of land situate near St. Georges Creek containing 150
acres, another 53 acres, another piece containing 39 acres and one piece of
marsh containing 3 acres. Also a messuage, being the late dwelling house of sd
Samuel Griffith, and a lott of ground belonging to it containing in breadth 45-
1/2 feet, in length 300 feet. This to a value of 313 pounds. Property sold to
Thomas Smith, merchant, as the highest bidder of all ye above for the sum of
120 pounds 5 shilling. The messuage property bounds land late of Anthony
Green, since of Margaret Williamson, now in possession of Elizabeth Waters,
land of Nicholas Meer and land of James Claypoole, dec'd.. Signed: Wm Read,
Sheriff. Wit: H Gonne, Bourn Ack: Aug term 1730. (I1 285)

202. Deed. 1 June 1730. Jacob Rogiers of White Clay Creek Hun. in Co. of New
Castle, yeoman, for the sum of 76 pounds 14 shillings, sold unto Francis Land
of Christeen Creek in sd Co., yeoman, all his plantation and tract of land
containing 151, situate on the south side of White Clay Crk.. It bounds the land

of Hugh Morrison, land late of Jacob Rogeirs Sen. and land of John Parker. Signed: Jacob Rogeirs, Johanna Rogeirs (mark). Wit: James James Jun., Jean Garison, ? Dollan. Ack: Aug Term 1730. (I1-287)

203. Deed. 8 May 1730. Isaiah Phipps of Pencadder Hun. in Co. of New Castle, yeoman, & Elinor his wife, for the sum of 20 pounds, sold unto Francis Land of Christeen Creek, yeoman, all their plantation and tract of land containing 127 acres, situate in sd Hun. & Co. It bounds the land of David Price and land lately sold by sd Phipps to David Merick. Signed: Isaiah Phipps (mark), Elinor Phipps (mark). Wit: Simon Hadly, Benj ?red. Ack: Aug Term 1730. (I1-289)

204. Deed. 11 Aug 1730. Nicholas Vandike of Georges Creek in Co. of New Castle, yeoman, for the sum of 70 pounds, sold unto Francis Land of Christeen Creek, yeoman, a tract of land containing 150 acres, situate in Red Lyon Hun. in sd Co. It begins on a branch of Georges Creek and bounds the lands of Thomas Morgan and John Gill. Signed: Nicholas VanDike. Wit: James Anderson, Brian McDonald. Ack: Aug Term 1730. (I1-290)

205. Deed. 8 May 1730. Garret Dushene of Apoquinenemy Creek in Co. of New Castle, yeoman, for the sum of 118 pounds, sold unto Francis Land of Christiana Creek, yeoman, his plantation and tract of land, containing 232 acres of fast land, and 112 acres 138 perches of marsh, situate on the north side of Apoquinemy Creek, called High Hook land. It bounds land of sd Dushene and land late of Isaiah Gooding, and marshes late of Samson Atkinson and Peter See. Signed: Garret Dushen, Elizabeth Dushen. Wit: James James Jun., John Thomas. Ack: Aug Term 1730. (I1-291)

206. Deed. 20 May 1730. William McDonald of Miln Creek Hun. in Co. of New Castle, yeoman, and Mary his wife, for the sum of 210 pounds, sold unto William McMechen of same place, a tract of land and premises in sd Hun. lying on the west side of White Clay Creek. It bounds the land of George Mankin, land late of Joseph Robison, land late of Morten Justis, land late of Justa Justis, to Red Clay Creek, and contains 253 acres. This is part of a larger tract that Bryan McDonald was granted by Patent under the hand of Griffith Owen, Thomas Story and James Logan, dated 8 Oct 1706, for a tract containing 593 acres. In sd Bryan's Last Will, dated 23 Feb 1707, he did bequeath unto his son, afsd William, 253 acres of sd land and premises that he then lived on. Signed: Wm McDonald, Mary McDonald (mark). Wit: Richard McDonald, James McMechen. Ack: Aug Term 1730. (I1-293)

207. Note. 10 Aug 1724. Know Ye that Thomas Rodgers of ye City of New Castle, merchant, and Thomas Rodgers of Boston in New England, merchant,

are firmly bound unto Patrick Reilly of ye City, Chyurgeon in the sum of 28 pounds. Conditions are that both or either of the Rodgers pay sd Reilly the sum of 14 pounds on or before 10 Sept next. Signed: Samuel Rodgers, Thos Rodgers. Wit: Rowl FitzGerald, Jos Fox. (I1-296)

208. Deed. 20 Aug 1730. Isabella Clement, widow, and Jacob Clement her son, both of Cecill Co. in Prov. of Maryland, planter, of one part, and William Williams of Pencader Hun. in Co. of New Castle, tanner, and Jean his wife, of the other part. Witnesseth that sd Williams and Jane his wife, for the sum of 70 pounds, paid by sd Clements, sell unto them a tract of land situate in Pencader Hun. It bounds the line of the Welsh Tract, and contains 232 acres 40 perches. This is part of a tract of 30,000 acres granted by William Penn on 9 Oct 1701, unto William Davis and David Evens. They then subdivided and surveyed by George Daikins, made over by deed dated 28 Dec 1721 unto Rees Evans; and from him by Deed unto William Rees, blacksmith; since transferred by Deed dated 10 Jan 1728 from sd William Rees and Mary his wife to afsd William Williams. Signed: Wm Williams, Jane Williams. Wit: Thos Strode, David Bevans. Ack: Aug Term 1730. (I1-297)

209. Deed. 18 Aug 1730. John Gooding of St. Georges Hun. in Co. of New Castle, gent., for the sum of 6 pounds, sold unto Enoch Cornwell of ye same place, carpenter, a lott of land situate near Georges Bridge in sd Co., between ye Cornwells house and ye street. It bounds the land of Jacob Bebbers and William Goforth. Signed: John Gooding. Wit: John Dunning, John Peterson. Ack: Aug Term 1730. (I1-298)

210. Deed. 25 May 1730. Daniel Meruer of ye Town & Co. of New Castle, carpenter, and Anne his wife, for the sum of 32 pounds, sold unto James Armitage of White Clay Creek Hun. in sd Co., yeoman, a lott of land in sd Town & Co., together with buildings etc. It bounds the lands of Thomas Smith, Hermanas Alricks and Francis Land. This was a lott of vacant land that Wm Penn did grant unto John Cann by order dated 5th day 7th mo 1682. It bounded land of James Williams and Sesquehanna St. Then sd Cann conveyed sd lott unto Peter Goddin by deed dated 10 Sept 1692. Then sd Goddin by his Last Will and Testament dated 20 Dec 1724 devised sd lott unto his wife Anne, now the wife of afsd Daniel Meruer, and his children. As all children dec'd but Elizabeth, and she with her husband William Wright did convey their part of sd lott unto sd Meruer by Deed. Signed: Dan Meruer (mark), Anna Maruer (mark). Wit: ? Gordon, David French. Ack: Aug Term 1730. (I1-299)

211. Deed. 15 Aug 1830. Samuel Johnson of White Clay Creek Hun. in Co. of New Castle, yeoman, and Annabella his wife, for the good will and natural

54

affection that they have unto their son, Samuel Johnson Jun., of same place, carpenter, and for the sum of 5 shillings, grant unto him a tract of land and premises. This is land they bought of David Loyd and Grace his wife, by deed dated 17 May 1720, excepting 7 acres out of sd tract sold to George Finley. It bounds lands of John King, Neal Cook and John Crawford and contains 103 acres. Signed: Samuel Johnson, Anabela Johnson (mark). Wit: John Ogle, Naphtilie Johnson, James Armitage. Ack: Aug Term 1730. (I1-301)

212. Deed. 11 Aug 1730. John Gooding of St. Georges Hun. in Co. of New Castle, gent., for the sum of 6 pounds, sold unto William Goforth of same place, yeoman, a lott of land situate near Georges Bridge in sd Co. It is situate between land of sd Goforth and the street and bounds the lott of Enoch Cornwell and Benj. Swett. Back runs 40 feet and 110 feet long. Signed: John Gooding. Wit: John Dunning, John Peterson. Ack: Aug Term 1730. (I1-302)

213. Deed. 17 Aug 1730. Stanley Vandike of St. Georges in Co. of New Castle, yeoman, and Margaret his wife, for the sum of 72 pounds, sold unto John McCoole, yeoman, a plantation and tract of land containing 130 acres, situate in sd Co. It begins by the road that goes from ye Meeting House to Jno Asltons to Doctors Swamp and land of John Anderson. This is part of a tract of 330 acres formerly laid out to Richard Scagg of Kent Co in Maryland by virtue of a warrent dated 6 Nov 1675. Then by Scraggs Deed dated 6 Oct 1707 was sold to Hermanas Alricks; and by Mary Alricks, widow and relict of sd Hermanas by her Deed dated 28 March 1709 did sell unto John Reece. Then sd Reece by his Deed dated 16 Nov 1713 sold same unto James Anderson, dec'd.; and by Francis Taylor and Mary his wife and John Anderson, son and daughter of sd James, the sd 130 acres confirmed unto afsd Stanley Vandike by Deed dated 6 May 1715. Signed: Standley Vandike, Margaret Vandike (mark). Wit: David Stewart, Fra Taylor. Ack: Aug Term 1730. (I1-303)

214. Deed. 12 Aug 1730. Jacob Bebber of St. Georges in Co. of New Castle, merchant, and Mary his wife, for the sum of 150 pounds, sold unto Valentine Dushene of same place, yeoman, his plantation and tract of land situate in same place. It begins at the foot of the new bridge and runs by Georges Creek and bounds the lands of Ann Anderson and James Anderson and contains 193 acres. This is part of a tract that formerly belonged to Uriah Anderson, dec'd, late of sd Co. and by his Last Will left to his surviving children to equally divided. In complience, the afsd 193 acres was the share unto Mouns Anderson by instrument dated 18 May 1719, from under hands and seals of James, John, Uriah, Jonas, John Priestly and Mary his wife. Then by sd Mouns Anderson's Deed dated 23 Nov 1721 unto afsd Jacob Bebber. Signed: Jacob Bebber, Mary Bebber. Wit: Hans Hanson, Thos Noxon. Ack: Aug Term 1730. (I1-305)

215. Deed. 26 June 1730. Richard Grafton of New Castle Co., merchant, for the sum of 38 pounds, sold unto John Richardson of Christiana Hun., a piece of land situate in same place. It is bounded by the lott late of Robert Robson on the south, on the west Otter St., on the north with house & lott of sd John Richardson and on the east with Beaver St. This is land that sd Grafton received by a Deed Poll, dated 19 May past, under the hand of William Read, Sheriff of sd Co. Signed: Richard Grafton. Wit: Robt Gordon, William Shaw. Ack: Aug Term 1730. (I1-307)

216. Deed. 14 May 1730. William Bennet of Co. of Chester in Prov. of Penn., yeoman, for the sum of 12 pounds, sold unto Thomas Yeatman of Co. of New Castle, yeoman, a piece of land situate part in Chester Co. and part in New Castle Co. It bounds the other land of sd Yeatman and sd Bennet and contains 20 acres. This is part of a larger tract of 100 acres that was granted sd Bennet by the James Logan and Rees Thomas. This is whereas Wm Penn, by patent dated 23 Oct 1701 granted his daughter Latitia 15,500 acres; sd Latitia intermarried with William Aubery of City of London merchant, who by their Letter of Attny dated 8 Feb 1713 authorized James Logan and Rees Thomas in their behalf to convey sd land. Sd Attny's by their indenture dated 19 June 1727 did grant unto afsd William Bennet two pieces of land - part in Chester Co. and part in New Castle Co. Signed: William Bennet. Wit: Simon Hadly, John Evans Jun. Ack: Aug Term 1730. (I1-308)

217. Deed. 8 Aug 1729. William Gregg of Co. of New Castle, yeoman, and Margery his wife, for the sum of 4 pounds, grant unto Samuel Grave of same place, yeoman, a piece of land containing 4-1/4 acres bounding both their lands. This is part of a larger tract of 200 acres. This is whereas Latitia Penn by her letter dated 21 Oct 1701 authorized Edward Pennington & James Logan on her behalf to sell her land; and they did convey 200 acres of it unto John Gregg, who did grant same unto his son, the afsd William Gregg. Signed: William Gregg, Magery Gregg. Wit: Simon Hadly, Henry Dixon. Ack: Aug Term 1730. (I1-310)

218. Judgement. 19 May 1730. William Read, Sheriff of Co. of New Castle send Greetings. Whereas Isaac Miranda at Court of Common Pleas on 21 May 1729, did recover against Jerome Dushene of Georges Hun. and Mary his wife, Admin. of Goods that were of Samuel Griffith, late of sd Co., merchant, dec'd, the sum of 139 pounds 13 shill & 9 pence. Goods & chattles of sd Griffith seized. Taken was two piece of land situate near Georges Creek, one about 150 acres, the other 53 acres. Also one other piece near same creek containing 39 acres, also one piece of marsh about 3 acres; also a messuage which was the late dwelling house of sd Griffith; and a lott belonging to it measuring 45-1/2 feet by

300 feet. At pubic sold to Anthony Dushane of Georges Hun., yeoman, as the highest bidder the 39 acres and marsh for the sum of 12 pounds 2 shill 6 pence. The 39 acres bound land of Thomas Morgan & land late of John Gill. Signed: Wm Read, Sheriff. Wit: H. Gonne. T. Bourn. Ack: Aug Term 1730. (I1-311)

219. Judgement. 19 May 1730. William Read, Sheriff of Co. of New Castle. (This is another part of remaining property of Samuel Griffith in suit by Isaac Miranda, record #218). Remaining unsold was the 150 acres, the 53 acres and the messuage. Sd Sheriff sold 150 acres unto Nicholas Vandike of Georges Hun., yeoman, as the highest bidder for the sum of 90 pounds. This land bounds land late of Thomas Morgan and land of John Gill. Signed: Wm Read, Sheriff. Wit: Jerome Dushane, David Howel (mark). Ack: Aug Term 1730. (I1-314)

220. Judgement. 19 May 1730. William Read, Sheriff of Co. of New Castle. (This is another part of remaining property of Samuel Griffith in suit by Isaac Miranda, records #218 and #219). Remaining unsold was the 53 acres and the messuage. Sd Sheriff sold the 53 acres unto David Howell of the Hun. of Pencader, yeoman, as the highest bidder for the sum of 24 pounds. This land bounds the land late of Bellarby Crums. Signed: Wm. Read, Sheriff. Wit: Jeroon Dushene, John Rice. Ack: Aug Term 1730. (I1-316)

221. Judgement. 19 May 1730. William Read, Sheriff of Co. of New Castle send Greetings. Whereas Thomas Littell, late of Appoquinominik Hun. in sd Co., yeoman, was seized of 300 acres of land in same place and under mortgage, dated 16 Aug 1727, unto John French, Joseph England and John Richardson, Gent., Trustees of the Gen. Loan Office. Default of sd mortgage to have been paid 16 Aug 1729. Sd Sheriff seized sd land with improvemnts and sold land and premises to Robert Miller for the sum of 40 pounds. This was part of a larger tract containing 400 acres. It bounded land late of James Beswicke, Michael Offley, William Skar and Thomas Bell. Signed: Wm Read, Sheriff. Wit: H. Gonne, Sigf. Alrich. Ack: Aug Term 1730. (I1-318)

222. Judgement. 19 May 1730. William Read, Sheriff of Co. of New Castle send Greetings. Whereas John French, late sd Co., gentleman dec'd., was seized of several lotts of land, bounded on the south by the burying ground, to west with Otter St., to north with house and lott of John Richardson, Esq., and to east with Beaver St. The premises under mortgage dated 17 July 1723, under his hand confirmed unto John Richardson and Joseph England, Trustees of the Gen. Loan Office. Sd Trustees lately before Justices for default of payment and recovery. Sd Sheriff seized land and conveyed to Richard Grafton, merchant, and Robert Robertson for the sum of 38 pounds 10 shill. Signed: Wm Read, Sheriff. Wit: William Shaw, Ro. Gordan. Ack: May Term 1730. (I1-320)

223. Judgement. 19 May 1730. William Read, Sheriff of Co. of New Castle send Greeting. Whereas by Patent dated 20 June 1716 by Philhard Hill, Isaac Norris and James Logan, Prop. deputies, granted unto John French, late of sd Co., a piece of fast land and marsh containing 11 acres. Sd French under mortgage dated 16 July 1723, unto John Richardson and Joseph England, gentlemen, Trustees of Gen. Load Office. Then sd French conveyed unto Robert Eyre a piece of sd 11 acres. Sd French then died and mortgage not released. Trustees in court to recover. Sd Sheriff for the sum of 30 pounds sold to Richard Grafton sd 11 acres. Signed: Wm Read, Sheriff. Wit: Thomas Janvier, Robt. Gordon. Ack: Aug Term 1730. (I1-322)

224. Deed. 13 Aug 1730. Mary Laicon of Co. of Philadelphia, widow, and John Rambo, yeoman, of same place, Exec. of the Last Will of Neils Laicon, late of ye No. Liberties of City of Phila., dec'd., of the first part; John Seeds of Christeen Hun. in Co. of New Castle, blacksmith, and Isaac Hershe of White Clay Creek in same Co., millwright, of the second part; and Solomon Creson of sd City of Phila., turner, of ye third part. Witness for the sum of 43 pounds to parties of the first part, they confirmed with the consent of sd Seeds and Hershe, do by the direction of sd Neill Laicon in his Last Will, grant and sell unto afsd Solomon Creson a messuage, water corn mill and a tract of land situate on the west side of Red Clay Creek. It bounds the land of Justa Justice and contains 147 acres. This is part of 290 acres taken in execution of the suite of Hipollitus Lefeaver, yeoman, against one Richard Rumsey for 36 pounds, by writ of late Queen Ann directed to John French, High Sheriff, sold by Deed dated 12 Aug 1708. Sd Lefeaver granted 294 acres unto sd Niels Laicon by Deed dated 16 July 1711. By sd Laicon's Last Will dated 3 Dec 1721, he devised Exec. to sell land. They sold but did not convey same unto afsd John Seeds, who likewise sold same unto afsd Isaac Hershe who erected a messuage and mill upon sd land. Signed: Mary Maicon (mark), John Rambo, John Seeds, Isaac Hershe. Wit: H. Hamilton, J. Gordon jun., Robert Dyer, Mor. Morgan. Ack: Aug Term 1730. (I1-324)

225. Judgement. 19 May 1730. William Read, Sheriff of Co. of New Castle send Greeting. Whereas Josias Littell, late of Apoquinimink Hun. in sd Co. was seized of 100 acres of land near Duck Creek in sd Co. under Mortgage with buildings and improvements unto John French, Joseph England and John Richardson, Gentlemen, Trustees of Gen. Loan Office. Sd Trustees in Court for default of sd mortgage. Sd Sheriff seized land and premises and sold same unto John Gooding of Georges Hun., gent., as highest bidder for 16 pounds 15 shill. This land bounds land of James Beswicke, Michael Offley, William Skar and Thomas Bell. Signed: Wm. Read, Sheriff. Wit: Edward Blake, John Dunning. Ack: Aug Term 1730. (I1-326)

58

226. Judgement. 20 July 1730. William Read, Sheriff of Co. of New Castle send Greetings. Whereas James Forster, yeoman, and Mary his wife for securing money did grant Trustees of Gen Loan Office their messuage & lott of ground lying in the Town of New Castle, now in the poss. of William Cox. It bounds Beaver St. and land formerly belonging to Thomas Spry, now in poss. of Elizabeth Silsboe. Payments defaulted and Trustees in Court to collect. Sd Sheriff for the sum of 34 pounds 10 shill paid by William Shaw of sd town, gent., as highest bidder, sold to him sd premises and land. Signed: Wm Read, Sheriff. Wit: David French, Ralph Hay. Ack: Aug Term 1730. (I1-330)

227. Deed. 29 July 1730. David Bevan of Penkader Hun. in Co. of New Castle, farmer, for the sum of 40 pounds 10 shill, grant unto William Evans of sd Co., taylor, a tract of land in sd Hun. containing 150 acres. It bounds the land of Simon James, Henry Bevan and Thomas Johns. This is land that sd Henry Bevan did grant unto his son, afsd David, by deed dated 10 May 1729. This was part of a larger tract where sd Henry now doth dwell. Signed: David Bevan. Wit: Jacobus Williams, John Hore. Ack: Aug Term 1730. (I1-331)

228. Gift Deed. 25 June 1730. 'John Land, bricklayer, of New Castle, and Rebeckah his wife, in consideration of the Natural Love & Affection we bear to our daughter, Dorcas McGhee, wife of John McGhee, taylor, for settling ye marriage Portion of ye sd Dorcan according to pursuance of a certain Agreement made before marriage; as for other divers good causes and valuable considerations, us John and Rebeckah thereunto moving; We, grant and confirm unto sd John and Dorcas McGhee a piece of ground lying in sd Co.' It bounds the lott of Moses Degonne and contains 4,500 sq. ft., together with improvements. This is land that was granted sd Land's by Richard Cantwell, Henry Garretson and Elizabeth Garretson his wife by Deed dated 6 March 1706. Signed: John Land, Rebekah Land. Wit: Wm Read, H. Gonne. Proved: Aug Term 1730. (I1-333)

229. Deed. 12 May 1730. David Loyd of Chester in Prov. of Penn, gent., and Grace his wife, for the sum of 31 pounds formerly received, and 33 pounds 12 shill now received grant and sell unto Joseph Smith of Hun. & Co. of New Castle, yeoman, a piece of land situate in Mill Creek Hun. in Co. of New Castle. It bounds the land of Thomas Ogle and contains 232-1/2 acres. This is whereas Justices of Comon Bench at Westminster did recover against John Guest, late juner London Gent. a debt of 240 pounds 40 shill. Sd Guest being dead it was made known to Samuel Manston and Susannah his wife of his testament that they should be before Justices in Co. of New Castle. Richard Clark, Sheriff of sd Co. seized goods and chattles that were sd Guest's. Seized a tract of land near where sd Guest or his under tenants had dwelled containing 1,250 acres, with

divers other land. This was sold unto afsd David Loyd but sheriff died before Deed passed to him so John French by Deed Poll dated 15 May 1716 did certify it. Signed: David Lloyd, Grace Lloyd. Wit: John Owen, Jane Tunn, William McMechen. Ack: Aug Term 1730. (I1-335)

230. Deed. 19 June 1730. Gilbert Falconar of Prov. of Maryland, gent., for the sum of 78 pounds, sold unto Joseph Parker of Town & Co. of New Castle, a messuage and lott of ground in sd town & Co. This is land that George Dakeyne was seized of. It bounded the River Delaware and land belonging to Edward Blake, dec'd., and land of Samuel Perry and was 300 feet long. Sd Dakeyne by Deed dated 2 Sept 1715 did sell lott & messuage unto Isaac Norris of City of Philadelphia, merchant. By sd Norris' deed dated 16 Oct 1716 did sell same unto afsd Gilbert Falconar. Signed: Gilbt. Falconar. Wit: David French, John Legate. (I1-338)

231. Release of Dower. 5 Aug 1730. Hannah Falconar, wife of Gilbert Falconar of Prov. of Maryland, gent., for a valuable consideration paid by Joseph Parker, have released unto him all estate claim of my dower on mentioned piece of ground and messuage. Signed: Hannah Falconar. Wit: Jane Falconar, Wm Coober. Ack Aug Term 1730. (I1-340)

232. Deed. 23 May 1730. John Gooding of Georges Hun. in Co. of New Castle, gent., for the sum of 25 pounds, sold unto Peter Staats of Apoquinimink Hun., yeoman, a tract of land situate in same Hun., near Duck Creek, containing 100 acres. This is land that sd Gooding received by Deed Poll from Wm Read, Sheriff of sd Co. It bounds the land late of James Beswick and Michael Offley, land late of William Skarr and land of Thomas Bell. Signed: John Gooding. Wit: Edward Blake, John Dunning. Ack: Aug Term 1730. (I1-340)

233. Deed. 8 April 1729. Abigal Alricks of New Castle Co., spinster, for the sum of 330 pounds, sold unto Jacob V Bebber sen., of sd Co., merchant, now in his actual possession, for the term of one year, one moiety of a tract of land called Groningen, situate on the east side of Augustine Creek. This is land that Edmond Andros by patent dated 25 March 1676 did grant unto Peter Alricks, late of sd Co. Sd Alricks by his Last Will dated 5 Jan 1697 did bequeath sd land unto his son, Hermanus Alricks; who died intestate leaving issue the afsd Abigal, Peter and Mary Alricks, since dec'd. Signed: Abigail Alricks (mark). Wit: Hans Hanson, Thos Noxon. Ack: Aug Term 1730. (I1-341)

234. Deed. 10 July 1730. Henry Dixon of Co. of New Castle, yeoman, and Ruth his wife, and William Dixon of sd Co. and Hannah his wife, John Dixon of sd Co., yeoman, and Sarah his wife, Thomas Dixon of sd Co., yeoman, and

Hannah his wife, George Dixon of sd Co., yeoman, and Ann his wife, and
William Hicklan of sd Co. and Dinah his wife, and Ann Dixon of sd Co.,
spinster, (sd Henry, William, John, Thomas, George, Dinah and Ann being the
children of Ann Houghton dec'd, by William Dixon her first husband), for the
sum of 280 pounds, sold to James Phillips of sd Co. yeoman, a messuage
plantation containing 295 acres. It bounds the lands of Thos Graves and George
Dixon. This is part of a 300 acre tract that was surveyed for afsd William Dixon
by Henry Hollingsworth, as directed by a warrent dated 13 Feb 1691. Sd Dixon
built the plantation thereon and then died intestate, as did Ann Houghton.
Signed: George Dixon, Ann Dixon, William Hicklen, Dina Hicklin (mark), Ann
Dixon, John Dixon, Sarah Dixon, Thomas Dixon, Hannah Dixon, Henry Dixon,
Ruth Dixon, William Dicon (mark), Hannah Dixon. Wit: Simon Hadly, Simon
Hadly Jun. Ack: Aug Term 1730. (I1-344)

235. Deed. 18 Sept 1730. Gideon Griffith of New Castle Co., gent., and
Margaret his wife, late widow and sole Exec. of Patrick Reilly, late of same
place, Chirurgeon, dec'd., for the sum of 130 pounds, sold to William Read, of
sd Co, now in his actual possession by virtue of agreement for the term of one
year, a messuage and bank lott situate on the River Delaware. It bounds bank lot
in tenure of Richard Grafton. This is property that Jonathan Howston, carpenter,
Jas Robinson, yeoman, and Wm Dixon, yeoman, Execs of the Last Will of
Anthony Howston, gent. dec'd., (sd Jonathan his son & Heir), by an indenture
dated 26 April 1726, granted unto afsd Patrick Reilly. Sd Reilly in his Last Will,
dated 28 Dec 1727, gave property and sole Exec. to his beloved wife, Margaret.
John French, then Regr. for Probate Court granted Admin to her. Signed:
Gideon Griffith, Margaret Griffith. Wit: David French, William Shaw. (I1-346)

236. Deed. 23 Sept 1730. Martha Edwards, wife of Richard Edwards, late of
Apoquinimink Hun. in Co. of New Castle, yeoman, sends Greeting. By Power
of Attny from sd Rich. Edwards dated 30 July 1725 (recorded Lib J, fol 273) for
the sum of 12 pounds 10 shill and causes me moving, and also the heirs of Jas
Askew, late of sd Hun. & Co., yeoman, dec'd, forever quit claim and release my
Dower as wife or widow of sd James Askew, to Wm Read being in his
possession, one messuage & piece of ground, situate in sd Co. It was formerly
released by sd James Askew to Anthony Howston, Gent., by deed dated 21 Aug
1712 (recorded Lib D pag 123) settled upon sd William Read. It is of equal
breadth to the burying ground or grave yard and bounds bank lotts of Joseph
Hill and Richard Grafton. Signed: Martha Edwards (mark). Wit: H. Gonne.
Bourn. Ack: Nov Term 1730. (I1-350)

237. Deed/mortgage. 2 Aug 1730. William Battell of ye Town & Co. of New
Castle, Gent., and Parnella his wife, for the sum of 885 pounds, discharge upon

Ashur Clayton and Robert Chapman, Gents., in their actual possession, for the term of one whole year, a tract of land and plantation situate in White Clay Creek Hun. in sd Co., containing 500 acres. It begins at Rum Branch to Lathams Run to Christiana Creek. (Men. indenture dated 7 April 1730 by sd Battell to David French and Andria Peterson, Gent., Trustees of the Gen. Loan Office for 60 pounds.) Signed: W. Battell, Parnella Battell. Wit: Sam Bakley, David French. Ack: Nov Term 1730. (I1-352)

238. Deed. 17 Sept 1730. Gideon Griffith of New Castle Co., Gent, and Margaret his wife, late widow and sole Exec. of Patrick Reilly, late of same place, Chyrurgeon, for the sum of 5 shillings and considerations them thereunto moving, sell unto William Read of sd Co., merchant, a messuage and Bank Lott now in his actual possession, for the term of one whole year. It is equal breadth of Burying Ground and bounds bank lotts of Joseph Hill and Richard Grafton. Signed: Gideon Griffith, Margt Griffith. Wit: David French, William Shaw. Ack: Nov Term 1730. (I1-354)

239. Judgement. 19 May 1730. William Read, Sheriff of Co. of New Castle sends Greetings. Appearing to John French, Joseph England and John Richardson, Gent. Trustees of Gen. Loan Office on 15 June 1728, was Cantwell Garretson, late of Appoquinimink Hun. in sd Co. for 200 acres of land, part of a tract called Red Clift, secured by Bill of Credit. Now surviving Trustees, sd England and sd Richardson, who outlived sd French, were lately in Court on default of payment of sd mortgage. Sheriff seized sd land and appurt. and sold ye land and premises to Richard Cantwell of sd Hun. as highest bidder for the sum of 35 pounds. It bounds the lands late of John Golden, Halliwell Garretson and Dyres. Signed: Wm Read, Sheriff. Wit: H. Gonne. Bourn. Ack: Nov Term 1730. (I1-355)

240. Deed. 12 Nov 1730. James Briggs of St. Georges Hun. in Co. of New Castle, carpenter, and Margery his wife, for the sum of 70 pounds, sold to William Cook of same place, bricklayer, a tract of land plantation, situate in sd Hun. & Co. It bounds the land of John Pullar, dec'd., and contains 30 acres. Signed: James Briggs, Margery Briggs (mark). Wit: Hans Hanson, David Ross, Thos Noxon. Ack: Nov Term 1730. (I1-357)

241. Deed. 16 Sept 1730. Henry Hartup of Black Birds Creek in Co. of New Castle, planter, for the sum of 52 pounds, sold to Francis Land of Christeen Creek in sd Co., yeoman, a tract of land premises situate on the NW side of Blackbird Creek. It bounds the lands of John Hartop and sd Henry Hartup and contains 186 acres of land. And also a tract of marsh, bounding a pasture called Cabin Point. Signed: Henry Hartup (mark). Wit: John Hill, Rose Hill (mark).

62

Ack Nov Term 1730. (I1-359)

242. Deed. 18 Nov 1730. Christopher Eaton of New Castle Hun. & Co., yeoman, for the sum of 318 pounds, sold to John Richardson of Christana Hun. in sd Co, merchant, all that Island and outlet called Hamburgh, situate on NW side of Delaware River, containing 450 acres. This was granted by Patent unto John Williams by Gov. Edmond Andros in 1680, and by Will devised to Jacobus Williams, son & heir; by Deed granted to John Richardson in 1710, and later signed over to Wm Battell, then to 'myself' (Eaton). Bounded by river and land formerly of Hendrick Clemens, branch called Mr.Thom's Run, land of Peter Alricks, to old path leading to Maryland. Signed: Christopher Eaton. Wit: W. Battell, John Rice. Ack: Nov Term 1730. (I1-361)

243. Deed. 20 April 1730. John Hartup and Henry Hartup, sons of Robert Hartup, late of Black Birds Creek in Apoquinimink Hun. in Co. of New Castle, dec'd., planter, send greetings. Whereas Hartup sen. left issue three sons, sd John, sd Henry and Robert Hartup (youngest), all being at full age, a mutual division of land, marsh and premises agreed upon. Afsd John and Henry for divers good reasons, them thereunto moving, and valuable consideration of sum of 5 pounds discharge unto sd Robert their claims on a tract of land and premises left by their father. It bounds the lands of Widow Haley and Richard Cantwell. Signed: John Hartup, Henry Hartup (mark). Wit: Jos Wood, Thos Rothwell, Thos Noxon. Ack: Nov Term 1730. (I1-362)

244. Deed. 20 April 1730. Henry Hartup and Robert Hartup (of above record #243) release their claim of inheritance on same land to their brother John Hartup for the sum of 5 pounds. Signed: Henry Hartup (mark), Robt Hartup (mark). Wit: Jos Wood, Thos Rothwell, Thos Noxon. Ack: Nov Term 1730. (I1-364)

245. Deed. 20 April 1730. John Hartup, eldest, and Robert Hartup, youngest sons of Robert Hartup (of records #243 and #244) release their claim of inheritance on same land to their brother Henry Hartup for the sum of 5 pounds. Signed: John Hartup, Robt Hartup (mark). Wit: Jos Wood, Thos Rothwell, Thos Noxon. Ack: Nov Term 1730. (I1-366)

246. Deed. 20 Oct 1730. Edward Nelson of the Town & Co. of New Castle, yeoman, and Mary his wife, for the sum of 15 pounds, sold to Thomas Smith of same place, merchant, a messuage and lott of ground situate in sd town. It bounds lott now in possession of sd Smith and lott of Wm Shaw, containing 62 feet in front, 47 feet back and 168 feet long. Signed: Edward Nelson (mark), Mary Nelson (mark). Wit: Margaret Williamson, John Legate, James Armitage.

Ack: Nov Term 1730. (I1-368)

247. Deed. 29 October 1730. Margaret Williamson of Town & Co. of New
Castle, for diverse good reasons, me thereunto moving, and sum of 10 shillings,
grant unto Thomas Smith a piece of my present lott whereon part of a new brick
tenement belonging to sd Smith is erected. The other part of sd tenement being
built on lot lately purchased of Wm Read, sheriff. My lott is now in the tenure
of John Champnes. It bounds the lott of Alexander Davis, sd Smith and marsh
of Nicholas Meers. Signed: Margaret Williamson. Wit: John Savage, John Rice.
(I1-369)

248. Deed. 28 April 1730. Richard Grafton of the Town & Co. of New Castle,
merchant, for the sum of 60 pounds, sold unto John VnGezell of same place,
sadler, a piece of marsh & meadow ground, below described. This is whereas by
Patent dated 15 Jan 1675 from Edmond Andros, was granted unto Hendrick
Jansen a lott of ground in sd town, containing 62-1/2 feet front, 54-1/2 feet
behind, 380 feet long. It bounded lotts of John Askues and Justs Andriesons. Sd
Hendrick Jansen then died and Samuel McBur and Johanna wife, surviving
daughter of sd Jansen, by their Deed Poll dated 21 Sept 1708 did grant sd lott
unto Thomas Trese of the City of Philadelphia, merchant. Sd Trese by his
indenture dated 18 March 1712 did sell unto Margaret Tenth and Thos Trese sd
lott. By their indenture dated 24 March 1714 granted same to Samuel
Monckton, of City of Phila. Sd Monkton then became seized of another lott on
the bank of Delaware River. It bounded lands of George Hoggs and James
Miller. Sd Monckton made his Last Will dated 27 Aug 1720. He bequeathed his
estate ("the wearing apparel, linnens & woolens of my late late wife excepted")
unto his loving wife Rachel and my brother Phillip. They by Lease & Release
dated 3/4 June 1723, sold unto John VnGezel, Phy., the sd two lotts of ground.
Whereas Richard Nicholle, Esq., by his Patent dated 1 Jan 1667, did grant unto
John Carr of New Castle, gent., 150 acres of marsh & meadow ground on No.
end of town of New Castle. Sd Carr made his Last Will dated 13 Jan 1675 &
bequeathed unto his wife & children to be equally divided. His son Richard Carr
of Cecil Co. in Prov. of Maryland, yeoman, by indenture dated 3 Aug 1696, sold
unto John Donaldson, Richard Halliwell and Robert French, afsd 150 acres of
marsh. Sd Donaldson by his Last Will dated 12 Feb 1701 bequeathed unto his
daughter, Mary, all his marshes. Whereas Peter Mainards and Petemella his
wife, one of the daughters of afsd John Carr, and John Bristow and Ann his wife
(another daughter) by their Deed Poll dated 4 Sept 1704 did sell unto afsd
Halliwell, French and heirs of sd John Donaldson, the 150 acres of marsh.
Whereas George Yeates and Mary his wife (daughter of sd Donaldson) by
indenture dated 12 Dec 1712 granted unto afsd John VnGezell part of the sd 150
acres of marsh, containing 3-3/4 acres. It bounds lands of Thos Elliot, John

Silsbee and Daniel Mertiery. Then sd VnGezel by Deed Poll dated 22 Jan 1729 did sell unto afsd Richard Grafton a piece of marsh, part of where sd VnGezel now liveth between sd John's dwelling house and the dwelling house of Ann Hogg. Signed: Richd Grafton. Wit: David French, Gideon Griffith. Ack Nov Term 1730. (I1-370)

249. Deed. John Lewden of Christiana Bridge in Co. of New Castle, yeoman, in consideration of the fatherly Love & Affection which I bear to my son in Law, Nicholas Callander as also for other considerations, me thereunto moving, grant unto him a piece of land situate on the south side of Christiana Bridge. It begins by a stake some distance from John Lewden's door to a stake by the Hen house, and contains 1-1/4 acre 5 perches. Signed: John Lewden. Wit: Nathaniel Pope, Abiah Gareson (mark). 20 July 1730. James James Jun. signs affidavit that sd Nathaniel Pope appeared before him and swore the deed afsd. (I1-374)

250. Deed. 15 Feb 1730. Wm Brachan of Mill Creek Hun. in Co. of New Castle, yeoman, and Hannah his wife, for the sum of 21 pounds, sold to Thomas Barr of same place, yeoman, a piece of land and premises containing 154 acres, situate in sd Co. It begins at Mill Creek and bounds land of Joseph Robinson and John McDonald. This is part of a tract of land purchased from Christopher White. Signed: William Brackan (mark) Hannah Brachan. Wit: Simon Hadly, Henry Dixon. Ack: Feb Term 1730. (I1-375)

251. Deed. 1 Feb 1730. David Miller of New Castle Co., yeoman, for the good will and natural affection he bears unto his son, Abraham Miller of same place, carpenter, and for valuable consideration, grants unto him a tract of land, containing 150 acres, bounding the land of Jas Miller by White Clay Creek. This is half of a tract containing 300 acres that was sold to sd Miller by Robert French, merchant, by deed, dated 20 April 1703. This is land that sd French acquired by a patent, dated 15 Dec 1702, under hands of Edward Shippen, Thomas Story and James Logan. Sd Miller empowers his friends Wm Read, Simon Hadly and James James jun. to make over the Deed in Court of Common Pleas. Signed: David Miller. Wit: Thomas John, James Armitage. Ack: Feb Term 1730. (I1-376)

252. Deed. 30 Jan 1730. David Miller of Co. of New Castle, yeoman, for the good will and natural affection he bears unto his son, James Miller, yeoman, of same place, and for valuable consideration, grants unto him a tract of land by White Clay Creek. (This is the other half of the same land described in record #251. Same provision for making over the Deed.) Signed: David Miller. Wit: Thomas John, Abraham Miller, James Armitage. Ack: Feb Term 1730. (I1-378)

253. Deed. 17 Feb 1730. Daniel Barker of Christiana Hun. in Co. of New Castle, farmer, and Elizabeth his wife, for the sum of 144 pounds, sold to Archibald Hamilton of sd Hun., farmer, a tract of land containing 150 acres (part of a larger tract). It bounds the lands of Wm Kirkpatrick, Wm Cleany, Patrick Dun and Wm Dixon. This land was surveyed and laid out by Thomas Pierson unto Wm Stockdale, but he was deprived of it for not improving it. It afterwards was granted by Wm Markham, Robert Turner and John Goodson, then Comm., unto Thos Sawyer on 13 Feb 1691. Sd Sawyer conveyed same to Edward Mathews, who by deed dated 17 Nov 1702, granted same to Herman Kenchy. Sd Kenchy and Margery his wife by Deed dated 21 May 1725, granted the 350 acres unto John Beard. Sd Beard with his wife, Rebeca, by Deed in 1729, granted same unto afsd Daniel Barker. Signed: Daniel Barker, Elizabeth Barker. Wit: John McDoul, William Allmond. Ack: Feb Term 1730. (I1-379)

254. Deed. 5 Nov 1730. Morgan Morgan of Mill Creek Hun. in Co. of New Castle, taylor, for the sum of 35 pounds, and for other good causes, him thereunto moving, sold to John Harris of New Castle Hun., farmer, his title, property claim on that acre of land with dwelling house thereon. Sd Morgan jointly bo(u)nd unto sd Harris in one penal Bond of 62 pounds 14 Shills conditioned for payment within 3 years. Signed: Morgan Morgan. Wit: Nathl Wainford, Jas Mills. Ack: Feb Term 1730. (I1-382)

255. Deed. 15 Feb 1730. Samuel Johnson jun., of Co. of New Castle, yeoman, for the sum of 125 pounds, sold to George Patty, weaver of same place, a piece of land situate on North side of White Clay Creek, containing 163 acres. It bounds the lands of John King, Neal Cook and John Crawford. Signed: Samuel Johnson jun. Wit: James Cannon, James Armitage. Ack: Feb Term 1730. (I1-383)

256. Deed. 16 Nov 1730. John Garret of Co of New Castle in Territory of Penn., yeoman, and Margaret his wife, for the sum of 4 pounds in Pennsilvania money, sold to Edmd. Butcher of Co. of Chester In Prov afsd., millwright, one equal fifth part of one tract of land "part of 135 acres" and premises. It bounds Red Clay Creek and contains 10 acres. This is whereas Wm Penn, lately dec'd, by a Patent dated 23 Oct 1701 did grant to his daughter Latitia a parcel of land called the Mannor of Stenning, situate on So. side of Brandywine Creek, part in New Castle & part in Chester, containing 15,500 acres. Sd Latitia intermarried with Wm Aubery who constituted Jas Logan, Rees Thomas as Attny's to sell sd land. The Attny's by indenture dated 2 June 1726 granted to Wm McMechen 3 parcels of sd land containing 961 acres at quit rent of 1 shilling per 100 acres. Sd McMechen and Jennet his wife by indenture dated 22 March 1726 granted unto sd John Garrett two tracts containing 35 acres (135(cg)) under ye Yearly

Quit rent as above to ye Lord on ye first Day of March forever, situate in New Castle Co. Signed: John Garret, Margaret Garrett (mark). Wit: Simon Hadly, Zach Butcher. Ack: Feb Term 1730. (I1-384)

257. Deed. 16 Nov 1730. John Garret of the County of New Castle & in Territories of Pensilvaia, yeo., and Margaret his wife, for the sum of 4 pounds, sold to William Cox, yeoman, of same place, one equal fifth part of one tract of land, situate on Red Clay creek, containing by est. 10 acres, in New Castle Co. (Same as Record #256 with correction that Wm McMechen sold John Garret two tracts of land containing 135 acres). Signed: John Garret, Margaret Garrett (mark). Wit: Simon Hadly, Zach Butcher. Ack: Feb Term 1730. (I1-386)

258. Deed. 16 Nov 1730. John Garret of the County of New Castle in the Territorys of ye Province of Pensylvania yeomn. & Margaret his wife, for the sum of 4 pounds, sold to Henry Dixon of ye same place, yeom., one equal fifth part of one tract of land, situate on Red Clay Creek, containing by est. 10 acres, in New Castle Co. (Same as Records #256 and 257). This is part of 135 acres sold sd Garrett by Wm McMechen. Signed: John Garret, Margaret Garrett (mark). Wit: Simon Hadly, Zach Butcher. Ack: Feb Term 1730. (I1-388)

259. Deed. 16 Nov 1730. John Garret of New Castle County in the Territorys of Pensylvania yeo; & Margaret his wife, for the sum of 4 pounds, sold to Francis Pullen of ye County of Chester & Province afsd, weaver, one equal fifth part of one tract of land, situate on Red Clay Creek, containing by est. 10 acres, in New Castle Co. (Same as Records #256, #257 and #258. John Garrett was establishing a five-part partnership for his Mill (cg)). Signed: John Garret, Margaret Garrett (mark). Wit: Simon Hadly, Zach Butcher. Ack: Feb Term 1730. (I1-390)

260. Deed. 9 Feb 1730. Hans Hans of Red Lyon Hun. in Co. of New Castle, yeom, for the sum of 8 pounds, sold to Edward Thomas of sd Co., yeom, a piece of marsh ground in sd Hun. on the west side of Delaware River. It bounds the marsh of Cornelius Truax' to the mouth of Cader Creek and contains 10 acres 60 perches. Signed: Hance Hans. Wit: Simon James, Samuel Clemt. Ack: Feb Term 1730. (I1-392)

261. Deed. 17 Feb 1730. John Vangezell of New Castle, sadler, & Mary his wife, for the sum of 26 pounds, sold to John McGhee of same place, taylor, a piece of ground & premises in sd place. It is bounded on NW with the Green or Market place, to the NE with fence, to SE with another fence, to SW with ye lott lately belonging to John French, Esq., dec'd. It contains 103 feet in length, 23 feet 9" in breadth. Sd lott was formerly granted by Rachel Munston, widow of

Samuel Munston, late of Philad., 'Chyurgeon', & Philip Munston, brother of ye sd Samuel, unto sd John VnGezell by indenture dated 3/4 June 1723. the same lott was formerly granted to Hendrick Jansen by Patent under the hand of Edmond Andros, dated 15 Jan 1705 (recorded Lib. Y, pp 130). Signed: John VnGezell, Mary Vangezell. Wit: Wm Read, Bourn. Ack: Feb Term 1730. (I1-393)

262. Deed. 20 Nov 1730. John Gooding and Ann Brooks, Exec. of ye Last Will of Augustine Cox, late of ye Co. of New Castle, yeom., dec'd, for the sum of 191 pounds sold to Jacob Gooding of ye sd Co., Gent., several tracts of land and marsh that sd Cox in his lifetime was seized of. One piece of marsh lies near Georges Creek, and contains 234 acres. It bounded the land late of John Cox by Dragons Run and land of Charlie Cox and (blanked out). Also another adjoining marsh and also a piece of land & premises that bounds land late of Wm Derrickson and land late of John Stout and contains 21 acres. Sd Cox's Last Will empowered Exec. to sell his land. Signed: John Gooding, Ann Brooks (mark). Wit: Timothy Collins (mark), Andw Peterson, Rd. Cantwell. Ack: Feb Term 1730. (I1-396)

263. Deed. 1 Feb 1730. To all people shall come we, Wm Chambers of White Clay Creek Hun. in Co. of New Castle, yeoman, Son & Heir and Exec. of the Last Will of John Chambers, late of the Hopp yard & Hun. in sd Co., Planter, dec'd, and Elizabeth Chambers, wife of sd Wm. Sd Will, dated 25 Oct 1730, proved 10 Dec last before Robert Gordon, Esq. Regr. for probate granted them Administration. Sd Will bequeathed all his Estate together with stock of cattle, household furniture, etc of ye Plantation unto his eldest son, afsd William Chambers. Now for the Natural Love & Affection they bear unto our Brother, Joseph Chambers of the Hopp Yard, yeom., other son of sd John, their right in the piece of Land called the Hopp Yard containing 430 acres; whereof sd John in his lifetime sold 100 acres to James Boggs. Signed: William Chambers, Elisabeth Chambers. Wit: Samuel Jackson, Edward Armstrong, Herm. Starr. Ack: Feb Term 1730. (I1-397)

264. Deed. 2 Feb 1730. Thomas Wollaston of Phila. in Prov. of Penn., cordwainer, & Eleanor his wife, for the sum of 260 pounds, sold to Jeramiah Wollaston of Co. of New Castle, yeoman, a tract of land situate on White Clay Creek in sd Co. It bounds the land of Wm Wollaston and contains 224 acres. Signed: Thomas Wollaston, Eleanor Wollaston (mark). Wit: Edward Roberts, Geo. Robinson, Jas. Lawrence. Ack: Feb Term 1730. (I1-399)

265. Judgement. 7 Feb 1730. William Read, Esq. Sheriff of Co. of New Castle send greetings. Whereas by a Writ of Fieri Facias dated 21 Aug last, the goods

& chattles of Patrick Reilly, late of sd Co., Chyrurgeon, dec'd., in the hands of
Gideon Griffith and Margaret his wife, Exe. of sd Reilly were seized for debt.
Taken in execution was a piece of land with ye Appurts. It bounded land late of
Thos Allet and contained 6 acres 73 perches of land valued at 60 pounds.
Jonathan Lee and James Pearson were lately in Court before Justices against sd
Griffith. Now sd Sheriff for the sum of 60 pounds 1 shilling sold same land unto
Richard Grafton, merchant of sd Co., as the highest bidder. Signed: Wm Read,
Sheriff. Wit: H. Gonne, Bourn. Ack: Feb Term 1730. (I1-401)

266. Deed. 2 Nov 1730. William Aubery of City of London in ye Kingdom of
G.B., merchant, & Latitia his wife, of the first part. James Logan of City of
Phila., in Prov. of Penn., merchant, & Rees Thomas of Co. of Phila., Gent. of
the second part. Archibald McDonald of Co. of New Castle, yeoman, of the
third part. Sd Aubery's by their attornies, sd Logan & sd Thomas, for the sum of
45 pounds, sold unto afsd Arch. McDonald a piece of land in sd Co. It bounds
the lands of Simon Hadly, sd McDonald, John Champion, Francis Bradley and
Josiah Ramage, and contains 99-1/2 acres. Signed: James Logan, Rees Thomas.
Wit: John Dixon, Henry Green. Ack: Feb 1730. (I1-402)

267. Deed. 2 Nov 1730. William Aubery of City of London in ye Kingdom of
G.B., merchant, & Latitia his wife, of the first part. James Logan of City of
Phila., in Prov. of Penn., merchant, & Rees Thomas of Co. of Phila., Gent. of
the second part. John Dixon of Co. of New Castle, yeoman, of the third part. Sd
Aubery's by their attornies, sd Logan & sd Thomas, for the sum of 47 pounds,
sold to afsd John Dixon a piece of land in sd Co. It bounds the lands of Simon
Hadly, sd Dixon and Wm Berkingham and contains 100 acres. Signed: James
Logan, Rees Thomas. Wit: Henry Green, Archibald McDaniel (mark), Jos.
Harrison. Ack: Feb 1730. (I1-405)

268. Deed. 15 Feb 1730. Gideon Griffith of the Town & Co. of New Castle,
Gent., & Margaret his wife, for the sum of 30 pounds, sold to John Musgang of
St. George Hun. in sd Co., 150 acres of land in sd Co. This is land that John
Bolton, late of sd Co., dec'd., was seized of, called Mill Branch, which lead into
the Head of Drawyers Creek. It bounded lands of Andw. Peterson, Esq. and
Andrew Brian. This was half of a tract of land called Chesterfield (other half
belonged to sd Brian). Afsd Bolton granted sd land unto Charles Crow of Cecil
Co. in Prov. of Maryland, planter, by Deed Poll dated 2 Oct 1694 (Lib B, page
192 & 193). Then sd Crow by his Deed Poll dated 1 Aug 1714 (Lib H, fol 129)
confirmed same land unto Patrick Reilly of Town of New Castle, Doctor. Sd
Reilly made his Last Will dated 28 Dec 1727 and bequeathed his Estate to his
dearly beloved wife, Margt. Reilly. Sd Will proved 11 Jan 1727 and sd Margt.
intermarried with ye above Gideon Griffith. Signed: Gideon Griffith, Margt.

Griffith. Wit: Rd. Cantwell, Thos Noxon. Ack: Feb Term 1730. (I1-407)

269. Deed/mortgage. 6 Feb 1730. Gertruy Vangezell of Co. of New Castle, widow, for the sum of 100 pounds, and for other causes her thereunto moving, releases unto Revrd. George Ross of sd Co., now in his actual possession by virtue of a bargain for the term of one year, all that messuage and piece of ground and part of a Bank Lott situate in sd Co. It bounds the front lott now in possession of Ann Hogg and John Hogg, on Front Street on NW, to NE with an alley laying between the present Shop & ground of Thomas Janvier junr. on SE and River Delaware on the SW., with bank lott right agst the present dwelling house of John VnGezell. Sd Bank Lott was formerly granted to George Hogg, senr., cordwainer, by a Patent under hands of Edw. Shippen, Thos. Story and Jas. Logan dated 29 June 1702. Sd Hogg granted same unto Cornlius VnGezell, merchant, late of sd Co. by Deed dated 11 June 1715 (Lib E, Pa 247). Sd VnGezell made his Last Will dated 8 Nov 1717 and bequeathed all his Estate to his mother, afsd Gertruy VnGezell, during her natural live and after her decease to be equally divided between his brother Joannes and his sister Catherine. Will proved 8 May 1718 before John French and estate confirmed unto sd Gertrug, Joannes & Catherine. Then sd John VnGeszell & Mary his wife & sd George Ross and Catherine his wife by indenture dated 31 March last did confirm sd land and messuage unto afsd Gertrug. Then sd Gertruy for securing 50 pounds unto Andrew Peterson and David French, Trustees of Gen. Loan Office entered into mortgage, trans. same to sd Ross. Signed: Gertruy Vangezel. Wit: Wm Read, John Lefever. Ack: Feb Term 1730. (I1-409)

270. Deed. 4 May 1730. Benjamin Price of Baltimore Co. in Prov. of Maryland, planter, & Elizabeth his wife, Heir apparent at Law of John Ogle, late of Co. of New Castle, yeoman, dec'd., and Thomas Harris of sd Co., yeoman, for the sum of 5 pounds, release unto James James jun., of Christiana Bridge in sd Co., Gent., a piece of land situate lying near sd Bridge. It bounds land of Nathanl. Pope and contains 3 acres. Signed: Benjamin Price (mark), Elizabeth Price, Thomas Harris (mark). Wit: So. Evans, Jno Thomas, Jno Ogle, John Herbert. James James jun. empowered John Ogle or John Dening to receive for him in Open Court, signed 20 May 1731. Sd Price's authorize Thos. Harry, yeoman, to make over this Deed, witness 4 May 1731. Ack: May Term 1731. (I1-412)

271. Deed 18 May 1731. Wm Goulden of Cap May Co. in Woot Jeroey, yeoman, brother & Heir to the Real Estate of John Goulden, late of Apoquimong, dec'd., for the sum of 200 pounds, sold unto Joseph Brown & Paul Allface of Co. of New Castle Co., a tract of land situate on the south side of Apoquimong Creek in sd Co. It bounds the land lately belonging to Wm Dyre, dec'd., and contains 300 acres. This is part of a greater tract formerly granted to

Capt. Edmond Cantwell by Patent under seal of Edmond Andros, Esq., dated 20 March 1679. By sd Cantwell's last Will dated 28 Oct 1679 bequeathed Estate to his children to divide equally. Richard Cantwell, only son of sd Edmond, on 18 May 1709 did release his right title part to Henry Garretson & Elizabeth Garretson, only daughter of sd Edmond. They conveyed their Right to John Goulden by a Deed dated 6 May 1715 to 250 acres. Afterwards they conveyed 50 more acres to him on 14 May 1725. On 7 March 1729, sd Goulden died intestate without issue and afsd Wm Goulden became Heir at Law. Signed: William Goulden (mark). Wit: Rd. Cantwell, Daniel Corbet. Ack: May Term 1731. (I1-413)

272. Deed. 20 May 1731. Benjamin Stout jun., of Hund. of Red Lyon in Co. of New Castle, yeoman, for the sum of 18 pounds, sold to Thomas Rees of same place, Doctor, a piece of land bordering upon Maryland Road that leads to Bohemia. It bounds the lands of sd Stout and John Goforth, and contains 15 acres 2 perches. Signed: Benjamin Stout jun. Wit: Jno VnGezell, Henry Newton. Ack: May Term 1731. (I1-415)

273. Deed. 26 April 1731. Henry Parker of Elk River in Cicol Co. in Prov. of Maryland, planter, for the sum of 35 pounds, sold to John Justis of Christiana Hun. in Co. of New Castle, farmer, one half a tract of land plantation containing 100 acres. This is half of a 200 acre tract that Conrade Constantine of sd Hun. by virtue of a Warrant from Wm Willeh, surv., had, called Cold Harbour, situate on the north side of Christiana Creek and west side of Delaware River. This was laid out (by Thos Pierson, Deputy) for sd Constantine, who did convey the 200 acres to sd Henry Parker. Signed: Henry Parker (mark). Wit: James McMullan, Gisebord Wollraven (mark). Ack: May Term 1731. (I1-416)

274. Deed. 27 March 1731. Elizabeth Garretson, daughter & co-heir of Edmond Cantwell of Apoquinemy Hun. in sd Co., dec'd, for the sum of 14 pounds 8 shilling 3 pence, grants unto Francis Land of Christeen Creek in Co. of New Castle, yeoman, one half part of a messuage & lott of ground lying on Front Street, now in ye tenor of Mary Carpenter, widow. It is bounded with house & lott of Isaack Gravenract and lott late of Gunning Bedford and Mathias Vanderhyden. Sd Eliza. Garretson appoints Richard Cantwell or Wm Read to be her lawful Attny. in ye open Court to deliver this. Signed: Elizabeth Garretson. Wit: John Legate, S. Bourn. Ack: May term 1731. (I1-417)

275. Deed. 22 April 1731. John Demerez of St. Georges Hun. in Co. of New Castle (one of the sons of John Demerez, dec'd), yeoman, for the sum of 5 pounds and other causes, he the sd John thereunto moving, granted to David Demerez of Appoquinamink in sd Co. (another son), yeoman, a tract of land

containing 144 acres situate in sd Hun. & Co. This is part of a larger tract of 300 acres that was owned by their father. It is bounded northward with the Mill Pond on St. Georges Creek, eastward with land of Dirick See and Jno McCool, southward with land of sd McCool and westward with land of James Anderson. Sd Demerez made his Last Will dated 6 March 1720 and bequeathed unto his sons John and David both half of sd land. Signed: John Demerest (mark). Wit: Jno McCool, Thos Noxon. Ack: May Term 1731. (I1-418)

276. Deed. 22 April 1731. David Demerez of Appoquinamink Hun. in Co. of New Castle (one of the sons of John Demerez, dec'd), yeoman, for the sum of 5 pounds and other causes & considerations him the sd David thereunto moving, grants unto John Demerez of St. Georges Hun. in sd Co. (another son), yeoman, a tract of land containing 144 acres. (same land as rec. #275). Signed: David Demerest (mark). Wit: John McCool, Thos. Noxon. Ack: May Term 1731. (I1-419)

277. Deed. 17 May 1731. William Chambers, Exec. of John Chambers, late, dec'd., and Joseph Chambers, both of Co. of New Castle, yeomen, for the sum of 98 pounds, 12 shilling, sold to Samuel Ruth of same place, farmer, a tract of land situate on the north side of White Clay Creek in sd Co. It bounds the lands of Jonathan Hog and Jas Boggs, and contains 120 acres. This is land that was taken up by Joseph Moore and patented to John Guest, Patent dated 19 April 1703. Signed: William Chambers, Joseph Chambers. Wit: Saml. Jackson, Daniel McLean. James Armitage. Ack: May Term 1731. (I1-421)

278. Deed. 27 Feb 1730. Joseph Smith of Mill Creek Hun. in Co. of New Castle, yeoman, & Mary his wife, for the sum of 57 pounds, sold to Wm McMechen of same place, Gent., a piece of land & premises situate in sd Co. It is bounded by the lands of James Cannon, Jas. Boggs, John Chambers and sd Smith, and contains 124-1/2 acres. This is part of a larger tract containing 232-1/2 acres. Signed: Joseph Smith, Mary Smith (mark). Wit: Margt. Creaghead, James Armitage. Ack: May Term 1731. (I1-422)

279. Deed. 15 March 1730. John VnGezell of the Town & Co. of New Castle, sadler, & Mary his wife, for the sum of 30 pounds, sold to Esther Glen of same place, widow, a piece of ground situate in sd Town. This is part of the Front lott whereon sd VnGezell now dwelleth. It is bounded NW with Market Place, to NE with lott now in tenure of George Hogg, to SE with a fence, to SW with part of lott lately released by sd VnGezell to John McGhee of sd town. It contains in lengh 103 feet & in breadth 23 feet 9 inches. Signed: Jno. VnGezell, Mary Vangesell. Wit: William Glen, John Legate. Ack: May Term 1731. (I1-424)

280. Deed. 24 March 1730/31. Esther Glen of the Town & Co. of New Castle, widow, for the sum of 5 shillings, confirms unto John Maggee of same place, taylor, a piece of ground situate in sd town. This is part of a lott purchased by sd Glen of John VnGezell. It bounds the Town Green, a corner of sd Glen's & Maggee's lott to stake in sd VnGezells line. Signed: Esther Glen (mark). Wit: John Hore, John Legate, William Glen. Ack: May term 1731. (I1-425)

281. Deed. 8 April 1730. Catherine Lefever, Admin. of All which were of Hippolatas Lefever, late of Co. of New Castle, yeoman, at the time of his death, and John Lefever of the same place, weaver, & Susannah his wife, for the sum of 50 pounds, sold to Philip VnLeuvenigh of sd Co., weaver, a lott of ground & premises, situate in sd town. This is land that Wm Penn, by Patent dated 16 Dec 1689 granted unto George Hogg. It contained in breadth 60 feet, and bounded E on Front St., on W by Bank St., to N by lott belonging to the prietor, and to S by lotts of Englebert. Sd Hogg by his Deed dated 18 June 1695, did confirm same unto afsd Hippolatas Lefever. Signed: Catherine Lefever (mark), John Lefever, Susannah Lefever (mark). Wit: James Merrewether, Robertson. Ack: May Term 1730. (I1-427)

282. Deed. 27 April 1730. Garret Packard of Apoquinamink Hun. in Co. of New Castle, yeoman, & Rachel his wife, Henry Packard of same place, yeoman, Catherine Packard of same place, spinster, Peter Packard of Georges Hun. in sd Co., yeoman, & Catharine his wife, for the sum of 270 pounds, sold to George Hadly of New York, mariner, in his actual possession now by virtue of indenture for the term of one whole year, a piece of land in sd Co. It bounds the lands late of Joseph Stoll and John Richards, and contains 200 acres. Also a piece of meadow land situate on the west side of Delaware River. It bounds marsh late of Henry Ward, now called Hanson's Marsh; also land of John Boyer & John Stout, and contains 15 acres. This land was granted by sd John Boyer unto afsd Henry Packard, (father of the sd Garret, Henry, Catherine & Peter) by Deed dated 17 May 1703 (rec: Lib B, Fo 655,656) Sd Packard made his Last Will dated 15 Feb 1710, and bequeathed same to his wife, Hannah, during her life and after her decease to be divided among his sd children. Signed: Garret Packard, Rachel Packard (mark), Henry Packard, Catherine Packard (mark), Peter Packard, Catherine Packard (mark). Wit: Wm Read, John Rice. 'Sealed & delivered by Rachel Packard in presence of H. Gonne, John Dunning'. 'May 26 1730 rec'd of George Hadley 270 pounds'. Ack: May Term 1731. (I1-428)

283. Deed. 3 May 1731. Jacob VanBebber of Red Lyon Hun. in Co. of New Castle, merchant, & Mary his wife, for the sum of 330 pounds, sold unto Valentine Dushene of St. Georges Hun. in sd Co., yeoman, one moiety of a tract of land and swamp containing 280 acres. It is situate on the NE side of

Augustine's Creek, called Groeningen, bounding the line of Mr Waly, now Ashton's. This is land that Abigail Allrich of sd Co., spinster, granted to sd Van Bebber by lease for the term of one year, dated 7 April 1729. On 8 April 1729, sd Allrichs granted release for same. Signed: Jacob VBebber, Mary VBebber. Wit: Abram. Gooding, Thos. Noxon. Ack: May Term 1731. (I1-432)

284. Deed. 20 May 1730. Isaac Gooding (one of the sons of Isaac Gooding, late of Rieden Island in Co. of New Castle, dec'd), for the sum of 55 pounds, sold unto Jacob Gooding of St. Georges Hun. in sd Co., yeoman, piece of land & premises containing 50 acres. It begins at the division line of both sd Isaac & sd Jacob, near sd Jacob's dwelling plantation, and bounds the land of Hans Hanson. This is part of a tract of 150 acres devised to sd Isaac by his father's Will. Signed: Isaac Gooding (mark). Wit: Abram. Gooding, Thos. Noxon. Ack: May Term 1731. (I1-434)

285. Deed. 10 May 1731. Thos. Basset of Apoquinamink Hun. in Co. of New Castle, and Jane his wife, & Benjamin Richardson of sd place, yeoman, and Mary his wife, for the sum of 30 pounds, sold to John Shaw of Red Lyon Hun. in sd Co., a tract of land containing 200 acres, situate in sd Co. This is whereas Mathew Corbet of sd Hun., dec'd., in his lifetime by virtue of two warrents was laid out two tracts of land (1st warrent dated 11th day 1st mo 1705 - no date for 2nd). By sd Corbet's Last Will, dated 10 Feb 1719, he did bequeath unto his two daughters, (afsd) Jane and Mary, each of them 100 acres. This land adjoins tract known by ye name of Old Plantation, which is since sold by James Corbitt (son, heir & Exe. of sd Will) to Co. John French of sd Co., dec'd. Sd French sold same to John Peel of sd Co., dec'd. Signed: Thomas Basset, Jane Basset (mark), Benja. Richardson (mark), Mary Richardson (mark). Wit: Andw. Peterson, Thos. Noxon. Ack: May term 1731. (I1-436)

286. Deed. 17 May 1731. David Demerest of Apquinaminck Hun. in Co. of New Castle, yeoman, for the sum of 126 pounds, sold to Jacobus See of St. Georges Hun. in sd Co., yeoman, a tract of land containing 144 acres and premises. This is whereas Wm Grant, late of sd Co. in his lifetime was granted a Patent, dated 25 March 1676, for a tract of land called the Task, containing 400 acres. It layed on the West side of Delaware & So. side of main branch of St. Georges Creek, above the land of John Scott. In sd Grant's Last Will, he bequeathed sd land unto his son, Wm. Sd Wm Grant by indenture dated 15 Jan 1708 (rec: Lib.C, fob 172/3/4/5 & 6) confirmed 300 acres of sd land unto John Demerest. Sd Demerest in his Last Will, dated 6 March 1720, bequeathed to his loving son, David, half of sd tract, lying between Creek & Scott's Run. (Other half given to his son John). It bounded lands of sd John and James Anderson. Then by indenture between sd John & sd David, dated 27 April 1731, sd David

became seized of sd 144 acres. Signed: David Demerest (mark). Wit: Jno
McCoole, Thos. Noxon. Affid: 'I, Golah Demarest, widow & relict of within
named John Demerest, dec'd, for good causes, me thereunto moving, and 5
pounds, relinquish my dower...' Signed: Golah Demerest (mark). Ack: May
Term 1731. (I1-438)

287. Deed. 17 May 1731. John Hartup of St. Georges Hun. in Co. of New
Castle, yeoman, and Ann his wife, for the sum of 75 pounds, sold to Richard
Wathinson of sd place, gent., a parcel of land containing 56 acres 114 perches in
sd Hun & Co. It bounds a tract called the Meeting House Land, and land of
Peter Branks. This is part of a larger tract of 205 acres that Johanis Schare of sd
place, dec'd, by virtue of a Patent from Edmond Andros was possessed of. It
bounded land of Andrew Anderson on St. Augustins Creek. Sd Schare by his
Last Will bequeathed same to his son, Martin Schare. Then by indenture dated
12 Feb 1723, sd Martin Schare of Salem Co. in Prov. of West New Jersey,
yeoman, & Mary his wife, sold same to Isaac VnDyke, yeoman, of sd Hun. &
Co. (Deed ack. in Court on 22 May 1724, rec: Lib G, pag 327). Then by
indenture dated 7 May 1729, Thos. VnDyke, son & heir of sd Isaac, sold same
land to Ann Brank, widow and relict of Peter Brank. And whereas sd Ann Brank
since intermarried with afsd John Hartup. Signed: John Hartup, Ann Hartup
(mark). Wit: Abram Gooding, Thos Noxon. Ack: May term 1731. (I1-440)

288. Deed. 15 Oct 1710. Susannah Guest of ye City of Phila. in Prov. of Penn,
Relict & widow of John Guest, late of sd City, gent., dec'd, send Greeting.
Whereas there is a tract of land called Pilgrims Place situate on the north side of
a branch Christiana Creek, called White Clay Creek in Co. of New Castle. It
bounded the land of John Ogle and contained 1,000 acres. This land was granted
by Warrent from Wm Penn dated 11th day of 12th mo. 1688; laid out by survey
unto Wm Welsh, dec'd, father of the above named Susannah Guest (only
daughter & heir of sd Welsh). Then Wm Welsh, in Right of Patent dated 23 Oct
1701 (Book A, Vol.e, pag 123 & 124) granted land unto sd John & Susannah
Guest. They then granted 400 acres of sd land unto Evan Rees. Know now that
sd Susannah Guest for the sum of 80 pounds 6 shillings, grant unto John
Campbell of sd prov., clothier, all the remaining 600 acres of land and Premises.
Signed: Susanna Guest. Wit: Geo. Duncan, Joseph Willer, Anthony Sto?ne. (I1-
442)

289. Notice: "Whereas 3 weeks ago information was brought to ye Custom
House at ye Port of New Castle on Delaware agst ye Brigantine Charming
Peggy Ellis Davy Commandr for illegible trade & forasmuch as Henry Newton,
Gent., Naval Officer of sd port thro ye malicious Insinntiony of his Enemiy
Stands Charged with giving ye sd Information not only at the request of Mr.

75

Newton but also out of a pure desure to do every man Justice. I do hereby
Certify that the charge above sd is altogether unjust & malicious altogether
groundless unreasonable & further that Mr. Newton neither spoke of Master
Cargo in any wise to me till I returned from Margarets Hook... 17 July 1731. ?
Keith" (I1-444)

290. Appointment. 9 July 1731. "George the second... To Hermanus Alrichs of
Co. of New Castle, Greetings. I appoint you to be Sheriff of County of New
Castle within our Government in Room and Stead of William Read, who has
voluntarily & formally resigned sd Office... P. Gordon". (I1-444)

291. 1 Sept 1731. "I, John Morgan of Pencadder Hun. in Co. of New Castle send
Greetings. For ye Consideration of my annual maintainance during my
remaining natural Life & of the Natural Affection wch I have to my Dear wife,
Margaret Morgan & Thos. Bowen, weaver of sd Co., I appoint them Trustee
over my Estate... for consideration of paying debts after the time of my death..
my Funeral.. and with other consideration me especially moving, grant unto
Thos. Bowen my goods, ready money & apparel utensils brass Pewter &
bedding, all other lumber as utensils for husbandry.. together with my horses,
hoggs & sheep...etc" Signed: John Morgan (mark). Wit: John Morgan jun.,
Reyd. Howell. (I1-445)

292. Deed. 24 Sept 1720. John Ellot of Carushook in Co. of Phila., yeoman, in
consideration of the intermarriage of his daughter Eliz. with Jonathan Hays of
ye Township of Newton in Co. of Chester, husbandman, and for the natural love
& affection toward his son in law, grants unto sd Hays a tract of land containing
135 acres situate in Co. of New Castle. This is land that Joseph More of White
Clay Creek in sd Co., millwright, did sell unto Joseph Wood of sd Co., gent., by
indenture dated 15 May 1703. Sd Wood sold same to afsd John Ellot by deed
dated 19 Aug 1703 (ack. in Court 21 Feb 1704). Signed: John Ellot. Wit: D.
Pearson, Sarah Pearson, Andrew Elliot, Enoch Elliot, John Peter (mark), Patar
Elliot. Deed proved by John McPeter Aug 1731. (I1-445)

293. Deed. 10 Sept 1689. William Guest of Co. of New Castle in Terr. of Penn.,
farmer, for the sum of 7 pounds paid by Hugh Symone of sd Co., husbandman,
grants unto sd Symone a tract of land lying on the north end of Richd. Mankins
line, containing 100 acres. Signed: Wm Guest. Wit: Rd Aynode, Thomas
Gasper. Ack: Sept 1689. Ja. Claypoole. (I1-446)

294. Deed. 17 Aug 1731. Wm Battell of the town & Co. of New Castle, gent.,
and Parnela his wife, for the sum of 51 pounds, sold to Robt Meers of White
Clay Creek Hun. in sd Co., cordwainer, two parcels of land and premises situate

on ye north side of main branch of Christiana Creek, containing 34 acres 66
perches. This is part of a tract formerly confirmed by Patent to Thomas
Langshane, and afterwards seized by sd Wm Battell. Also one tract adjoining,
both surveyed into one tract. It bounds the mouth of Lathan's Run along Mr
Claytons line, and contains 91 acres 11 perches. Signed: W. Battell, Parnellah
Battell. Wit: H. Keith, Jno. VnGezell, James Armitage. Ack: Aug 1731. (I1-447)

295. Deed. 24 May 1731. Robt. Hartup of BlackBird Creek in Co. of New
Castle, planter, for the sum of 35 pounds 8 shilling, sold unto Francis Land of
Christeen Creek in sd Co., yeoman, a tract of land premises, situate on Black
Bird Creek in sd Co. It bounds the lands of Widow Haley and Richd. Cantwell,
and contains 172 acres. Also the Right Claim that sd Hartup may have in 76
acres of land adjoining thereunto belonging. Signed: Robert Hartup (mark). Wit:
John Hill, Rose Hill (her mark). Ack: Aug 1731. (I1-448)

296. Deed. 4 June 1731. Duncan Drumond of Mill Creek Hun. in Co. of New
Castle, merchant, for the sum of 59 pounds, sold unto Francis Land of Christeen
Creek in sd Co., yeoman, a plantation & tract of land situate in sd Co.,
containing 110 acres. It begins at Mill Creek, a branch of White Clay Creek and
bounds land late of John Conn. This together with improvements except 10
acres, part of ye same which was conveyed by Jas Robinson to 'ye Honble
London protestant Society for ye Propagacun of ye Gospel'. Signed: Duncan
Drumond. Wit: David Lewis, John Hill. Ack: Aug term 1731. (I1-449)

297. Deed. 30 July 1731. John Allen of White Clay Creek Hun. in Co. of New
Castle, fuller, for the sum of 71 pounds 19 shill. 6 pence, sold to Francis Land of
Christeen Creek in sd Co., yeoman, a tract of land situate on the north side of
Christeen Cr., containing 200 acres. Signed: Jon. Allen, Agnes Allen (mark).
Wit: John Stevenson, John Miller. Ack: Aug term 1731. (I1-450)

298. Deed. 29 July 1731. Francis Land of Christeen Creek in Co. of New Castle,
yeom., send Greetings. Whereas there is a tract of land situate on the north side
of Christeen Cr. near the bridge, containing 76 acres. This tract was taken in
Execution from Ann Letort by George Dakeyn, Coroner of sd Co., by Deed Poll
from sd Dakeyn dated 17 May 1711. It was assigned over unto John Ogle, late
of d Co., dec'd. Then sd Ogle by indenture dated 15 Feb 1717 did confirm same
unto afsd Francis Land -- all this land, except 11 acres sold by sd Ogle to Alex.
Frasier, now in possession of James James Esq.; six acres of same sold to Nath.
Pope; 4 acres of same sold unto Danl. Mercier; 3 acres of same sold to Saml.
Patterson, and 2-1/2 acres of same sold to Aaren Jordine. (Lib E. pag 198). Now
sd Land for the sum of 53 pounds sold unto Rees Jones of Christeen Bridge,
Practioner of Phisick, his interest in sd tract of land above recited. Signed: Fra.

Land, Christian Land. Wit: Asher Clayton, Sam Bickley, James Armitage. Ack: Aug 1731. (I1-451)

299. Deed. 14 Aug 1731. John Stevenson of NewCastle Co., weaver, & Grace his wife, for the sum of 135 pounds, sold unto John Miller of sd Co., farmer, a tract of land & plantation he now liveth upon, lying on ye north side of Christeen Creek, containing 152 acres. This is part of a larger tract formerly patented to Israel Harrison & John Ellice, patented at Phila. 31 Sept 1692. Signed: John Stevenson, Grace Stevenson (mark). Wit: James Armitage, Lewis Howell, John Allen. Ack: Aug term 1731. (I1-452)

300. Power of Attny. 10 May 1731. Abraham Santford, Johannes Hardenbrook & Jeremiah Tothill, all of the City of New York have appointed in our place, Abraham Depeyster of sd city, merchant, our true & lawful Attny ... for that piece of land in Co. of New Castle on South side & N/NW of Christiana Creek, on West with 'foart Nutten Island', on SW with Spring called Bessey, on East with Ferne Hook, containing 500 acres. Also marsh ground bounding Plantation of John Clasen containing 100 acres. Also two lotts of ground situate on East end of Town of New Castle. We grant to sd Abraham Depeyster the right to sell afsd in our name. Signed: Abrah. Santford, Johannes Hardenbrook, Jere. Tothill. Wit: John Clark, John Clark jun. Affidavit by John Clark Jun. (I1-453)

301. Deed. 15 Aug 1730. Thomas Vandike of East Jersey, weaver, for the sum of 210 pounds, sold unto William Cuerton of New Castle Co., a messuage & tenement of land situate on the south side of Georges Creek. It bounds the land of Saml. Clements and contains 242 acres of land and marsh. Signed: Thomas Vandyck. Wit: Valentin Dushene, Mary Cannon. Ack: Aug Term 1731. (I1-454)

302. Deed. 23 July 1731. William Goforth of the Town of St. Georges in Co. of New Castle, weaver, & Ann his wife, for the sum of 50 pounds, sold unto Andrew Jubarr of Red Lyon Hun. in sd Co., weaver, a tract of land situate near sd Town, containing 330 acres. It bounds the lands of James Anderson, David Stoats, John Cox and Floren Sorency's garden. Signed: William Goforth, Ann Goforth (mark). Wit: Abram. Gooding, Thos. Noxon. Ack: Aug Term 1731. (I1-455)

303. Deed. 23 July 1731. Andrew Jubar of Red Lyon Hun. in Co. of New Castle, weaver, for the sum of 50 pounds, sold unto William Goforth of ye Town of St. Georges, weaver, a messuage land & tenement situate in sd Town, containing 3 acres. It bounds the lands of Enoch Conway, sd Wm Goforth, Benja. Swett and Jacob VanBebber, merchant. Signed: Andrew Jubar (mark). Wit: Abram. Gooding, Thos. Noxon. Ack: Aug Term 1731. (I1-456)

304. Deed. 31 July 1730. Robert Robertson of ye Town & Co. of New Castle, Gent., & Hernelea his wife, for the sum of 40 pounds, sold unto William Battell of same place, Gent., a piece of ground situate in the Town of New Castle (part of a larger lott, late in ye tenure of Col. John French, dec'd.). It begins on north side of Beaver Street at SE corner of ye Quaker Meeting ground, and contains 1 acre of ground. Signed: Robertson, Harnulah Robertson. Wit: James Floyd (mark), William Allmond, George Graham (mark). Ack: Aug term 1731. (I1-459)

305. Deed. 18 Aug 1731. Thomas Gray, Exr. of Last Will of John Renzey, late of New Castle Co., merchant, dec'd., for the sum of 100 pounds, 15 shillings, sold to James Hutchinson of sd Co., Mariner, a messuage and 12 acres of land situate lying at White Clay Creek in sd Co., together with all barns stables mills store houses and outhouses. Sd Will of sd Renzey, was dated 11 April 1731 and named sd Execr. Signed: Thomas Gray. Wit: Thomas Creaghead, Wm. Patterson. Ack: Aug Term 1731. (I1-460)

306. Deed. 19 Aug 1731. James Hutchinson of New Castle Co., mariner, for the sum of 101 pounds, sold unto Thos Gray of sd Co., merchant, a messuage and 12 acres of land situate lying at White Clay Creek in sd Co. Signed: James Hutchinson. Wit: Thomas Creaghead, Wm. Patterson. Ack: Aug Term 1731. (I1-461)

307. Deed. 28 June 1731. Peter Dollan of New Castle Co., Mariner, and Catharine his wife, for the sum of 149 pounds, sold unto John Richardson of Christiana Hun. in sd Co., merchant, and John McCoole of Georges Hun. in sd Co., yeoman, Execs. of ye Last Will & Testament of John Ashton, late of Georges Hun., yeoman, dec'd., two pieces of land. One piece of land containing 143 acres is situate in New Castle Hun. in sd Co. It bounds the land formerly of Henry Land, land late of John Reynolds & Arthur Fairis, land of Thos Dakeyne and Wm Patterson, formerly of Thos Midriff, and land late of Wm Parsons. The second piece is a messuage and piece of ground situate on the south side of Christiana Bridge. It begins by the door of John Lewden sen.'s dwelling house, and contains 1-1/4 acre 25 perches. (Wife of sd Dollan named 'Mary' at one time). Sd Peter Dollan and his wife Catherine appoint Robt Gordon, Chars. Springer & Simon Hadly their Attny to deliver this Deed in Court. Signed: Pr. Dollan, Catharine Dollan. Wit: Wm Read, Bourn, Sigfs. Alrich. (I1-462)

308. Deed. 8 Feb 1731. Aves French and Wm. Battell, Exec. of the Testament of John French of New Castle Co., Gent., dec'd., for the sum of 320 pounds sold unto John Renolds, yeoman, of sd Co., three tracts of land situate in sd Co. One of them contains 240 acres 64 perches. It begins by the Maryland Road and

bounds the lands of John Grantom & Peter Anderson, of John Garretson now Arthur Fairis' land, of Cathern Garretson now Peter Dolands land and John Granthams. One other tract contains 80 acres. It begins by Elk River Road and bounds the land of John Renolds, formerly of Henry Lands. The third piece of land contains 69 acres 96 perches. It bounds the lands of Peter Anderson and John Renolds, and island formerly belonging to John William Neering. Also a piece of marsh bounding marshes of Peter Alrichs and Joseph Roads, containing 400 acres. Afsd John French by deed dated 20 May 1720 became bound unto sd John Renolds in ye sum of 320 pounds for ye messuage plantation, formerly belonging to Cornelius Tobey containing 400 acres. Signed: Aves French, W. Battell. Wit: John Hore Jun., VnGezell. Ack: Aug term 1731. (I1-465)

309. Deed. 8 April 1731. Philip James of Pencader Hun. in Co. of New Castle and Ann his wife, for the sum of 98 pounds, sold unto John Jones of Philadelphia in Prov. of Penn., Bolster, 200 acres of land situate on Christiana Creek in sd Co. It bounds the lands of Howell James, land late of Jas. James and David Thomas. This piece of land & premises was formerly mortgaged (not yet released) to Francis Land, yeoman, to sd Philip James & Ann by Deed dated 6 Jan 1729. Signed: Philip James, Ann James. Wit: Wm. Becke, Bourn. Affidavid signed by Jno. Richardson. Ack May Term 1731. (I1-467)

310. Deed. 2 Nov 1730. William Aubery of City of London in ye Kingdom of GB, merchant & Latitia his wife, of the 1st part, by their Attorneys James Logan of City of Philad. in Prov. of Penn., merchant, and Rees Thomas of Co. of Phila, Gent., grant unto Henry Green of Co. of New Castle, carpenter, a parcel of land containing 100 acres, situate in sd Co. It bounds the lands of John Montgomery, Thos. Dickson and Thos. Hollingsworth. This is part of 15,000 acres sd Latitia received from her father, Wm. Penn. Signed: James Logan, Rees Thomas. Wit: John Dixon, Archibald McDonald (mark). Ack: Aug Term 1731. (I1-469)

311. New Castle Co. Decembr 2 1731. Joseph England, late of sd Co., Gent., personally appeared before me, David French Esq. Justice for sd Co. and declared that he was present & saw Richard Edwards in the within Power of Attny, named sign seal & deliver the same & subscribe the same Joseph England. Witness also write these same John Philips. Signed: Jos. England. Signed: Da. French. noted: "see page 273 for Power". (I1-471)

END OF DEED RECORDS - VOLUME I-1

BEGINNING OF DEED RECORDS - VOLUME K-1

Note: Pages 1 through 212 missing, badly torn incomplete records begin at page 213 and continue bad through 216. (Records #312-316 below)

312. Deed. (half missing). James Moor and his wife Rebecca grant a parcel of meadow ground and premises unto Zacharias Kettle. Signed: James Moore. Wit: Lucas Stidham, John Wood (mark). 'New Castle May 4th 1734 received of Zacharias Kettle the sum of 20 pounds consideration money being one Iron Gray Horse formerly sold me for the sum of 20 pounds'. Proved by Lucas Stidham in Court May Term 1734. (K1-213)

313. Deed. 20 April 1721. John Campbell of White Clay Creek in Co. of New Castle, yeoman, for the sum of 48 pounds & for good causes, sd Campbell thereunto moving, sold unto Joseph Ramage of same place, yeoman, a parcel of land & premises. (torn document) names: Susanna Guest, widow & relict of John Guest, William Welsh... Part of a larger tract of 1,000 acres by Patent from William Penn dated 23 Oct 1701 confirmed to John Guest. Signed: John Campbell. Wit: Charles Campbell, Josias Ramage. Proved: May 1734. (K1-213)

314. Deed. 26 .. 1734. William Goforth of Town ?, weaver, and Ann his wife, for the sum of 90 pounds, sold unto John Daniel Tony, miller, (torn fragmented rec.) .. bounding land of Jacob Rogers, formerly James Claypools, containing 185 acres. Part of 200 acres granted to Edward Green of Co. of New Castle by Warrant dated 27th day 5th mo. 1685. Sd Green conveyd to sd Jacob Rogers, late of sd Co., dec'd, by deed dated 17 Nov 1696... Sd 185 acres to James James Jun. (missing signature) Wit: Wm Patterson, John Herbert. (K1-214)

315. Deed. 25 April 1734. William McMechen of Co. of New Castle, yeoman, & Jennet his wife, for the sum of 54 pounds, sold to John Withrow, yeoman, of sd Co., a tract of land containing 90 acres, situate on so. side of Brandywine Cr. in sd Co. This is part of a larger tract sold to sd McMechen by James Logan & Rees Thomas, Attny's for Wm Aubery & Latitia his wife, by Deed dated 1 June 172? (Rec: Liber H/page 58). It begins by Red Clay Creek and bounds John Garret's land, and lands of Thomas Wilson and Thomas Hollingsworth, Jeremia Lochrey and Samuel Ruth. (Torn) mentions: Lots of Cor?, John Gooding to William Goforth, sd Goforth and Ann his wife..(end of rec) (K1-2..)

316. Deed. 25 Sept .. William Dixon of Mill Creek Hun. and Hannah his wife, for the sum of 3 pounds, sold to William Pasemore of Co. of Chester in Prov. of Pen., yeoman, one equal fourth part of a tract of land, situate in Christiana Hun. (torn doc.) mentions: part of 221 acres and land of James Morton. Signed:

William Dixon (mark), Hannah Dixon. Wit: Simon Hadly, James James Jun.
Ack: May term 1734. David French (K1-2..)

317. Deed. 25 Sept 1733. William Dixon of Mill Creek Hun. in Co. of New
Castle, yeoman, and Hannah his wife, for the sum of 3 pounds, sold unto John
Sasmore of Township of Kennet in Co. of Chester, yeoman, one equal fourth
part of a tract of land & premises, situate in Christiana Hun. This is part of a
larger tract of 221 acres that sd Dixson bought from Henry Smitker and
Catherine his wife by Deed dated 18 Sept 1729. (Book I/page 122). It bounds
land of James Morton and contains 13 acres. Signed: William Dixson (mark),
Hannah Dixson. Wit: Simon Hadly, James James Jun. Ack: May Term 1734.
David French. (K1-217)

318. Deed. 18 Feb 1733/4. John Grigg of Christiana Hun. in Co. of New Castle,
yeo., & Elizabeth his wife, for the sum of 30 pounds, sold unto Jonathan Strange
of same place, clothworker, a parcel of land containing 50 acres, situate in sd
Hun. & Co.. It bounds the land of Joseph Underwood & sd Strange. This is part
of a larger tract of 124 acres, that was granted along with another tract
containing 94 acres, by Patent dated 31 Dec last from John Penn, Thomas Penn
and Richard Penn. (Rec. Phila. Patent Book A/Vo 6/page 243). Signed: John
Gregg, Elizabeth Gregg (mark). Wit: William Allen, Zach. Butcher. Ack: May
Term 1734. David French pro. (K1-218)

319. Deed. 18 Feb 1733/4. Samuel Underwood of Christiana Hun. in Co. of
New Castle, yeoman, eldest son & heir at Law of Samuel Underwood lately
dec'd., and Mary his wife, and Joseph Underwood, and Benjamin Underwood,
Exec., of the Last Will of sd Saml., for the sum of 45 pounds, sold unto
Jonathan Strange of same place, clothworker, a tract of land & premises
containing 50 acres, situated by Brandywine Cr. This is part of a larger tract of
200 acres that was granted unto John Grigg of same place, oldrenter, by virtue
of a Warrant from Thomas Holms, Surveyor, dated 20th day 3rd mo. 1685. It
was then by Patent under Wm Penn's Comm. of Property (Wm Markham,
Robert Turner & John Goodson) conveyed to sd Saml Underwood dec'd..
Signed: Saml. Underwood (mark), Mary Underwood (mark), Joseph
Underwood, Beng. C. Underwood. Wit: Thomas Willsoon, Zach. Butcher.
'Proved by Charles Springer May Term 1734'. (K1-219)

320. Deed. 15 April (torn document). Joseph Chambers and William Chambers
of.., for the sum of 1..(?), sold to David Nivin of same place, part of a tract of
land called the Hop Yard situate on No. side of White Clay Creek. This part was
sold to sd John Chambers by David Loyd by Deed dated 4 May 1720. It bounds
the land of Andrew Neils, Charles Bryans, Moses Kenny, sd Joseph Chambers,

Wm McCreas and James Boggs. It contains 200 acres 36 perches of land. (end of record). (K1-223)

Note: pages 225 and 226 missing.

321. (front of document missing). Mentions granting to Mathias Sereck. Signed: James Anderson, Anne Anderson (mark). Wit: Andrew Peterson, R. Cantwell. Ack: May Term 1734. David French pro. (K1-227)

322. Deed. 22 May 1734. Samuel Vance of St. Georges Hun. in Co. of New Castle, yeoman, for the sum of 51 pounds, sold unto Anne Heally of Appoquinimink Hun. in sd Co., widow, and William Harroway, son and heir of Samuel Harroway, dec'd., a tract of land containing 100 acres. It is situate on the north side of Blackbirds Creek, binding upon Beaver Dam, and bounds land of Robert Hartup. This is land that sd Vance was seized of by virtue of a Deed Poll dated 20 Aug 1719 from Rowland Fitz-Gerald, Esq. High Sheriff of sd Co., under direction of the Justices of Court of Common Pleas. Signed: Samuel Vance. Wit: David French, John Legate. Ack: May Term 1734. (K1-227)

323. Deed. 20 May 1734. Peter Davis of St. Georges Hun. in Co. of New Castle, yeoman, and Hannah his wife, for the sum of 66 pounds, sold unto Abraham Goulden of same place, yeoman, a one third part of 200 acres containing 66 acres of land and premises. This is whereas Daniel Smith, late of sd Co., dec'd., obtained a Warrant for 200 acres of land dated 1st day 5th mo. 1684. Thomas Pierson, Surveyed sd land 31st day 3rd mo. 1685. It bounded land of Casparius Hermanus on the Canoe Branch of the Delaware River. Sd Smith died leaving issue one son named Casparus Smith. Sd son by his Deed Poll dated 20 Nov 1705 granted sd land & premises unto Richard Davis. (Lib C/fol:128/129). Sd property called Strawberry Hill. Sd Davis' Last Will dated 9 April 1719, directed sd land should be equally divided in between his sons in three parts. One third part for Philip Davis dec'd. & by his heirs bought of afsd Peter Davis. One third part for Richard Davis, dec'd. Signed: Peter Davis, Hannah Davis. Wit: Abram Gooding, Thos. Noxon. Ack: May Term 1734. (K1-228)

324. Deed. 22 May 1734. Thomas Sawyer of St. Georges Hun. in Co. of New Castle, yeoman, and Guardian to the Heir of Peter Brank of sd Hun., dec'd., for the sum of 160 pounds, sold unto Richard Walkinson of same place, cloathier, a plantation and tract of land situate in sd Hun. & Co. It contains 101 acres of land and 10 acres of marsh, and bounds the land of Lawrence Skeer. Sd Peter Brank by indenture dated 11 May 1726 did convey sd land & marsh to Francis Land of Christiana Creek (with certain condition of redemption in writing). (Lib H/page 213). Soon after Exec. of sd Deed, sd Peter Brank died and afsd Thomas Sawyer

83

appointed by Orphans Court as Guardian to children of sd Brank. Sd Sawyer redeemed sd land & marsh for benefit of sd children by Deed of Release dated 29 May 1733 from sd Land. Signed: Thomas Sawyer. Wit: Francis Land, Thomas Noxon, Cha. Robinson. Ack: May Term 1734. (K1-230)

325. Deed. 3 July 1732. Andrew Justason of Christiana Hun. in Co. of New Castle, farmer, and Breta his wife, for the sum of 10 pounds, sold unto Joseph Way off sd Hun. & Co., a piece of ground containing 4 acres 35 perches, lying on the no. side of Christiana Cr. within the Town of Willingtown in sd Co.. It bounds the land of Charles Empson and Doctor James Milner. Signed: Andrew Justason (mark), Breta Justason (mark). Tho. Willing, Samuel Milner, Charles Empson. Ack: May Term 1734. (K1-232)

326. Deed. 3 July 1732. Andrew Justason of Christiana Hun. in Co. of New Castle, farmer, and Breta his wife, for the sum of 5(?) pounds, sold to Charles Empson of sd Hun. & Co., mariner, a lott of ground situate within the Town of Willing Town on the north side of Christiana Cr. It bounds the lotts of Samuel Scott, Doctor Milner and Joseph Way. Signed: Andrew Justason (mark), Breta Justason (mark). Wit: Tho. Willing, Samuel Milner. Ack: May Term 1734. (K1-233)

327. Deed. 3 July 1732. Andrew Justason of Christiana Hun. in Co. of New Castle, farmer, and Breta his wife, for the sum of (?) pounds, sold to James Milner of sd Hun. & Co., 'Chirurgoon', two lotts of ground lying on the no. side of Christiana Creek within the Town of Willingtown. One lott bounds lotts of Charles Empson, Samuel Scott and Joseph Ways, and contains 2 acres 5 perches. The other lott bounds sd Justason's dwelling house and lott of Joseph Ways, and contains 1 acre 152 perches. Signed: Andrew Justason (mark), Breta Justason. Wit: Tho. Willing, Joseph Way. Cha. Empson. Ack: May Term 1734. (K1-234)

328. Deed of Release. 15 May 1734. Francis Land of Christiana Creek in Co. of New Castle, yeoman, for the sum of 46 pounds 12 shilling paid by Thomas Sawyer of St. Georges Hun. in sd Co., yeoman and Guardian to the Children of Peter Brank of sd Hun., dec'd., release and forever quit claim all my right of property that I have by virtue of an Indenture of Mortgage made between Brank, dec'd, and sd Francis Land, bearing date 11 May 1726. This is a plantation tract of land containing 101 acres. Signed: Fr. Land. Wit: Chas. Robinson, Thos. Noxon. Ack: May Term 1734. (K1-236)

329. Deed. 22 Feb 1733. Michael Myre of New Castle Co. & Brandywine Hun., yeoman, for the sum of 46 pounds, sold unto David McMullen of sd Hun. &

Co., yeoman, a tract of land containing 100 acres lying on the West side of Delaware in the Mannor or Rockland. This is land that Lawrence Hendrickson, late of Shillpot Creek in sd Hun. & Co. in his lifetime was seized of. (It was surveyed by Henry Hollingsworth, dep. surv. on 9th day 6th mo. 1689). Sd Hendrickson died leaving issue two daughters, Elizabeth and Rebeccah who inherited land. Sd daughters then granted sd land unto afsd Michael Myre. Signed: Michael Myre (mark), Ann Myre (mark). Wit: Tho. Cartmell, John Campbell. Ack: May Term 1734. (K1-237)

330. Deed. 7 March 1733. John VnGezel of New Castle, sadler, and Mary his wife, for the sum of 77 pounds 10 shill., sold unto Henry Gonne of same place, shopkeeper, two lotts of ground situate in the Town of New Castle. One of them contains 30 feet in breadth 150 feet in length. It is bounded by the orchard of Mosses Degonne, land bequeathed by John Land to his son Joseph, land late of John McGhee now of Philip Janvier. The other lott contains 25 feet in breadth & behind bordering on the lott sold by sd John VnGezel and Mary his wife to Hester Glen. Signed: Jno. VnGezell, Mary Vangessell. Wit: Richd. Grafton, Richd. Bermingham. Ack: May Term 1734. (K1-238)

331. Deed. 6 March 1733. Henry Gonne of New Castle, shopkeeper, and Elizabeth his wife, for the sum of 10 pounds, sold unto John VnGezell of same place, sadler, a part of a lott of ground & premises, situate in Minquaa's St. in New Castle, containing 30 feet breadth 150 feet length. It bounds the lott of Moses Degone, land bequeathed by John Land to his son Joseph Land and ground late of John McChee now of Philip Janvier. Sd Gonne and wife appoint Wm Read and John Legate as their Attny to ack. this deed. Signed: H. Gonne, Elizabeth Gonne. Wit: Richd. Grafton, Richd. Bermingham. Ack: May Term 1734. (K1-239)

332. Deed. 12 Dec 1733. Parnellah Battell, Widow Relict & Exec. of William Battell, late of Co. of New Castle, Gent. dec'd., for the sum of 30 pounds sold unto George Monroe of sd Co., Innholder & glazier, a piece of a lott of ground & premises, situate in the Town of New Castle. It begins at the house late of Roelof Dehaes, now possessed by John Russell, to the Church, to lott late of Doctor Reily, now of Gideon Griffith. This lott formerly belonged to Gunning Bedford, then sd Bedford and his wife Mary granted same unto afsd Wm Battell, by Deed dated 18 May 1720. Signed: Parnellah Battell. Wit: Henry Newton, Stephen Lewis, Robertson. Ack: May term 1734. (K1-241)

333. Deed. 26 March 1733. George Ross of Co. of New Castle, Gent., surviving Exec. of the Last Will of Richard Halliwell, late of sd Co., merchant, dec'd., for the sum of 24 pounds 5 shill (being the highest price), sold unto Robert Gordon

of sd Co., Gent., a parcel of marsh situate on the west side of Horse Dyke. It contains 40 acres, and bounds the marsh late of Robert French, dec'd.. The sd Will of sd Halliwell, dated 4 Dec 1716, directed that his Execs were to sell his 400 acres of land that were lately granted him by Patent, also his marsh containing 40 acres and also 17 acres of land adjoining sd marsh. (John Moore was his other Exec. but has died). Signed: Geo. Ross. Wit: Richd. Bermingham, Anthony Dowdall, H. Gonne. Ack: May Term 1734. (K1-242)

334. Deed. 28 May 1734. Emphraim Titus of Hunterdon Co. in Prov. of West New Jersey, sole heir of George Hadley, late of Co. of New Castle, dec'd., for the sum of 30 pounds, sold unto Thomas Noxon a plantation & tract of land late belonging to afsd Hadley, dec'd., an Uncle of afsd Titus. Sd property now in the tenure of John Clark and is situate in Red Lyon Hun. in sd Co. It bounds the Dragon Swamp, the lands of John Tilton, Hans Hans, dec'd., and Henry Ward, dec'd. It contains 200 acres, together with a parcel of marsh containing 15 acres. Sd Titus appoints William Shaw and Gideon Griffith as Attny. Signed: Ephraim Titus. Wit: Mary Titus, John Titus, Edward Hart. Affidavit dated 4 June 1734 signed James James Jun. (K1-244)

335. Promissory Note. "I promise to pay to Henry Gonne on Order three months after Date hereof Two merchantable Fat six year old Steers of the value of three pounds each...27th Day of June 1733. William Hamilton". Testis S. Bourn. "Sampson Bourn appeared before two Justices & deposeth the note in company with Wm Hamilton (sd William was a resident in Co. of New Castle & was frequently called & known by the name of Jockey Hamilton) & Henry Gonne & this Dept. as Evidence of note. Oct 15 1734". Sworn before us R. Gordon, Richd. Grafton. (K1-245)

336. Appointment. 15 Aug. "George Phenny, Esq. Surveyor Gent. of His Majesties Customs in the So. District on the Continent of America, send Greeting. Know that by Authority granted me, I appoint Sergeant Smithies, Gent. & Searcher of all Rates, Dutys & Impositions arising within Crecks Harbours & costs from Cape Henlopen to Christian Creek upon Delaware...." Signed: G. Phenney. (K1-246)

337. Deed. 20 May 1734. Benjamin Stout of Redlyon Hun. in Co. of New Castle, yeom., and Elizabeth his wife, for the sum of 150 pounds, sold unto John Goforth of sd Hun. & Co., tanner, a messuage and 135 acres of land, situate in sd Hun. & Co. It bounds Kings Road that leads to Bohemia. This land and marsh was granted by Benjamin Stout Senr., dec'd., to afsd Benjamin Stout by his Deed dated 6 Sept 1731. Also another piece of marsh adjoining afsd land & premises, containing 5 acres. This bounds the line of Thomas Morgan's marsh.

This 5 acres is part of 250 acres that was sold by John Hales, late of sd Co. unto Stephen Lewis in 1724, and added to sd 135 acres. Signed: Benjamin Stout, Elizabeth Stout. Wit: John Campbell, Josiah Lewis. Examination of Elizabeth Stout by Andw. Peterson. Ack: Aug Term 1734. (K1-246)

338. Deed. 18 May 1734. John Garretson of White Clay Creek Hun. in Co. of New Castle, yeom., son of Paul Garretson, dec'd., and Elizabeth his wife, for the sum of 15 pounds, sold unto Nicholas Hayman of Christiana Bridge in sd Co., merchant, a parcel of land containing 13 acres and also two acres of marsh, situate at Fish Point in sd Co. The first bounds land of Peter Anderson. The marsh bounds Red Lyon Creek. This is land that Jacobus Williams Neering was seized of by Deed dated 28 Dec 1720. Sd Neering granted same two parcels unto Valentine Cork, late of Co. of Phila. in Prov. of Penn., dec'd. and Elizabeth his wife. Signed: John Garretson (mark), Elizabeth Garretson (mark). Wit: George McKay, Elinor Wintor (mark). Elizabeth was examined by James James Jun. Ack: Aug Term 1734. (K1-248)

339. Deed. 17 Aug 1734. Andrew Jubart of Red Lyon Hun. in Co. of New Castle, weaver, for the sum of 95 pounds, sold unto Egbord Egbordson of same place, yeoman, part of a tract of land containing 80 acres, situate in sd Hun. & Co. It bounds the lands of Peter Leforgos and Peter Anderson. This is whereas Edmond Andros by his Patent dated 5 Nov 1675 did grant unto Joseph Young of sd Co. a parcel of land bounding St. Georges and Dragon Creeks, containing 1,280 acres. Sd Jacob (named) Young dyed leaving two sons, Jacob & Joseph; who by their Deeds dated 20 Aug 1706 and 10 Nov 1700 conveyed unto Charles Anderson and John Cox sd land. Sd Anderson & sd Cox by their Deed dated 20 July 1708 did confirm unto Joseph Neale of Salom in New England the uppermost part of sd land, containing 437 acres. Then sd Neale dyed leaving one son, Joseph Neale, who by his indenture dated 18 May 1714 did grant unto David Stout of Freehold in Prov. of East New Jersey, 330 acres of sd land. Then sd Stout by his indenture dated 13 April 1715 granted unto Francis King of Appoquinimink in afsd Co. sd 330 acres. Then sd King by indenture dated 13 May 1718 did confirm unto Peter Jubart, Jacob Jubart, Maudlin Jubart, Andrew Jubart and Abraham Jubart sd 330 acres. Whereas afsd Andrew Jubart became seized of sd land as the sole survivor and heir. Signed: Andrew Jubart (mark). Wit: Enoch Cornwall, Thos. Noxon. (K1-250)

340. Deed. 19 Aug 1734. Abraham Gouldon of St. Georges Hun. in Co. of New Castle, yeoman, and Ann his wife, for the sum of 8 pounds, sold unto John Sands of sd Hun. & Co., taylor, a parcel of land containing 10 acres, situate in sd Hun. & Co. This is part of a larger tract that Alexander Adams, dec'd., was seized of. It bounded the Maxwour Road and lands of sd Alexander Adams,

John Rice and Cornelius King. Then sd Adams by Deed Poll dated 14 May 1705 granted unto Peter King sd tract containing 250 acres. Sd King by indenture dated 9 Dec 1710 granted same unto Mathias Borkolls of the City of New York, yeoman. Sd Borkhole by indenture dated 9 Dec 1711 did sell same land unto afsd Abraham Gouldon. Signed: Abram. Golden, Ann Golden (mark). Wit: Hans Hanson, T. Noxon. Ann Golden examined by Hans Hanson. (K1-252)

341. Deed. 10 May 1734. Henry Packard of Appoquinimink Hun. in Co. of New Castle, yeoman, and Ann his wife, for the sum 75 pounds, sold to Peter Packard of St. Georges Hun. in sd Co., yeoman, a tract of land containing 110 acres, situate in Appoquinimink Hun. This is part of a larger tract of 300 acres that William Penn by his Warrant dated 5 Sept 1684 did grant unto William Clark. Sd Clark then assigned his Right & Interest of sd Warrent to Isaac Wheeldon. Thomas Pierson surveyed sd land on a branch called Sasafrass. Then sd land passed to sd Wheeldon's son & heir Joseph Wheeldon; who by his Deed Poll dated 19 Sept 1711 did grant same land and premises unto Cornelius Williams. Then sd Williams by indenture dated 8 April 1730 did grant same unto afsd Henry Packard. Signed: Henry Packard, Ann Packard (mark). Wit: Richard Rogers. Ann Packard was examined by Andw. Peterson. Ack: Aug Term 1734. (K1-254)

342. "Recd from Mr. Richard Grafton 148 penny weight & 4 grains wt of gould 148 penny weight & 12 grains wt of silver & 12 shill & 6 pence sherd? silver to be laid out in sundry goods agreeable to his orders abroad & to be remitted him New Castle 24th July 1732. Nathal. Patterson". (K1-256)

343. "Recd from Mr. Richard Grafton 17 pounds Barbadoes Curry to be laid out in Ozenburghs & Garlick to be remitted him from abroad New Castle 28 July 1732. Nathal. Patterson". (K1-256)

344. Deed. 19 Aug 1734. William Pattison of St. Georges Hun. in Co. of New Castle, yeoman, and Mary his wife, for the sum of 250 pounds, sold unto Elias Naudain of same place, mariner, a tract of land containing 200 acres and plantation that was bequeathed him by his father. This is part of a larger tract whereas Edmund Andros by his Patent dated 1 Dec 1675 did Grant unto Caspares Herman. It was called St. Augustine, and layed opposite to Reeden Island on the Delaware River, bounding the land of Claes Kirston. Then sd Herman by his Deed dated 17 March 1686/7 did convey 400 acres, part of sd land to William Pattison. Then sd Pattison made his Last Will dated 17 Jan 1696, he gave to his daughter Elizabeth Pattison 100 acres, and unto his son, afsd William, the remainder of the Plantation when they come of age. Signed: William Pattison (mark), Mary Pattison (mark). Wit: Hans Hanson, Thos.

Noxon. Mary Pattison was examined by Hans Hanson. Ack: Aug Term 1734. (K1-256)

345. Judgement. 17 May 1734. Henry Newton, Esq. High Sheriff of Co. of New Castle, send Greeting. Whereas Edward Jones of St. Georges Hun., merchant, was lately in Court and recovered against Peter Davis Exe. of the Last Will of Philip Davis, late of sd Hun, dec'd., a debt of 20 pounds & damages. Whereas by a writ dated 17 Aug, John Gooding, late Sheriff was commanded to seize goods & chattles of sd Davis. Seized & taken in Execution from the hands of Peter Davis, Exe. was a tract of land containing 200 acres at value of 50 pounds. Writ witnessed by Robert Gordon, Esq. Sd tract of land was divided and part sold to Abraham Goulden for the sum of 47 pounds 10 shilling. It bounds the now dwelling place of John Sands and contains 60 acres. Signed: Henry Newton, sheriff. Wit: John Vance, Thos. Noxon. Ack: Aug term 1734. (K1-258)

346. Deed. 11 Aug 1734. Francis Land of Christeen in Co. of New Castle, yeoman, for the sum of 31 pounds, release to Richard Smith and Margary his wife, heirs of George Williams, a tract of land. Signed: Fr. Land. Wit: John Price, James Anderson. Ack: Aug Term 1734. (K1-260)

347. Deed. 23 Aug 1734. James Thompson of Mill Creek Hun. in Co. of New Castle, for the sum of 38 pounds 10 shilling, confirm unto Thos. Berry of Christiana Hun. in sd Co., cordwainer, a parcel of land containing 34 acres, situate in Christiana Hun. It bounds the lands of La? Tomlinson, Peter Hendrickson and sd Berry. This is part of a tract taken up by Warrant from Wm Penn in 1684 unto Adam Stedham. Sd Stedham bequeathed sd land unto his children; and land sold unto Andrew Cock by Henry Stedham, eldest son of Adam. Sd Cock by Deed confirmed 34 acres and 6 more to Arthur Faires, who by Deed dated 19 Feb 1733/4 granted sd 34 acres to afsd Jas. Thompson. Signed: James Thompson (mark). Wit: Jas. Hamilton, Thos. Gray. Ack: Aug 1734. (K1-260)

348. Deed. 20 Aug 1734. Edmund Shaw of Red Lyon Hun. in Co. of New Castle, yeoman & surviving Adm. of the Estate of John Shaw, dec'd., for the sum of 39 pounds, sold unto William Whillet of St. Georges Hun. in sd Co., merchant, 200 acres of land, situate in Appoquinimink Hun. This is whereas Mathew Corbit, dec'd, in his lifetime, by virtue of two Warrants (one dated 11th dy 1st mo 1705), was seized of two pieces of land. Sd Corbit's Last Will dated 10 Feb 1719, bequeathed to his two daughters, Jane and Mary, each 100 acres out of the tract, called the old Plantation, late in possession of John Peele, dec'd. Sd Jane Corbit intermarried with Thomas Bassett and sd Mary intermarried with Benj. Richardson. The two couples sold the adjoined 200 acres unto John Shaw,

dec'd., by Deed dated 10 May 1731 (Lib J/page 436). Sd John Shaw died without leaving sufficient to pay debts. Orphans Court on 16 July 1734 before John Richardson, Charles Springer, Richard Grafton, James Armitage, James James and Thomas James, sd Edmund Shaw said he overpaid Estate himself 20 pounds and petitions for reimbursement. Signed: Edmond Shaw. Wit: Thos. Noxon, Rodger Shennan. Ack: Aug Term 1734. (K1-261)

349. Deed. 20 Aug 1734. Adam Peterson of Appoquinimink Hun. in Co. of New Castle, yeoman, and Mary his wife, for the sum of 100 pounds, sold unto Andrew Peterson of St. Georges Hun. in sd Co., Esq., a tract of land containing 200 acres. It bounds the plantation now in tenure of Edward Best. This is part of a larger tract of 400 acres that Lewis Johnson, dec'd., by virtue of a Patent was seized of. It was situate on the south side of Appoquinimink Creek, opposite to land of Barent Hendrickson, and bounding land of Cornelius Bays & Camps. Sd Johnson, by Deed Poll dated 30 Jan 1673, sold same to Henry Touls and Robert Money. Then sd Touls set over his share unto sd Money, dated 21 Nov 1674 (written on bottom of Deed). Sd Money dyed and in his Last Will he appointed Edward Larimore of Maryland, Exec. Sd Larimore by his Deed Poll dated 20 June 1692 sold sd land & premises unto Roelof Anderson. Sd Anderson made his Last Will dated 18 Aug 1685 and bequeathed to his wife, Hilleka, all his real estate. Then sd Hilleka, widow, made her Last Will dated 20 July 1708 and bequeathed to her cousin, Adam Peterson, son of her brother Adam Peterson, dec'd., the sd 400 acres. Signed: Adam Peterson, Mary Peterson (mark). Wit: Thos. Noxon, John Day. Ack: Aug Term 1734. (K1-263)

350. Deed. 20 Aug 1734. Abraham Vandike and Andrew Vandike of St. Georges Hun. in Co. of New Castle, yomen and sons of Andrew Vandike, dec'd., and Joseph Miller of New Castle Hun., carpenter and Mary his wife, daughter of afsd Vandike, for the sum of 40 pounds and also for affection which they bear to their brother, John Vandike of St. Georges Hun., yeoman & elder son of afsd Vandike, grant unto him their interest in the Plantation & tract of land, now in sd John's possession. It is situate on the north side of Drawyers Creek, bounding land of Thomas Hyet, Abraham Gooding and Garrit Dushene, and contains 160 acres. This is land Andrew Vandike sen. owned. He made his Last Will dated 20 May 1730 and bequeathed sd property to be equally divided amoung his sons, afsd Abraham, Andrew and John, and Jacob, and his daughters, afsd Mary and also Elizabeth and the child his wife was then bigg with. Signed: Abraham Vandike, Andrew Vandike, Joseph Miller, Mary Miller. Wit: Jacob Gooding, Thos. Noxon. Mary Miller examined by James Armitage. Ack: Aug Term 1734. (K1-264)

351. Deed. 12 Aug 1734. Richard Smith of Cecil Co. in Prov. of Maryland,

yeoman, & Margaret his wife, heirs of George Williams, dec'd., for the sum of 130 pounds, sold unto James Creags of Red Lyon Hun. in Co. of New Castle, farmer, a tract of land containing 125 acres, situate in Red Lyon Hun. It bounds Georges Creek and land of Benjamin Stout. This is part of a larger tract of 550 acres, once belonging to Joseph Wood of the town of New Castle, gent., who by indenture of Lease & Release dated 19/20 Feb 1707, did convey same to John Lewis. Sd Lewis by his Last Will dated 1 Sept 1708 did devise 250 acres unto his Exec. to be sold to pay his debts. Then Sarah Lewis, relict & Exec. by her L&R dated 23/24 Dec 1724, did convey 125 acres of sd land unto afsd George Williams, lately dec'd. Signed: Signed: Richard Smith, Margret Smith. Wit: James Anderson, John Price. Margaret Smith examined by James Armitage. Ack: Aug Term 1734. (K1-266)

352. Gift Deed. 20 Nov 1734. John Garretson of New Castle Hun., yeoman, send Greeting. For consideration of the natural Love & Affection which he beareth unto his son & heir apparent, John Garretson junr., and for other causes him, the father especially moving, doth grant to his son one part of a tract of land & plantation, situate on Christiana Creek, now in possession of the father. It contains 200 acres, part of 300 acres. Also one half part of the orchard. Signed: John Garretson (mark). Wit: James James junr., John Herbert. Ack: Nov Term 1734. David French. (K1-267)

353. Deed. 8 June 1734. Michael Butcher of Red Lyon Hun. in Co. of New Castle, yeom, and Maudlean his wife, for the sum of 91 pounds, sold unto Francis Land of Christeen Creek, yeoman, all their Plantation and parcels of land situate in sd Hun. & Co. One parcel, called Beverly, part of a tract called the Exchange, bounds Dragon Swamp & Beaver Dam, and contains 100 acres. Also another called Hansons Marsh contains 50 acres. It bounds the land of John Stout and Cedar Creek. Also a part of marsh in Peter Hanson's land belonging to sd Butcher. Signed: Michael Butcher, Maudlean Butcher (mark). Wit: James James Junr., Jean Garison. Maudlin Butcher was examined on 10 July 1734 by James James Junr. Ack: Aug Term 1734. (K1-268)

354. Deed. 13 Nov 1734. John Garretson of Christeen Creek in Co. of New Castle, yeoman, for the sum of 19 pounds 16 shilling, sold to Francis Land of same place, yeoman, a parcel of land containing 20 acres, situate in New Castle Hun. in sd Co. It bounds the land of John Hill and land sd Hill lately purchased of sd Garretson, land formerly belonging to Major John Donaldson in the tenure of Peter Alrichs, Benjamin Dors and Tho. Turner. This is part of the land formerly granted to sd Garretson by Warrant and laid out for 60 acres. Signed: John Garretson (mark). Wit: John Hill, Rose Hill, Saml. Land. Ack: Nov Term 1734. (K1-269)

355. Deed. 13 Nov 1734. John Garretson of Christeen Creek in Co. of New Castle, yeoman, for the sum of 30 pounds, sold unto John Hill of Mill Creek in sd Co., wheelwright, a parcel of land containing 40 acres, situate in New Castle Hun. in sd Co. It bounds the land of John Harris by Elk River and land of Francis Land. Signed: John Garretson (mark). Wit: Fr. Land, Saml. Land, Christan Land. Ack: Nov Term 1734. (K1-270)

356. Deed. 18 Nov 1734. Francis Graham, Executor of the Estate of Elizabeth Ogle, Relict of Thomas Ogle of Mill Creek Hun. in Co. of New Castle, yeoman, lately deceased, sendeth Greeting. There is a parcel of land containing 140 acres 30 perches, situate in sd Hun. & Co. It bounds the land of George Patty by White Clay Creek, lands of Archibald Howe and William Gaulaghord. This is part of a tract called (?) brothers, granted by Patent dated 28th day 1st mo 1684 from Gov. Penn. Land surveyed 6 Feb 1733/4 and Thomas Ogle sold same to his son James Ogle, but he died before land was confirmed unto sd son. By Thomas Ogle's Last Will dated 13 July 1734, he ordered his Exec. to confirm same, which this instrument does. Signed: Francis Graham. Wit: Fr. Land, Saml. Land. Ack: Nov Term 1734. (K1-271)

357. Deed. 7 Nov 1734. Thomas Hathorn of White Clay Creek Hun. in Co. of New Castle, yeoman, and Jennet his wife, for the sum of 176 pounds, sold unto Hugh Stewart of London Township in Co. of Chester, a tract of land containing 100 acres. This is land that James Claypoole and James Turner by their Patent dated 7 March 1686 did grant unto Broer Sonexon. It was called Waters Land, and situate on No. & So. side of White Clay Creek. Sd Sonexon conveyed his Right Title of sd land on the south side containing 100 acres unto Thomas Ogle Sen, by Deed dated 1 March 1698. Sd Ogle by Deed dated 26 Aug 1732 granted same unto James Ogle. Signed Thos. Hathorn, Jennet Hathorn (mark). Wit: William McMechen, James McMechen. 20 Nov 1734 Jennet Hathorn examined by James James Jun. Ack: Nov Term 1734. (K1-272)

358. Deed. 19 Aug 1734. Egbord Egbordson of Red Lyon Hun. in Co. of New Castle, yeoman, for the sum of 90 pounds, sold unto Abraham Goulden and Lewis Geton, both of St. Georges Hun. in sd Co., yeomen, two tracts of land. One is a Plantation and land containing 80 acres, situate in St. Georges neck in Red Lyon Hun. It bounds the lands of Peter Lforges and Peter Anderson. The other is a point of land lying contiguous, containing 20 acres. Signed: Egbort Egbortson (mark), Mary Egbortson (mark). Wit: Hans Hanson, Jab. VBebber. Mary Egberdson examined by Hans Hanson. (K1-274)

359. Deed. 14 Sept 1734. Sarah James, the daughter of John James, dec'd, of Pencader Hun. in Co. of New Castle, spinster, for the sum of 40 pounds, sold

unto John Lindsay of the same place, yeoman, a parcel of land containing 207 acres 147 perches, situate in sd Hun. & Co. It bounds the lands of Benjamin Underwood, Thomas James, Henry Bevan and Robert Harris. This is part of a larger tract of 525 acres sold by William Davis and David Evans to Richard Prigg, and conveyed by sd Prigg to afsd John James by Deed dated 27 March 1716. Condition is that sd John Lindsay will pay to Prop. of Prov. of Penn. money due by Agreement between the Prop and William Davis and David Evans dated 15 Oct 1701. Signed: Sarah James. Wit: Hannah Armitage, James Armitage. Ack: Nov Term 1734. (K1-275)

360. Deed. 19 Aug 1734. Thomas Jones of Brandywine Hun. in Co. of New Castle, for consideration of sum of 40 pounds paid by William Derrickson and John Wilder of sd Hun & Co., grant unto them a messuage or tract of land containing 91 acres, situate in sd Hun. & Co. Signed: Thomas Jones (mark). Wit: George Robinson, Valentine Robinson. Proved Aug Term 1734. (K1-276)

361. Power of Attny. 20 Aug 1734. Thomas Jones of Brandywine Hun. in Co. of New Castle have ordained my well beloved Friend, Andrew Hudson of sd Hun. & Co. to be my true Attorney in my name to recover such debts due me, and Authority to make over in open Court of Common Pleas, to deliver to William Derrickson and John Wilder a Deed of 91 acres. Signed: Thomas Jones (mark). Wit: George Robinson, Valentine Robinson. (K1-277)

362. Deed. 7 Sept 1734. John Hore of the town & Co. of New Castle, Surveyor, for the sum of 35 pounds, grant unto Mary Stewart, widdow & relict of James Stewart, late of sd Co., dec'd., a parcel of land containing 84 acres. This is land that sd James Stewart became seized of by virtue of a Patent dated 6 Sept in year afsd. It is situate on the north side of Christiana Creek in sd Co., and bounds the land of Matthias VnBebber. Signed: John Hore. Wit: George Monro, Benj. Gibbs. Ack: Nov Term 1734. (K1-277)

363. Deed. 25 Aug 1734. Thomas Willing of Christiana Hun. in Co. of New Castle, cooper, and Catherine his wife, and Andrew Justis and Bridget his wife, for the sum of 11 pounds, sold unto Samuel Kirk of the same place, storekeeper, a lott of ground situate in Willingstown on the north side of Christiana Creek in sd Co. It bounds Market Square. Signed: Andrew Justason (mark), Bridget Justason (mark), Thos. Willian, Catherine Willing (mark). Wit: Charles Springer, Mork Justason (mark). Bridget Justis and Catherine Willing were examined privately by Charles Springer. Ack: Nov Term 1734. (K1-278)

364. Judgement. 21 Sept 1734. Henry Newton, Esq. High Sheriff of Co. of New Castle send Greetings. Whereas John Richardson and John McCoole, Exec. of

the Last Will of John Ashton of sd Co., dec'd., of all and singular the Goods (etc) which were of Fristeram Sholand of sd Co. dec'd., lately were at Court and recovered against John Bishop, Exec. of the Last Will of afsd Fristeram Sholand, a debt of 7 pounds 5 shilling & damages. Seized of sd Fristeram Sholand, otherwise lately called Thrushurum Shorum, in the hands of sd John Bishop, was a plantation in St. Georges Hun. in sd Co. It contains 125 acres and appraised at 35 pounds. Robert Gordon witnesses Writ on 24 Aug, and sd Sheriff sold property for the sum of 21 pounds to John McCool of sd Hun. & Co. Signed: Henry Newton, Sherif. Wit: Thos. Noxon, Samuel Clement, Saml. James. Ack: Nov Term 1734. (K1-280)

365. Deed. 9 Oct 1734. Harmanus Alrichs, late of New Castle, now of the City of Philadelphia, Gent., and Peter Alrichs of New Castle Co., farmer, Exec. of the Last Will of Wessell Alrichs, dec'd., for the sum of 95 pounds, sold unto Jacobus Alrichs of sd Co., yeoman, a house & lott premises, situate in sd Co. It contains in breadth 120 feet and in length 300 feet. This is property that Francis Lovelance by his Deed at Fort James in New York, dated 1 May 1671, did grant unto Cornelius Winhart "I was then in the tenure of sd Winhart". Then Winhart by writing dated 14 April 1672, did sign over sd property to Dirick Albertson. Sd Albertson made over same to Casparus Herman, who signed over the same unto Peter Alrichs. Sd Alrichs by his Deed dated 23 March 1713, conveyed same to afsd Wessell Alrichs, gent., who made his Last Will and appointed afsd Hermanus and Peter as Exec. Signed: Harms. Alrichs, Peter Alrichs. Wit: Jos. Hill, Jacobus Williams, Robertson. Ack: Nov Term 1734. (K1-281)

366. Judgement. 20 Dec 1734. Henry Newton, Esq. Sheriff of Co. of New Castle, sendeth Greetings. Whereas David French and Andrew Peterson, Trustees of Gen. Load Office of sd Co., lately in Court against Agnes Shennan and Hugh Shennan, Exec. of the Last Will of Samuel Shennan, late of sd Co., a debt of 120 pounds and damages. Seized against estate of sd Shennan is a tract of land & tenement, situate in White Clay Creek Hun. containing 150 acres. Land appraised by Benjamin Gibbs and Abel Armstrong for 105 pounds. Sd Sheriff for the sum of 101 pounds, sold sd land to David French. Signed: Henry Newton, Sheriff. Wit: Willm. Shaw, James James jun. Ack: 21 Jan 1734. (K1-283)

367. Transfer of Title. 20 Dec 1734. David French of Co. of New Castle, Gent., acknowledges that his name was used in the Deed Poll (rec #366) by special Nomination of William Patterson of sd Co., mariner, and in trust for him -- that the 150 pounds already paid to Henry Newton, sheriff, for a tract of land was the proper money's of afsd William Patterson. Therefore by trust put in him by sd Patterson, sd French turns over to him the sd parcel of land, containing 150

acres of land, that was granted him by Deed dated 20 Dec 1734. This land bounds land of John French and John Kale. Signed: David French. Wit: James Armitage, Henry Newton. Ack: 21 Jan 1734. (K1-284)

368. Judgement. 20 Dec 1734. Henry Newton, Esq. Sheriff of Co. of New Castle send greetings. Whereas David French and Andrew Peterson, Trustees of Gen. Loan Office of sd Co., lately in Court recovered against Gideon Griffith a debt of 120 pounds and damages. Taken in execution was a parcel of land containing 12 acres, situate on the west end of Town of New Castle. Also a piece of a bank lott lying opposite the present dwelling house of sd Griffith. It is 600 feet in length and in breadth the width of the wharf thereon eraected. Land appraised by Anthony Palmer and Jehu Curtis for the sum of 90 pounds and offered for sale. Land purchased by John Finney as the highest bidder for 65 pounds 1 shilling. Signed: Henry Newton, Shff. Wit: Willm. Shaw, James James jun. Ack: 21 Jan 1734. (K1-285)

369. Judgement. 20 Dec 1734. Henry Newton, Esq. Sheriff of Co. of New Castle send greetings. Whereas David French and Andrew Peterson, Trustees of Gen. Loan Office of sd Co., lately in Court recovered against Joseph Wood, Admin. of All which were of Latitia Lowman, late of sd Co., widow, dec'd., a debt of 120 pounds 40 shill and damages. Taken in Execution was a dwelling house, lott of ground, outhouses situate in the Town of New Castle. Property appraised by Gideon Griffith and John Gooding for the sum of 225 pounds. Property purchased by John Finney as highest bidder for the sum of 165 pounds. Sd lott bounds the land late of Patrick Reilly, dec'd., and land in the tenure of Robert Gordon. Signed: Henry Newton, Shff. Wit: Willm. Shaw, James James Junr. Ack: 21 Dec 1734. (K1-286)

370. Appointment. 21 Feb 1734/5. 'John Penn, Thomas Penn, Esq... To Richard Sanderson of our Mannor of Rocklands in Co. of New Castle. We have rec'd information that great Spoil hath been committed by persons yet unknown to us on our Lands within our Mannor.. destroying & carrying away great quantities of Wood & timber... We appoint Richard Sanderson to be Keeper & Ranger, giving him Power & Authority to oversee...' Signed: John Penn, Thos. Penn. (K1-287)

371. Deed. 21 Feb 1734. Thomas Gray, Exec. of the Last Will of John Henzey, late of Co. of New Castle, merchant, dec'd., for the sum of 211 pounds, sold unto Thomas Campbell of Philada., merchant, and Daniel McFarson of sd Co., yeoman, a messuage and 385 acres of land situate in White Clay Creek Hun. in sd Co., bounding Muscle Cripple. Sd Henzey's Last Will, dated 11 April 1731, "devised all Real & Personal Estate to be sold to pay debts first and sums

remaining bequeathed to my dearly beloved wife, Elisabeth Henzey, and I appoint my well beloved Friend Thomas Gray as my sole Exec". Signed: Thomas Gray. Wit: John Gooding, John Legate. Ack: Feb Term 1734. (K1-287)

372. Deed. 20 Feb 1716/17. John Garretson of Christeen in Co. of New Castle, farmer, for the sum of 7 pounds, sold unto James Moire, a lott of land premises, situate in the Town of New Castle. It joins to Samuel Silsbee on No. side, on So. to lott of Peter Johnson, 67 foot in front of Beaver Street, and east to sd Garretson's lott. Signed: John Garretson (mark), Abiah Garretson (mark). Wit: John Silsbee, Moses Degon. Ack: 19 Feb 1716. Rowld. FizGerald, Db Com. (K1-288)

373. Deed. 29 Jan 1734. James Moore of NewTown in Maryland, and Rebecca his wife, for the sum of 9 pounds, sold unto Nathaniel Silsbee of Town of New Castle, bricklayer, a lott of ground premises, situate in sd Town. It joins the lot that was Samuel Silsbee's, dec'd., on No., to lott formerly Peter Johnston's, dec'd, on So. Beaver St., and East to lotts formerly of John Garretson senr. Signed: James Moore, Rebeckah Moore (mark). Wit: Isaac Janvier, Richard Edwards (mark). Sd Moore's impowered Philip Janvier as their Attny. Proved: Feb Term 1734. (K1-289)

374. Deed. 19 March 1734. James Merrewether of the Town & Co. of New Castle, curryer, and Elizabeth his wife, for the sum of 70 pounds, sold unto Nathaniel Silsbee of same place, bricklayer, a parcel of marsh, situate in sd Town. It bounds the marshes formerly of William Battell (now John Potts, dec'd), formerly of Daniel Merciers (now Doctor John Finneys), and formerly of John VanGezell (now sd Finney). This marsh was purchased by indenture dated 8 Aug 1726 from John VanGezell, sadler. Signed: James Merrewether, Elisabeth Merrewether. Wit: John Floyd, Benja. Swett. Elizabeth Merrewether was examined by James Armitage. Ack: 20 March 1734. (K1-290)

375. Deed. 20 Oct 1734. John Parkinson of Red Lyon Hun. in Co. of New Castle, Diapr weaver, for the sum of 185 pounds, sold unto William Murphey, of sd Co., a tract of land & premises, situate in sd Hun. & Co., commonly called Grubby Neck. It bounds a branch of Red Lyon and contains 200 acres. Signed: Jon. Parkenson. Wit: Fr. Land, Archibald Murphey. Ack: Feb Term 1734. (K1-291)

376. Deed. 21 Dec 1734. John Embly and Thomas Embly, both of Co. of New Castle, for the sum of 35 pounds, sold unto William Cox of the Town of New Castle, labourer, a tract of land situate on West side of Delaware & No. side Christiana Creek. This is land that Henry Dull of Christiana Hun. in sd Co. by

his Deed dated 14 Nov 1783 (1683), sold unto Henry Vanderburgh; who by his
Deed dated 19 ? 1694 did convey same unto Reyneer VnCoolin; who by his
Deed dated 17 Dec 1695 did convey same Luke Embly, late of White Clay
Creek, dec'd. Then sd Embly by his Deed dated 17 May 1697 did convey same
land unto James Read. Sd Read by his Deed dated 19 June 1701 did convey
same unto afsd Luke Embly, father of afsd John and Thomas Embly (who are
Exec. of their father's Will). Signed: John Embly (mark), Thomas Embly
(mark). Wit: John VanLeuvenigh, Robertson. Ack: Feb Term 1734. (K1-293)

377. Deed/Mortgage. 11 Jan 1734. George Yeates of Co. of New Castle, Gent.,
for the sum of 280 pounds, sold unto George McCall of City of Philada. in Prov.
of Penn., merchant, a plantation tract of land situate in New Castle Hun. It
begins at Mill Creek to Little Duck Creek to Beaver Dam to a place called Hell
Hole. It contains 782 acres 90 perches of land & cripple, and 48 acres 97
perches of improved marsh. Signed: Geo. Yeates. Wit: A. Hamilton, Harms.
Alrichs. Ack: Feb Term 1734. (noted: page 461 has release of mortgage of Geo.
McCall) (K1-294)

378. Deed. 19 Feb 1734. William Cox of New Castle Co., yeoman, and Amy his
wife, for the sum of 15 pounds, sold unto William Cox of Casson in sd Co.,
farmer, a tract of land containing 100 acres, situate on the No. side of Christiana
Creek. This land formerly belonged to Henry Dull of Christiana Hun. and by
him sold to Henry Vanderburgh, by Deed dated 14 Nov 1683. Sd Vanderburgh
by Deed dated 19 ? 1694 did sell same to Reyneer VanCoolin; and by his Deed
dated 17 Dec 1695 sold same to Luke Embly, late of White Clay Creek, dec'd.
Sd Embly by his Deed dated 17 May 1697 did convey same to James Read; who
by his Deed dated 19 June 1701 did covey same again to sd Luke Embly; who
dyed leaving his sons, Luke and John Embly as co-heirs & co-Exec -- who by
their Deed dated 31 Dec last, did convey same unto afsd William Cox. Signed:
William Cox (mark), Amy Cox (mark). Wit: Richard Rogers, Robt. Pertson.
Amy Cox examined by James Armitage. Ack: Feb Term 1734. (K1-295)

379. Deed. 4 Jan 1734. William Cox of NewCastle Town, labourer, and Amy
his wife, for the sum of 35 pounds and for other diverse reason, them thereunto
moving, sold unto John Vanleavenigh of same town, freeholder, two lotts of
land and premises, situate in sd town. They are bounded on the SE with Beaver
St, and lott late of Mr. Shaw, now in possession of Stephen Lewis, tanner, and
lott late of Hermah Reynerts, now in possession of Thomas Smith, merchant.
These lotts were granted unto Mathias & Emilius D'king by Gov. Francis
Lovelace by Patent dated 7 April 1673, then sold to Nicholas Daniel Price on 2
Jan 1682; and by Daniel Price & Johanes Price, sons of sd Nicholas, sold to
Adam Short on 8 April 1700; and by sd Adam Short by his Deed dated 17 Feb

1702 unto Richard Reynolds, dec'd. Sd Reynolds left two children, Richard and Mary Reynolds, his heirs. Sd Mary Reynolds then intermarried with Wm. Kellum, and together with her brother and husband by Deed dated 16 May 1732, did confirms sd lotts unto afsd William Cox. William Cox (mark), Amy Cox (mark). Wit: William Griffith, Robertson. Amy Cox examined by James Armitage. Ack: Feb Term 1734. (K1-297)

380. Deed. 18 Feb 1729. John Edward of Penkadaire Hun. in Co. of New Castle, yeoman, and Mary his wife, for the sum of 145 pounds, sold unto Benjamin Underwood of the Township of London Grove in Co. of Chester in Prov. of Penn., yeoman, a messuage and tract of land, situate in sd Hun. & Co. It begins at William William's Run, along King's road, to land of Col. French, to land of James James', by John James' line to beginnning, and contains 200 acres. Condition clause mentions an indenture made and executed between William Davis of Radnor in Co. of Chester, and David Evans of Penkadaire of one part and afsd John Edward of the other part. Signed: John Edward (mark), Mary Edward (mark). Wit: Evan Evan, Thomas Edward (mark), John David. Mary Edward examined by Thos. James. Ack: Feb term 1734. (K1-298)

381. Deed. 18 Feb 1734. Mathias Screek of Red Lyon Hun. in Co. of New Castle, yeoman, and Elizabeth his wife, for the sum of 9 pounds, sold unto Anthony Dushene, late of sd Co. but now of Cecil Co. in Prov. of Maryland, yeoman, a small parcel of land and marsh, containing 7 acres & 140 perches, situate in sd Hun. & Co. It bounds the land sold by sd Screek to John Daniel Thony, land belonging to afsd Dushene, and land of James Anderson. (This land left sd Screek by his dec'd father). Also another parcel of land containing 2 acres & 20 perches. It bounds afsd Dushene, land formerly of Gabriel Cox and land of David Howell. Signed: Matthias Shricke, Elizabeth Skreek (mark). Wit: Richard Cantwell, Thos. Noxon. Elizabeth Skreek examined by R. Cantwell. Ack: Feb Term 1734. (K1-299)

382. Deed. 15 Feb 1734. William McMechen of Co. of New Castle, yeoman, and Rebecca his wife, for the sum of 95 pounds, 8 shilling, sold unto John Baldwin of sd place, wheelright, part of a tract of land containing 192 acres. It bounds Red Clay Creek at a corner of John Garret's land, the lands of Richard Barry, Thomas Nichols, Jeremia Loehary and sd McMechen. Thirty acres of sd 192 acres were sold by sd McMechen to John Baldwin by Deed dated 22 March 1726. This is part of the land that William Penn by his Patent granted unto his daughter Latitia. Signed: William McMechen, Rebecca McMechen (mark). Wit: Hannah Armitage, James Armitage. Rebecca McMechen examined by James Armitage. Ack: Feb Term 1734. (K1-301)

383. Deed. 21 Feb 1734. Sylvanus Hussey of Town & Co. of New Castle, tanner & currier, for the sum of 70 pounds, sold unto Moses Hadley of sd place, weaver, a messuage and lott of ground, situate in sd town. It bounds land late of Claus Daniel Price, now in possession of William Cox, and land formerly belonging to Thomas Spry, now in possession of Elizabeth Silsby and Nathaniel Silsby. This is property that William Read, late sheriff of sd Co. by his Deed Poll dated 26 July 1730, did grant unto William Shaw of sd Co., gent.. Sd Shaw by his Deed dated 23 May 1733 did confirm same unto Stephen Lewis, tanner & currier, of sd town. Sd Lewis by his Deed dated 17 Jan 1734 did grant same to afsd Sylvanus Hussey. Signed: Sylvanus Hussey. Wit: Daniel Mercier (mark), Robertson. Ack: Feb Term 1734. (K1-302)

384. Deed. 21 Jan 1734. Edmund Shaw of Red Lyon Hun. in Co. of New Castle, yeoman, and Rebecca his wife, Relict & Exec. of the Last Will of her late husband, John Cox of sd Hun. & Co., and Gabriel Cox, Exec. also, for the sum of 117 pounds, sold unto William Goforth of sd place, weaver, a tract of land containing 234 acres, situate in sd Hun. & Co. This is part of 1,280 acres of land that Edmund Andros, Esq. by Patent dated 5 Nov 1675, granted unto Jacob Young, dec'd. It was situate between St. Georges Creek and Dragon Swamp, and was commonly called St. George's Neck. Sd Young died leaving issue two sons, Jacob and Joseph Young. Sd sons by two Deeds (one dated 10 Nov 1700, other dated 21 Aug 1706) did grant unto Charles Anderson and John Cox sd land. Sd John Cox's last Will, dated 3 Dec 1713, bequeathed all his land to be equally divided between his sons, Charles, John and Augustine Cox. Division of land made by George Dakeyne, surveyor, on 12 Oct 1720. By indenture of Release dated 1 Nov 1720 between sd Charles and Augustine on one part and sd John on the other for 234 acres. Father John Cox died possessed and by his Last Will dated 15 Jan 1731 ordained his wife Rebecca and Gabriel Cox as his Exec. Signed: Edmond Shaw, Rebeckah Shaw, Gabriel Cox (mark). Wit: Ja. VnBebber, Samuel Tillson, Thos. Noxon. Rebeccah Shaw examined by Rd. Cantwell. Ack: Feb Term 1734. (K1-304)

385. Deed. 18 Feb 1734/5. William Cuerton senr., of New Castle Co., yeoman, and Susannah his wife, for the sum of 50 pounds, sold unto Samuel Clement of sd Co., yeoman, a parcel of land & premises, containing 51 acres, situate on the south side of Georges Creek. It bounds the lines of sd Cuerton and sd Clement, lying between sd Cuerton & sd Clement. Signed: William Cuerton, Susannah Cuerton. Wit: John Dodd, Elizabeth Dodd (mark). Ack: Feb Term 1734. (K1-306)

386. Deed/mortgage. 20 March 1730. John Craig of Co. of Kent, yeoman, and Elizabeth his wife, for the sum of 88 pounds, sold unto Francis Woods of

Chester Co. of Prov. of Penn., yeoman, a parcel of land & premises, containing 110 acres, situate in White Clay Creek Hun. in Co. of New Castle. This land is now in sd Woods possession by virtue of an indenture for one year. It bounds the lands of John Cross and Samuel Johnson. Signed: John Craig, Elizabeth Craig (mark). Wit: George Monro, James Black. Elizabeth Craig examined by James Armitage. Ack: 20 March 1734. (K1-307)

387. Deed. 9 May 1721. John Pagett, late of White Clay Creek Hun. in Co. of New Castle but now of Cohanzey in New Jersey, carpenter, for the sum of 22 pounds 12 shilling, sold unto John Cross of sd Hun. & Co., weaver, a parcel of land & premises, containing 100 acres. It is situate on the south side of sd creek and bounds the land of Thomas Ogles. This is part of a larger tract of 400 acres that sd Pagett was granted from John French, late sheriff of sd Co. by his Deed Poll dated 15 May 1716, for the sum of 60 pounds. Signed: John Pagett. Wit: Da. Lloyd, Jo. Parker, James Craig, Elston Wallis, A. Hamilton, Anw. Hamilton junr. Ack: 16 Apr 1734. (K1-309)

388. Deed. 25 Nov 1734. William Murphey of Red Lyon Hun. in Co. of New Castle, yeoman, for the sum of 118 pounds, sold unto Francis Land of Christeen Creek in sd Co., yeoman, his plantation & tract of land situate in sd Hun. & Co., known by the name Grubby Neck. It bounds Red Lyon Creek's branches, and contains 200 acres of land. Signed: William Murphey, Jean Murphey (mark). Jane Murphey examined by James Armitage. (both Jean/Jane used). Ack: Feb Term 1734. (K1-310)

389. Deed. 10 Jan 1734. George McCall and Samuel Carpenter, both of the City of Philadelphia, gent., for the sum of 333 pounds, grant unto George Yeates of Co. of New Castle, son of Jasper Yeates of sd Co., dec'd., gent., all that plantation and tract of 782 acres of land, and 48 acres of marsh, situate in sd Co. This is whereas in 1720, all the lands of sd Jasper Yeates which were devised by him to his sons, George and Jasper Yeates, were vested in William Trent, Joshua Carpenter and Andrew Hamilton of sd City as Administrators of his estate. Sd Jasper by his indenture of Lease & Release, dated 14 March 1722, devised 991 acres of land and marsh unto sd McCall and Samuel Carpenter senr., merchants. (Sd McCall and Sd Carpenter are brothers in Law to sd Jasper, the son). Sd McCall & Sd Carpenter granted 160 acres of sd land unto Thomas Fenton for the sum of 110 pounds. Sd Jasper Yeates junr. for the sum of 550 pounds, granted unto George Yeates the 782 acres, by his indenture between him and George Yeates dated 13 Jan 1701. Signed: Geo. McCall, Samuel Carpenter. A. Hamilton, Harm. Alrichs. David French, Esq, appointed to acknowledge in Court. (K1-311)

100

390. Land Patent. 24 March 1668/9. Francis Lovelace grants a piece of land at Delaware to Jurien Jansen, now in his possession. It lies above the town of New Castle. It bounds the west side by Matthy Eschelson and contains 640 acres. Signed: Francis Lovelace. Mathias Nicholls, Secr. (K1-314)

391. Transfer of Patent. 10 Aug 1697. "Know all man that we, Hendrick and Jurien Jansen, the heirs & survivors of Jurien Jansen, for a valuable sum of money to us paid (by) Peter & Pwell Jaquet, Adm of Jurien Jansen, dec'd., grant unto the Heirs of John Jaquet, late of Co. of New Castle, all our Right Title in within Patent..." Signed: Hendrick Jansen (mark), Jurien Jansen (mark). Wit: John Grubb, Jno Smith. Ack: 20 May 1705. Certified Jan 10 1735 by Will Tong, Prot. Will Shaw, Rec. of Deeds. (K1-314)

392. Deed. 15 May 1735. John Bryan of Co. of New Castle, yeoman, for the good will and natural affection he feels for Nathaniel Bryan, his son, yeoman, and also for the consideration that sd son will pay the remainder of purchase money which is still due the Loan Office on Bond of 23 pounds, grants unto him a tract of land. It is situate on the south side of White Clay Creek in sd Co. and contains 212 acres. It bounds the lands of Samuel Johnson, John Craig and John Cross. Afsd John Bryan purchased this land from James Craig and Elizabeth his wife by Deed of Lease & Release. Signed: John Bryan. Wit: James Bryon, James Armitage. Ack: May Term 1735. David French, prot. (K1-314)

393. Deed. 23 May 1735. John Finney of New Castle in same Co., Chyurgeon, acknowledges that his name was used on the Deed Poll, dated 20 Dec 1734, by the special appointment of Gideon Griffith of same place. This was whereas Henry Newton, Sheriff of sd Co., for the sum of 65 pounds 1 shilling, granted unto sd Finney a parcel of land situate in sd Co. containing 12 acres. And also a parcel of a bank lott opposite to the dwelling house of sd Griffith, containing in length 600, in breadth the width of the wharf thereon erected. Now sd Finney grants same property to sd Griffith. Signed: Jno Finney. Wit: John Hore, Antho Palmer. Ack: May Term 1735. (K1-316)

394. Slave Sale. 17 May 1735. Samuel Kirk of Christiana Hun. in Co. of New Castle, gent., for the sum of 15 pounds, sold unto Gideon Griffith of sd Co., gent., a certain Indian Slave named Jack aged 3 years, son of my Indian woman Slave named Nancy. This for the full end term of 28 years at which sd Slave Jack will attain the age of 31 years. Signed: Saml Kirke. Wit: Joshua Way, Robert Read. Ack: May Term 1735. (K1-317)

395. Deed. 19 May 1735. Ellis Lewis of the Township of Kennet in Co. of Chester, yeoman, and Mary his wife, for the sum of 225 pounds, sold unto John

Hendrickson junr., of Christiana Hun. in Co. of New Castle, yeoman, two messuages and parcels of land and marsh, situate in sd Hun. & Co. It lies between Christiana and Brandywine Creek. This is property that John Jonas Stalcop, late of sd Hun., yeoman, dec'd., by virtue of a Release from his elder brother Israel Stalcop, dated 30 Nov 1722, was seized of. One contains 38 acres and the other contains 101 acres. Sd Stalcop, by his Deed of Lease & Release dated 20 Aug 1728, did grant same two properties unto afsd Ellis Lewis. Signed: Ellis Lewis, Mary Lewis. Wit: Simon Hadly, Joseph Hadly. Mary Lewis was examined by Simon Hadly. Ack: May Term 1735. (K1-317)

396. Deed. 21 May 1735. James James Junr. of Christiana Bridge in Co. of New Castle, Esq., and Francis his wife, for the sum of 46 pounds, sold unto John Faires of the City & Co. of Philadelphia, cordwainer, two acres of land, part of a parcel called Popes Lott situate on Christina creek, bounding line of Robert Morton. It is 100 feet front on sd creek and 6 miles in length. This is whereas Wm Penn by Warrant dated 5th day 5th mo 1683, directed Thomas Pierson, then Co. Surveyor, to lay a tract of land called Eagles Point, unto John Ogle Sen., dec'd. It was situate on the north side of Christiana Bridge and contained 75 acres. Sd Ogle conveyed sd land and premises in 1696 unto John Latham; likewise Aaron Latham, son and heir, conveyed the same unto Anna Letort by deed, dated 21 Oct 1706. Sd Anna Letort for non-payment of a debt due to John French, then Sheriff of sd Co., directed sd property to George Dakeyne, then Coroner for sd Co. to direct sale. Deed of conveyence made to John Ogle Junr., dated 17 May 1711. Sd Ogle sold one lott of sd land, containing 6 acres to Nathaniel Pope, now in his possession. Then sd Pope conveyed sd lott unto Benjamin Burleigh; then sd Burleigh conveyed same to afsd James James Junr. by Deed dated 27 Jan 1729/30. Signed: James James Jun., Frances James. Wit: ?ey Howell, Edwd Edwards, David Williams, John Harris. Frances James examined by Thomas James. Ack: May term 1735. (K1-319)

397. Deed. 22 May 1735. Robert Miller of New Castle Hun. & Co., carpenter, for the sum of 50 pounds, sold unto Elias Bonine of St. George's Hun. in sd Co., yeoman, a moiety of a tract of land, situate in Appoquinimink Hun. in sd Co. It bounds the lands of John Currey, Isaac Morris and Jacob Staats, and contains 50 acres. This is part of a larger tract that William Read, late High Sheriff of sd Co. by his Deed Poll dated 19 May 1730 did grant unto afsd Robert Miller. It bounded the land late of James Beswike, and lands of Michael Offley, William Skarrs and Thomas Bell. Signed: Robert Miller. Wit: Benj. Gibbs, Nathaniel Wainsford. Ack: 12 Jan 1735/6. David French Pro. Examined: Will. Shaw. (K1-321)

398. Deed. 17 May 1735. Richard Cantwell of Appoquinimink Hun. in Co. of

New Castle, Gent., and Elinor his wife, for the sum of 100 pounds, sold unto John Scot of same place, yeoman, a tract of land containing 200 acres, situate in sd Hun. (part of a larger tract called Red Clift), now in the possession of sd Scot. It bounds the land late of John Gouldon, dec'd., and lands of Rebecca Dyer and Halliwell Garretson. Signed: Rd. Cantwell, Elinor Cantwell. Wit: John Riddick, Sam Cartwright. Elinor Cantwell examined by And. Peterson. Ack: May term 1735. (K1-322)

399. Judgement. May 1735. Henry Newton, Esq. High Sheriff of New Castle send Greetings. Whereas Margaret Wiliamson lately in Court has recovered against Agnes Sherman and Hugh Sherman, Exers of the Last Will of Samuel Sherman, late of sd Co., dec'd., 18 pounds 14 shilling 2 pence. This for non performance of a promise by sd Samuel in his lifetime. Sd Sheriff ordered to seize goods & chattles in sd Exer's hands. Taken in execution was a tract of land containing 100 acres and Plantation situate in White Clay Creek Hun. in sd Co. It bounds the land of Andrew Tilly. Property was appraised by Lewis Howell and William Paterson at 130 pounds. Premises offered to publick vendue and purchased by Roger Sherman, taylor, of sd Hun., as the highest bidder for the sum of 137 pounds. Signed: Henry Newton, Shff. Wit: William Paterson, H. Gonne. Ack: May Term 1735. (K1-323)

400. Deed. 24 Feb 1734. George Ret of New Castle Town & Co., taylor, and Dorothy his wife, for the sum of 145 pounds, sold unto Thomas Lawrence of Philadelphia in Prov. of Penn., merchant, a messuage and lott of ground where the sd Ret now dwelleth. It bounds the Quakers Meeting ground on Beaver St. and contains one acre. Signed: George Ret, Dorothy Ret (mark). Wit: Will Read, Peter Bard. Proved: May term 1735. Dorothy Ret was examined by Richd. Grafton. (K1-325)

401. Deed. 16 May 1735. John Hardin of Appoquinimink Hun. in Co. of New Castle, Exec. in Right of his wife, and Sarah his wife, late widow and Exec. of Johanis Wardiman of sd place, dec'd., for the sum of 25 pounds, sold to Mary Taylor of sd Hun. & Co., widow, a tract of land containing 200 acres. It bounds Gilprins Run, a branch of sd Creek, and the late dwelling place of sd Wardiman. This is part of a larger tract, whereas by a Patent from Edmond Andros dated 15 Jan 1675, was granted to Percifel Washton, dec'd, John Barber, James Williams and Edward Williams. It contained 1,200 acres and was situate on Black Birds Creek in sd Hun. & Co. One moiety of sd land, the SW part, was alloted to sd James & Edward Williams. Sd James then died Intestate leaving no issue and afsd brother was his survivor and heir. Then sd Edward died leaving issue one son, named Edward Williams; who by his indenture dated Feb 1732, did grant 450 acres of sd land unto afsd Johanis Wardiman. Signed: John Hardin, Sarah

Hardin (mark). Wit: Cha. Robinson, Tho. Noxon. Sarah Hardin examined by James Armitage. Ack: May Term 1735. (K1-327)

402. Deed. 22 May 1735. Robert Miller of New Castle Hun. & Co., carpenter, for the sum of 50 pounds, sold unto Jacob Staats of Appoquinimink Hun. in sd Co., yeoman, a tract of land containing 150 acres situate in Appoq. Hun. It bounds lands of Michal Offley, Isaac Norris and Isaac Staats, and part of the tract that sd Miller sold to Elias Bonine. This is part of 300 acres of land that William Read, late High Sheriff of sd Co., by his Deed Poll dated 19 May 1730, did grant unto afsd Miller. (It was the SW part of a 400 acre tract). It bounded the land late of James Beswicke and lands of sd Offley, William Skarr and Thomas Bell. Signed: Robert Miller. Wit: Benj. Gibbs. Nathal Wainsford. Ack: May term 1735. (K1-328)

403. Deed/mortgage. 27 March 1735. Thomas Chandler of the Township of Burmingham in Co. of Chester in Prov. of Penn., yeoman, and Mary his wife, for the sum of 50 pounds, sold unto John Heath of Christiana Hun. in Co. of New Castle in Terr. of Penn., yeoman, a messuage and 88 acres of land situate in Christiana Hun. It bounds the land late of John Scot, and lands of Joshia Baker, William Denny and Thos Nichols. This is land that was granted unto afsd Chandler by Patent dated 20 Dec last from John Penn, Thomas Penn and Richard Penn. This was to make good deficiencies in a late resurvey of two tracts of land now holden by sd Thomas and Swithin Chandler, his brother, (who conveyed his right to Thomas). Mentions obligation of equal date for the payment of 28 pounds 16 shilling upon demand within two years. Signed: Thomas Chandler, Mary Chandler. Wit: Rachel Thomas, Mary Nichols (mark), Zack Butcher, Benjamin Heath. Ack: May Term 1735. (K1-330)

404. Deed. 20 May 1735. Samuel Kirk of Christiana Hun. in Co. of New Castle, store keeper, and Margaret his wife, for the sum of 20 pounds, sold unto William Shipley of Redly in Co. of Chester in Prov. of Penn., yeoman, a lott of land and premises, situate in Willingtown on the north side of Christiana Creek. This is land that sd Kirk purchased by an indenture dated 25 Aug 1734, from Thomas Willing of sd Hun. & Co., cooper, and Catherine his wife, and Andrew Justis of the same place, planter, and Bridget his wife. Signed: Saml. Kirk, Margret Kirk. Wit: Charles Springer, Thomas Willing. Ack: 12 Jan 1735/6. Sd Kirks appointed David French as Attny. Margaret Kirk was examined by Charles Springer. (K1-332)

405. Deed. 24 Feb 1734. Richard Grafton of New Castle Town & Co., gent., and Mary his wife, for the sum of 55 pounds, sold unto George Ret of the same place, shop keeper, a lott of ground late in the tenure and occupation of Col.

John French, dec'd., situate in sd town. It bounds the Quaker Meeting ground on Beaver St. and contains one acre. Signed: Richd. Grafton, Mary Grafton. Wit: Peter Bard, Willm. Shaw. Mary Grafton examined by Willm. Shaw. (K1-333)

406. Deed. 21 May 1735. James James Junr. of Christiana Bridge in Co. of New Castle, merchant, and Frances his wife, for the sum of 307 pounds, sold unto John Welsh of New Castle Hun. & Co., blacksmith, a messuage and parcel of land near sd bridge. It bounds land late of John Ogle and contains one acre 15 perches. Signed: James James Junr., Frances James. Wit: David Williams, John Harris. Frances James examined by Thomas James. Ack: May Term 1735. (K1-335)

407. Judgement. 1 May 1735. Henry Newton, Esq. Sheriff of Co. of New Castle send greeting. Whereas William Allen lately in Court and by his plaint recovered against Parnell Battell, Exec. of the Last Will of William Battell, Gent., dec'd., late of sd Co., a debt of 161 pounds and damages. Sheriff ordered to seize goods and chattles of sd Battell. Taken in execution was a dwelling house and lott of land situate in the Town of New Castle (then in the tenure of sd Parnell Battell). It was appraised by Gideon Griffith and John Curtis for the value of 400 pounds. Publick vendue notice given and property was sold unto David French, Esq., as the highest bidder for the sum of 320 pounds. The property bounds the land late of Alexander Davis, dec'd., part of Margaret Williams lott, and marsh late in possession of Nicholas Meers. Signed: Henry Newton, Shff. Wit: Auth. Palmer, Keith. Ack: 12 Jan 1735. (K1-336)

408. Deed. 5 May 1735. John Pasmore and Elizabeth his wife of the Township of Kennet in Co. of Chester in Prov. of Penn., yeoman, for the sum of 100 pounds, sold unto Thomas Hollingsworth of Christiana Hun. in Co. of New Castle, yeoman, one equal fourth part of a tract of land situate in sd Hun. & Co. It bounds the land of James Morton and contains 13 acres. This is part of a larger tract of 221 acres that was purchased by sd Pasomre and William Dixon by a Deed from Henry Snicker and Kathren his wife, dated 18 Sept 1729. (Book I pp 122). Then sd Dixon and Jamiah his wife by their Deed granted afsd Pasmore one equal fourth part of 13 acres (part of sd 221 acres). (Book K pp 217). Signed: John Pasmore, Eliz. Pasmore (mark). Wit: Simon Hadly, William Lewis. Elizabeth pasmore examined by Simon Hadly. Ack: 12 Jan 1735. (K1-337)

409. Deed. 12 May 1735. Nathan Hussey of Christiana Hun. in Co. of New Castle, and Ann his wife, for the sum of 100 pounds, sold unto David McComb of sd Co., yeoman, a parcel of land and of marsh, situate in New Castle Hun. & Co. The land contains 80 acres. The marsh bounds marsh of Stephen Lewis and

contains 10 acres 70 perches. Signed: Nathan Hussey, Ann Hussey (mark). Wit: Charles Springer, Ann Springer (mark). Sd Hussey's appointed John Garretson Junr. as Attorny. Ann Hussey examined by Charles Springer. Ack: 13 Feb 1735/6. (K1-338)

410. Deed. 20 May 1735. James Angew and Margaret his wife of Milln Creek Hun. in Co. of New Castle, cooper, for the sum of 40 pounds, sold unto William Miller of sd Hun. & Co., weaver, a tract of land containing 45-3/4 acres, situate in same place. It is bounded on the east with John McDonald's land, on the north by John Hughy's land, on the west by William Brackin's land, and on the south with Thomas Barr's land. This is part of a tract before purchased of Christifor White by William Brackin, and purchased of sd Brackin by afsd James Agnew. Signed: James Agnew, Margrit Agnew (mark). Wit: Simon Hadly, Joseph Greer. Margret Agnew examined by Simon Hadly. Ack: 15 Jan 1735/6. (K1-340)

411. Judgement. 21 May 1735. Henry Newton, Esq. Sheriff of Co. of New Castle send greetings. Whereas John Richardson of sd Co., merchant, lately in Court by his plaint and recovered against Gideon Griffith, Adm. of all Goods and Chattles which were of Patrick Reilly, late of sd Co., Chyrurgeon, dec'd., not adm by Margaret Reilly, Excr. of the Last Will of sd Patrick, a debt of 111 pounds 8 shilling and damages. Seized and taken in execution was a large brick house and lott, situate on Front St. in Town of New Castle. It was valued at 200 pounds and in possession of sd Griffith. Sd Sheriff sold sd house and lott unto John Finney, Chyrurgeon, at Publick vendue, as the highest bidder for the sum of 150 pounds 5 shilling. It bounds the lotts of George Monroe and sd Finney. Signed: Henry Newton, Shff. Wit: John Curtis, Jno McCoole. Ack: 15 Dec 1735. (K1-341)

412. Deed. 21 May 1735. Augustine Constantine of Christiana Hun. in Co. of New Castle, yeoman, for the sum of two pounds, confirm unto Jonas Walraven of the same place, weaver, a piece of marsh or cripple ground, situate on the north side of Christiana Creek in sd Hun. It bounds the marsh of sd Walraven and contains 40 acres. Signed: Augustine Constantine (mark). Wit: Jas. Hamilton, Joseph Robinson, Jas. McMullan. Ack: 15 Jan 1735/6. (K1-342)

413. Deed. 5 March 1734/5. Augustine Constantine of Christiana Hun. in Co. of New Castle, yeoman, for the sum of 86 pounds, sold unto Jonas Walraven of sd Hun. & Co., a parcel of land and premises, situate on the west side of Delaware River on the north side of Christiana Creek. It bounds the land of John Richardson and contains 100 acres. Signed: Augustine Constantine (mark). Wit: Mathias Morten, Neils Justis, Jas. McMullan. Ack: 15 Jan 1735/6. (K1-343)

414. Deed/mortgage. 22 May 1735. Augustine Constantine of Co. of New Castle, yeoman, for the sum of five pounds, confirm unto David French of sd Co., Gent. and Mathias Morton of sd Co., yeoman, a parcel of marsh now in their actual possession by virtue of a sale to them made for one whole year by indenture dated the day before date hereof. It is situate in Christiana Hun. in sd Co., on the NE side of Morton's Gutt to Christiana Creek. It bounds line of John Richardson and contains 128 acres. This was part of a larger parcel called Conrades Cripply, by survey dated 6 March 1734. Signed: Augustine Constantine. Wit: Robt. Gordon, Robertson. Ack: 15 Jan 1735/6. (K1-344)

415. Deed. 14 Nov 1733. Andrew Cock of Christiana Hun. in New Castle Co., husbandman, for the sum of 6 pounds, sold unto Pietter Hendrickson of sd Hun. & Co., husbandman, two parcels of land. They are situate in sd Co. at the west end of land thas afsd Cock now liveth (part of sd tract formerly taken up by Adam Stedham, dec'd.). One bounds the land and house of Robert Pearse, and land of Benedictus Stedham, and contains 15-1/2 acres & 20 perches. Another small tract close to the first, lies between Arthur Faires' land and sd Pearse's, and contains 5 acres. Signed: Andrew Cox. Wit: Charles Springer, Charles Springer jun. (mark). Rec: 3 Feb 1735/6. (K1-345)

416. Deed/mortgage. 25 March 1735. Samuel Johnson of New Castle Co., yeoman, for the sum of 117 pounds 15 shilling, sold unto Francis Graham of sd. Co., blacksmith, a tract of land containing 173 acres 126 perches. It is situate on the north side of White Clay Creek in Mill Creek Hun. in sd Co. It bounds the lands of Archibald Homes, Jonathan Kay, Samuel Ruth and James Boggs. (Terms are that 76 pounds 6 shilling to sd Johnson now, and 41 pounds 9 shilling unto the Loan Office at New Castle as principal and interest.) Signed: Samuel Johnson. Wit: Adam Egget, James Armitage. Rec: 3 Feb 1735/6. (K1-346)

417. Gift Deed. 19 May 1735. Elizabeth Gerritson of Appoquinimink Hun. in Co. of New Castle, widow, send greetings. 'In consideration of the natural Love & Affection I bear unto by son, Halliwell Gerritson, and also for the sum of five shillings, I grant unto him a parcel of land containing 200 acres, situate in sd Co.' It is part of a larger tract called Red Clift. It bounds the lands of John Golden, sd Eliz. Gerritson, and Dyer's land. Signed: Elizabeth Gerritson. Wit: Rich. Colegate, Ellenor Cantwell. She empowers Richard Cantwell, Esq. as her attorney. Rec: 3 Feb 1735/6. Will Shaw, Rec. David French, Pr. (K1-347)

418. Deed. 29 April 1735. John Ball of Milln Creek Hun. in Co. of New Castle, blacksmith, for the sum of 255 pounds, sold unto William Ball of same place, blacksmith, a tract of land and premises, containing 42 acres, situate in sd Hun.

& Co. It bounds the lands of afsd John Ball and Simon Parson. This is part of a tract of 202 acres of land, which is part of a tract of 400 acres, called the New Design, situate on the west side of Delaware River, or on the west side of Milln Creek (a branch of White Clay Cr.), between land formerly belonging to sd Ball and Joseph Barns. Signed: John Ball. Wit: Willm. Shaw, Saml. Bourn. Rec: 3 Feb 1735/6. (K1-348)

419. Deed. 29 April 1735. John Ball sen. of Mill Creek Hun. in Co. of New Castle, blacksmith, for the sum of 60 pounds, grants unto William Ball of same place, blacksmith, a tract of land containing 100 acres, situate in sd Hun. & Co.. It bounds the land formerly of Richard Lewis. This is land that afsd John Ball purchased from William Anderson of Octerara Creek in Co. of Chester in Prov. of Penn.. Sd Anderson became seized of sd land by virtue of a warrant from the Commissioners, and it had been laid out by George Dakyne for the use of Joshua Morgan, dec'd. Signed: John Ball. Wit: Edward Blake, Robertson. Rec: 15 Jan. 1735/6. (K1-349)

420. Deed. 10 May 1735. John Hendrickson junr., of Co. of New Castle & Christiana Hun., husbandman, for the sum of 140 pounds, sold unto Christiffer Springer of sd Co. & Hun., farmer, two tracts of land lying in sd Hun. & Co., on the west side of Mill Creek. The first is part of a tract of land that Richard Robinson had a Grant for in 1685, but sd Robinson threw the land up and John Hendreckson senr. got a Grant for sd tract and gave part of it to his son (afsd) by a Deed of Gift dated 11 May 1733. This tract bounds sd creek and land of Jacob Hilley where he now liveth, unto land formerly belonging to George Read and now in possession of sd Hilley, unto land formerly of John Anderson Cock. It contains 80 acres. The other tract is the plantation & land formerly belonging to sd John Anderson Cock which Hendrickson Senr. bought of my Grandfather, afsd Cock, by Deed dated 30 Dec 1710. It was conveyed by his son, Justas Cock. It lies in sd Hun., called Oak Hill, and contains 100 acres. It bounds the land of Charles Springer, land formerly belonging to Stephen Cornelius and now in the tenure of Joseph Springer, land that sd Springer bought of Richard Manken, and land of sd Reed, Robinson and Hilley. Signed: John Hendrickson junr (mark). Wit: Charles Springer, Bu. Sinnixen. Rec: 13 Feb 1735/6. Will Shaw, rec. David French, pro. (K1-350)

421. Deed, 12 May 1735. Nathan Hussey and Ann his wife of Christiana Hun. in Co. of New Castle, for the sum of 40 pounds, sold unto John McComb of Mill Creek Hun. in sd Co., yeoman, a messuage plantation & parcel of land containing 100 acres 6 perches. It is situate in Letitia Penn's Mannor adjoining to London Tract. This is land that sd Hussey became seized of by a Deed dated 18 Aug 1726 (Lib H, pp213). Signed: Nathan Hussey, Ann Hussey (mark). Wit:

Charles Springer, Ann Springer (mark). Sd Hussey's appoint John Garretson junr. as their Attny. Proved: May Term 1735. (K1-351)

422. Deed. 8 May 1735. John Hussey of Co. of New Castle, yeoman, and Margaret his wife, for the sum of 80 pounds, sold unto Stephen Lewis of Town of New Castle, tanner, a parcel of land containing 110 acres, commonly called John Hussey's plantation. It bounds the land that John Morton now holds by Christiana Creek, and land of John McComb. Signed: John Hussey, Margaret Hussey. Wit: Sylvana Hussey, Hannah Cox. Ack: May Term 1735. (K1-353)

423. Deed. 1 May 1735. Edward Edwards and Mary his wife of Co. of New Castle, for the sum of 16 pounds, sold unto John Johnson and Mathew Fosster, a tenement or tract of land situate in the Welsh Tract. This is part of a great tract taken by William Davids & Company by Warrant of the Proprietor. It bounds the lands of Thomas Grifith, Henry Davis and Thomas Johns, and land that was John Wilds. It was surveyed 50 acres but no more than 48 acres 144 perches. It lays in the tract of land that sd Thomas Johns doth now dwell, part of great tract now called Pencader. Signed: Edward Edwards, Mary Edwards (mark). Wit: Richard Blackborn, Elizabeth Toby. Mary Edwards examined by Charles Springer. Rec: 12 Jan 1735/6. (K1-354)

424. Deed. 2 Dec 1734. Samuel David of Duck Creek Hun. in Kent Co., farmer, for the sum of 70 pounds, sold unto Thomas Neal of Pencader Hun. in Co. of New Castle, farmer, all his Right & Title to 200 acres of land located in Pencader Hun. in sd Co. It is now in occupation of John David, son of afsd Samuel David. It was bought of David Merick, who bought it of Elinor Phipps, wife and then Attny of Isaiah Phipps. It bounds the lands of David Price and Samuel James and contains 200 acres. Signed: Samuel David (mark). Wit: Frs Evan, Philip Davis. Jane David, wife of sd Samuel was examined by Thomas Neal. Signed: Jane David (mark). Ack: by Thos James. Rec: 12 Jan 1735/6. (K1-355)

425. Deed. 5 May 1735. John Neal of Brandywine Hun. in Co. of New Castle, yeoman, and Margory his wife, in consideration of a Release from John Bird of the same place, yeoman, dated even date, grants unto sd Bird three parcels of land situate in sd Hun. & Co. One contains 100 acres 64 perches. Another contains 60 acres. The last contains 9 acres. This is whereas Charles Empson and Mary his wife, by their Deed dated 12 Feb 1727 did sell unto sd John Neal and sd John Bird, two parcels of land in sd Co. One of sd parcels formerly belonged to John Nelson. It is bounded by the river Delaware and the lands of Jacob Clemontson and Hans Peterson and contains 165-1/2 acres. The other parcel formerly belonged to sd Clemontson, and is bounded by sd river and land

of sd Nelson and land late of Annake Lawson and contains 165-1/2 acres. These are 2/5 part of a 82-1/2 acre tract, commonly knows as Vertringo Tract. Then sd Neal and sd Bird made further divisions of sd land. Signed: John Neal, Margery Neal (mark). Wit: H. Gonne, Sam. Bourn. Rec: 12 Jan 1735/6. (K1-356)

426. Deed. 5 May 1735. John Bird of Brandywine Hun. in Co. of New Castle, yeoman, and Margaret his wife, in consideration of another Indenture of Release bearing even date, confirm unto John Neal of same place, yeoman, a parcel of land containing 170 acres 60 perches, situate in sd Hun. & Co. (See record #425) Signed: John Bird, Margaret Bird (mark). Wit: H. Gonne, Sam Bourn. Rec: 3 Feb 1735/6. (K1-357)

427. Deed. 8 May 1735. Francis Land of Christiana Creek in Co. of New Castle, yeoman, for the sum of 124 pounds, sold unto Charles Robinson of Georges Hun. in sd Co., cordwainer, a parcel of land and premises, situate in Georges Hun. in sd Co. It bounds the lands of John Ashton and James Anderson and contains 200 acres (except reserved 100 acres formerly sold by John Grant to James Atkinson). This tract of land was granted to Daniel Corbet by a Warrant dated 16 March 1789 (1689?), and surveyed by George Dakeyne. Sd Corbet by a Deed of Release dated 29 March 1726 conveyed same unto afsd John Grant; who by Deed dated 12 April 1726 did convey same to afsd Francis Land. Signed: Fr. Land, Christian Land. Wit: Jno Butcher (mark), Jacob Gooding, Michel Butcher (mark). Rec: 12 Jan 1735/6. (K1-359)

428. Deed. 30 May 1733. Samuel Vance of St. Georges Hun. in Co. of New Castle, carpenter, for the sum of 50 pounds, and other reasons him moving, and for the natural love and affection he bears his son, John Vance of same place, yeoman, grants unto sd son a tract of land and plantation, situate on St. Georges Creek in sd Hun. & Co. It bounds the land of Garret Dushane and land formerly of Alex Adams, and contains 170 acres 21 perches. Signed: Samuel Vance. Wit: Abram Gooding, Thos. Noxon. Rec: 3 Feb 1735/6. (K1-360)

429. Deed/mortgage. 10 March 1734. Francis Graham of Co. of New Castle, blacksmith, for the sum of 170 pounds 15 shillings (26 pounds 6 shilling now, and 41 pounds 9 shilling to the Loan Office), sold unto Samuel Johnson, yeoman, of sd Co., a tract of land containing 100 acres. It bounds the lands of Samuel Ruth, James Boggs and Archibald Homoo. This is part of the land surveyed for 200 acres situate on the north side of White Clay Creek, formerly the land of John Guest which was taken in Execution for paying his debts. This together with several other tracts of land sold by the Sheriff of sd Co. to David Loyd of Chester, gentleman, dated 15 May 1716. Then sd Loyd and Grace his wife sold sd 200 acres unto Thomas Ogle of sd Co. by deed dated 17 May 1720;

then sd Ogle by deed dated 15 Aug 1726, sold 100 acres of sd land to Archibald Homes. The remainder of sd land was mortgaged by sd Ogle in the Land Office. In sd Ogle's Last Will dated 30 July 1734, he empowered his wife Elizabeth Ogle, as Exec. Then she died and by her Will dated 18 Sept 1734, gave Exec. to Francis Graham and William Armstrong, who sold sd land at Publick Vendue on 8 March 1734/5 unto afsd Samuel Johnson. Signed: Francis Graham. Wit: Adam Egger, James Armitage. Ack: May Term 1735. (K1-361)

430. Deed. 4 March 1733/4. Andrew Cock and Johannes Cock, his son, of Christiana Hun. in Co. of New Castle, yeomen, for the sum of 32 pounds, sold unto Thomas Berry of the same place, cordwainer, a tract of land containing 40 acres, situate in sd Hun. & Co. It bounds the lands of Lucy Tomlinson, sd Cock, Robert Pierce and James Thompson. This is part of a 100 acre tract that was granted Adam Stedham by virtue of a Warrant from William Penn, called Adams Garden. Sd Adam died without a Will and his children, viz: Henry, Christopher, and Mary (who is ye wife of Jacob Vandervier) were heirs. They granted same land by release dated 16 May 1720 unto afsd Andrew Cock. Signed: Andrew Cock (mark), Johannes Cock (mark). Wit: J. Ferguson, William Clensay, James Morton. Rec: 12 Jan 1735/6. (K1-363)

431. Deed. 20 May 1735. Andrew Justason of Christiana Hun. in Co. of New Castle, yeoman, and Britta his wife, for the sum of 26 pounds, sold unto Charles Empson of the same place, yeoman, a piece of meadow ground containing 1 acre 104 perches, situate in sd Hun & Co. This is part of a larger plantation lying on Christiana Creek, that John Anderson, late of sd Hun. by deed dated 10th day 8th mo 1674 did grant unto Samuel Peterson and Lars Cornelison. Then sd Peterson's Last Will (dated 20th day 9th mo 1689) did bequeath that which of his sons whom is longest with his loving wife shall have his now dwelling plantation. Later Mathias Peterson, eldest son of Samuel, did by Deed dated 1st day 10 mo 1702, confirm unto his brother, Peter Peterson (as the longest liver with his mother) all Title of sd plantation (called the Old Land). Later sd Peter by his Last Will dated 29 Jan 1714/5, did give to his eldest son, Peter, after his wife's decease, his now dwelling plantation. Then sd son Peter and his wife Magdalan by Deed dated 8 May 1727 did grant 105 acres (part of 211 acres) unto afsd Andrew Justason. Signed: Andrew Justis (mark), Britta Justis (mark). Wit: Charles Springer, Tho. Willing. Britta Justis examined by Charles Springer. Rec: 12 Jan 1735/6. (K1-364)

432. Deed. 4 Aug 1735. 'Know all men that I, Charles Empson for the sum of 40 pounds do forever discharge Wm Shipley of Redly in Chester Co... and make over my Right and title of within mentioned piece of meadow ground.' Signed: Cha: Empson. Wit: Joshua Way, Jas McMullan. Rec 12 Jan 1735/6. (K1-366)

433. Deed. 16 May 1735. Joseph Robinson, John Robinson and Pricilla Robinson, all of Mill Creek Hun. in Co. of New Castle, for the sum of 11 pounds 10 shilling, sold unto Morton Justus of same place, yeoman, a lott of land containing 60 square feet, situate in Bread & Cheese Island (on the west side of Red Clay Cr.) in sd Co. It contains a store house, wharf and landing & appurt. Mentions protecting against lawful suits, troubles, evictions of Bryan McDonald or Catherine his wife, Stephen Hollingsworth and Ann his wife, George Robinson, David Robinson & Phebe Robinson, claims. Signed: Joseph Robinon, John Robinson, Priscillah Robinson, Wit: William Graham, Jas McMullan. Ack: May term 1735. (K1-366)

434. Deed/mortgage. 19 Aug 1735. John Hussey of Kent Co., planter, for the sum of 6 pounds, confirm unto Thomas Johnson of Co. of New Castle, farmer, his plantation and tract of land containing 109 acres, lying on the branches of Duck Creek. It bounds the lands of Patrick Broomfield and Wm Hackett. (This formerly belonged to Caleb Hussey, afsd John's father) Mentions the space of seven years. Signed: John Hussey (mark). Wit: John Holliday, Chas. King. Rec: 12 Jan 1735/6. (K1-367)

435. Gift Deed. 16 Aug 1735. Isabella French of Kent Co., relict of Caleb Hussey, late of same place. 'For the natural Love & Affection which I bear unto my loving Son, John Hussey..' release unto him all manner of Dower and Right which I have unto that plantation situate on the branches of Duck Creek.. formerly belonging to Caleb Hussey, father of John and husband of Isabella. Signed: Isabell French (mark). Wit: John Holliday, Chas. King. Rec: 12 Jan 1735/6. Wm Shaw, Rec. (K1-368)

436. Deed. 14 Aug 1735. Edmund Gerritson of Appoquinamink Hun. in Co. of New Castle, yeoman, for the sum of 40 shillings, forever discharges Thomas Noxon of St. Georges Hun. in sd Co., yeoman, a small parcel of land, situate in sd Hun. & Co. It is a point of land on the SE side of the southernmost branch of Appoq. Creek, called Sasifrass Branch, opposite to Lucas' Landing, from which there is a bridge. It contains one acre together with the right of digging away all earth for making a Mill Dam intended to be joined to the afsd point. Signed: Edmd. Gerritson. Wit: John VanLeuvenigh (mark), George Oens (mark). Rec: 12 Jan 1735/6. (K1-369)

437. Deed. 28 Jan 1701. Isaack Hansen of Flatbush in Kings Co. on the Island of Nasaia in Prov. of New York, by and with the consent of Annike his wife, and for the sum of two & forty pounds 16 shilling, sold unto Jacob Rycker of the same place, a half part of a third part of land described here. This is whereas sd Hansen in partnership with James Symson for the sum of 257 pounds, lately

purchased of Henry Garretson and Elizabeth his wife of Apoquinamy Creek in Co. of New Castle, a tract of land called Mountain Neck situate in sd Co. It contains 1,185 acres as of Deed dated 16 June 1701. It is bounded by land formerly belonging to Humphrah Ketly and 800 acres formerly granted unto Edmund Cantwell by Patent from Edmund Andros bearing date 25 March 1676. Then sd Hansen by agreement with sd Symson has since purchased all right to sd land. Signed: Isaack Hansen (mark), Anke Hansen. Wit: Peter Stryker, Denny Kegeman. June 3 1735. Saml. Garretson Esq. Judge said the named Pieter Stryker, aged about 80 years, appeared before him & declared he subscribed his name as evidence to this indenture and believes he saw sd Isaac and Annt Hansen sign this. Signed: Pieter Stryker. Rec: 12 Jan 1735/6. (K1-370)

438. Deed. 3 June 1735. Jacob Ryke of Flatbush on the Island of Nasaw in Prov. of New York, blacksmith, and Sytie his wife, for the sum of 150 pounds, sold unto Thomas Noxon of St. Georges Hun. in Co. of New Castle, yeoman, half part of one third part of herein land. This is whereas Edmund Andros by his Patent dated 25 March 1676 did grant unto Edmund Cantwell a tract of land containing 1,185 acres, called Mountain Neck, situate on the west side of Delaware River by the head of Appoq. Creek in the fork between the main creek and a branch called Sasafrass. Sd Cantwell made his Last Will dated 28 Oct 1679 and bequeathed for his daughter Elizabeth's use, his upermost plantation. Then by a Deed of partition between sd Elizabeth Cantwell, and her brother Richard Cantwell, dated 18 May 1709, she stood seized of it all. Then she intermarried with Henry Garretson and by their Deed Poll dated 16 June 1701, they did grant unto Isaac Hansen of Staten Island and James Sympson of Nasaw Island, both of Prov. of NY., the sd land. The sd Sympson by indenture datd 10 Jan 1712, did grant unto afsd Hansen one third of whole tract of sd land. Whereas sd Hansen by indenture dated 25 Jan 1712 did grant same unto afsd Jacob Rykeer. Signed: Jacob Ryke, Sytie Rycker (mark). Wit: Canul Menfient, S. Gerritson, John Suydam. Note: 3 June 1735. Sytie Rycker examined by S. Gerritson. Signed: Jacob Gomes. Rec: 6 Jan 1735/6. Will Shaw, rec. (K1-371)

439. Judgement. 22 Aug 1735. Henry Newton, Sheriff of Co. of New Castle send Greetings. Whereas Thomas Grome was lately in Court of Common Pleas and recovered against Parmehah Battell, Exec. of the Last Will of William Battell, late of sd Co., dec'd., 9 pounds 15 shillings and damages. Sheriff seized goods and lands of sd Battell at the time of his death. Taken was a bank or water lott of ground which was appraised by George Monroe and John Russell for 4 pounds. On 14 July last notice was given and sold to Robert Spicer of Philadelphia in Prov. of Penn, merchant, as the highest bidder for 13 pounds. Sd lott is situate in sd Co. and is 60 feet in breadth & 600 feet in length. It bounds lands of Richard Cantwell, Elizabeth Garretson, widow, now in tenure of Mary

Carpenter, widow, and the free wharf. Signed; Henry Newton, Shff. Wit: James Armitage, H. Gonne. Ack: Aug Term 1735. (K1-374)

440. Judgement. 18 April 1735. Henry Newton, Sheriff of Co. of New Castle send Greetings. Whereas William Goodard was lately in Court of Common Pleas and recovered against Anthony Dowdall of sd Co., yeoman, a debt of 60 pounds and damages. Sheriff ordered to seize of goods and lands of sd Dowdall. Taken in execution was one Bank Lott valued at 30 pounds. On 17 April instant at publick vendue, sd lott was sold to William Attwood as the highest bidder for 23 pounds. This bank lott is part of John VnGezell's bank lott and by him sold to sd Dowdall. It lies opposite sotts of sd VnGezell and Henry Gonne. Signed: Henry Newton, Shff. Wit: John VnGezell, Wm, Beeke, Nathl. Palmer. Ack: Aug Term 1735. (K1-376)

441. Deed. 21 Aug 1735. Joseph Brown, mariner, for 160 pounds, sold unto Paul Allfree of New Castle Co., his parcel of land which is one moiety of the plantation that sd Allfree now lives on. This they both bought of William Golden by Deed dated 18 May 1731. Signed: Joseph Brown. Wit: Richd. Colegate, Hall Gerritson, John Allfree. Rec: 12 Jan 1735/6. (K1-377)

442. Deed. 14 Jan 1734. John Hore of the Town & Co. of New Castle, gent., for the sum of 50 pounds, sold unto Sarah Edwards, widow of Edward Edwards, late of sd Co., dec'd., a parcel of land containing 150 acres, situate on the north side of Duck Creek. It bounds lands of James Hyatt, Dakeyne and James Hackett. This is land that sd Hore became seized of by virtue of a Patent from the Proprietors. Signed: John Hore. Wit: Jehu Curtis, Stephen Sykes. Rec: 12 Jan 1735/6. (K1-378)

443. Deed. 25 June 1715. Griffith Nicholas of Co. of New Castle, miller, and Margaret his wife, for the sum of 12 pounds, grant unto Thomas Rees of the same place, carpenter, a tract of land containing 182 acres 118 perches, situate between the Welsh tract and Elk river in sd Co. This land belonged to sd Nicholas by virtue of a Warrant, dated 10th day 4th mo 1713. It was surveyed by George Dakeyne on 12th day 5th mo 1713. Signed: Griffith Nicholas (mark). Wit: Elisha Thomas, Wm Williams, Saml Wilds (mark), Jno David. Rec 12 Jan 1735/6. (K1-380)

444. Deed. 12 Aug 1735. John Finney of New Castle and Co., chyrurgeon, acknowledges that his name was used on the Deed Poll by special nomination of Gideon Griffith of same place, gent., and in Trust for him, and the 150 pounds 5 shillings paid to Henry Newton, Sheriff of sd Co. was sd Griffith's. This Deed Poll was dated 21 May 1735, for a certain house and lott situate in the town of

New Castle. This property is bounded on S. with house & lott of sd Finney, on the W. with the Green or Market plact, on the N. with house & lott of George Monroe, and to the E. with Front or Water St. Signed: Jno Finney. Wit: Will Shaw, Jehu Curtins. Rec: 12 Jan 1735/6. (K1-381)

445. Deed. 21 Aug 1735. Hugh Watson of Red Lyon Hun. in Co. of New Castle, innholder, and Mary his wife, for the sum of 33 shillings, grant unto Samuel Clement of St. Georges Hun. in sd Co., yeoman, a parcel of land containing one acre 32 perches, situate in Red Lyon Hun., on the north side of St. Georges Branch, on the road to New Castle. Mentions secured to be paid by sd Clements for every acre of land and marsh, and also part of the land and plantation whereon afsd Hugh Watson now dwells, which hereafter shall be overflowed or drowned by means of a mill pond intended to be made by afsd Clement. Signed: Hugh Watson, Mary Watson. Wit: Thos. James, Thos. Noxon. Mary Watson examined by Thos. James. Rec: 12 Jan 1735/6. (K1-382)

446. Deed. 9 Aug 1735. Charles Empson of Christiana Hun. in Co. of New Castle, yeoman, and Mary his wife, for the sum of 40 pounds, sold unto William Shipley of Reyley in Co. of Chester in Prov. of Penn., yeoman, a parcel of meadow ground containing one acre 104 perches. This is whereas John Anderson, late of sd Hun. & Co. by indenture dated 10th day 8th mo 1674, did grant unto Samuel Peterson and Lars Cornelison a plantation lying on Christiana Creek. Then sd Peterson by virtue of afsd writing became possessed of every part of sd property. In sd Peterson's Last Will, dated 20th day 9th mo 1689, he bequeathed that whichever of his sons is longest with their mother (his wife) shall have afsd plantation. Then Mathias Peterson, his eldest son by writing dated 1st day of 10th mo 1702 did confirm unto his brother Peter Peterson the Title to property (as sd Peter stayed longest). Then sd Peter Peterson by his Last Will dated 29 Jan 1713, did give his dwelling plantation to his eldest son, Peter, after his wife's decease. Then the son, Peter, and his wife Magdalen by indenture dated 8 May 1727, did grant 105 acres of sd tract of 211 acres unto Andrew Justis. Then sd Justis and Britta his wife by indenture dated 20 May 1725 did grant afsd Charles Empson the afsd piece of meadow ground. Signed: Char. Empson, Mary Empson (mark). Wit: Adam Buckley, Rd. Sanderson. Mary Empson examined by Charles Springer. Rec: 23 Jan 1735/6. (K1-383)

447. Deed. 20 May 1735. Rees Jones of Christiana Bridge in Co. of New Castle, surgeon, and Sarah his wife, for the sum of 60 pounds, sold unto Benjamin Cook of the same place, merchant, a corner lott now in the actual possession of sd Cook, situated on N. side of sd bridge. It bounds the garden poles of Lewis Howell. This is part of a larger tract of 75 acres that Wm Penn by his Warrant dated 5th day 5th mo 1683, directed to Thomas Pierson (then Surveyor) to lay

out unto John Ogle senr. It was called Eagles Point and was situate on Christiana Creek. Sd Ogle conveyed same in 1696 unto John Latham, his son & heir Aaron Lathom conveyed the same land unto Anne Margaret Sotort by Deed dated 21 Oct 1706. Then sd Sotort was in Court for non-payment of a debt then due to John french, then Sheriff of sd Co. Sd Sheriff directed George Dakeyne, then Coron. of sd Co. to seize sd land for sale. On 17 May 1711, Deed of Conveyance made to John Ogle Jun. Then sd Ogle and Elizabeth his wife conveyed same tract of land and premises to Francis Land by Deed. Then sd Land with Christiana his wife conveyed same unto afsd Rees Jones. Signed: Rees Jones, Sarah Jones. Wit: Joseph Weldon, Andrew Coulbrtson, Sarah Jones Examined by James Armitage. Rec: 12 Jan 1735/6. (K1-385)

448. Deed. 28 June 1735. Jacobus Williams Neering of New Castle & Co., farmer, and Barbara his wife, for the sum of 20 pounds, sold unto Christopher Eaton of sd Co., farmer, a tract of land and marsh in sd Co., commonly called Hamburgh Island. It bounds the land of Peter Alrich and contains 500 acres. Signed: Jacobus Williams Neering, Barbara Williams Neering. Wit: Rich. Grafton, David French. Barbara Williams Neering examined by R. Grafton. Rec: 10 Jan 1735/6. (K1-387)

449. Judgement. 10 May 1733. John Gooding, Esq. Sheriff of Co. of New Castle send greetings. Whereas John French, John Richardson and Joseph England, Trustees of the late Loan Office were in court to recover against John Hore, Admin. of All which were of John Peele at the time of his death, to cover debt. This is whereas John Peele, late of sd Co., yeoman, did on 3 Feb 1723, take out a Indenture of Mortgage on a piece of land containing 126 acres with improvements, situate near Duck Creek and Black Bird Creek in sd Co. This was part of two tracts containing 476 acres. Sd Sheriff ordered to seize sd land. It was sold unto Jacob Gooding, farmer of sd Co., as the highest bidder, for the sum of 20 pounds. Signed: John Gooding, Shf. Wit: David French, Gideon Griffith. Rec: 10 Jan 1735/6. (K1-389)

450. Deed. 1735. William Whittet of St. Georges Hun. in Co. of New Castle, mariner, for a consideration in hand paid by Robert Jonathan Osborn of Philadelphia, gent., on the behalf of Jacob Martin of sd Hun. & Co., yeoman, sold unto sd Jacob Martin a plantation and tract of land in sd Hun. & Co. It is situate on the NW of Appoquinimink Creek, bounding land of John Peterson and Drawyers Creek, and contains 183 acres. Signed: William Whittet. Wit: Abraham Martin, Solomon Demrest. Rec: 10 Jan 1735/6. (K1-391)

451. Deed. 23 Aug 1735. Jacob Martin of Georges Hun. in Co. of New Castle, yeoman, and Eleanor his wife, for the sum of 250 pounds, sold unto Robert

Jonathan Osborn of Philadelphia, gent., a parcel of land containing 183 acres. This is land that Garrett Otto by a Patent from Francis Lovelace, dated 26 Feb 1671, (recorded by Mathias Nichols, then Sec. of Rolls office 1678) was siezed of, situate on Delaware River and NW side of Appoquinimink Creek. It bounded the lands of Hans Hanson and John Sherrick. Sd Otto's only son, Walraven Otto (after his father's death) by Deed Poll dated 30 Oct 1694 did convey sd land to James Read. Sd Read by his Deed Poll dated 7 Nov 1694 conveyed sd land unto Jeffery Martin. Sd Martin found out that sd Otto had reserved to himself 40 acres of land before granting land to sd Read. Then John Willson, Exec. of the Last Will of afsd Walraven Otto, by his Deed Poll dated 15 May 1697 did confirm sd 40 acres unto sd Martin. Sd Jeffery Martin's Last Will, dated 1 Jan 1726/7, willed that his land be equally divided between his three sons, Peter, Jacob and Abraham Martin. Sd Peter died intestate without issue, so afsd Jacob, surviving eldest brother, was his heir. Sd Abraham and Jamima his wife by indenture dated 27 Jan 1733/4, released their share to Jacob also. Then sd Jacob and Eleanor confirmed sd land to William Whittet, mariner of sd Hun. & Co. by Deed Poll bearing even date. Signed: Jacob Martin, Eleanor Martin (mark). Wit: Rd. Cantwell, William Whittet, Abraham Martin. Eleanor Martin examined by Rd. Cantwell. Exam: 10 Dec 1735. (K1-392)

452. Deed. 6 Aug 1735. Isaac Janvier of New Castle Co., joiner, and Rebecca his wife, and Francis Janvier of sd place, cordwainer, for the sum of 200 pounds, sold unto Jacob Gooding of St. Georges in sd Co., shopkeeper, seven pieces of land upon Reedon Island Neck, in sd Co. This is land that they inherited from their father, Thomas Janvier, late of sd Co., gent., by his Last Will dated 27 March 1728. (Sd Will directed the land, containing 350 acres total, be divided equally between his sons, afsd Isaac and Francis.) #1 called Home Lott, bounds land of Isaac Gooding and contains 17-1/4 acres. #2 bounds lands of John Hanson junr., land late of John Hanson senr., land late of Peter Stryker and contains 34 acres. #3 bounds sd Hanson's, William Pattison and sd Gooding and contains 150 acres. #4, #5 and #6 all contain 8 acres of marsh and bounds marsh late of John Berges & sd Hanson's. #7 marsh contains 201 acres. Signed: Isaac Janvier, Rebecca Janvier, Francis Janvier. Wit: David French, H. Gonne. Rebecca Janvier examined by David French. Rec 10 Jan 1735/6. (K1-395)

453. Appointment. Oct 1735. John Penn, Thomas Penn & Richard Penn proclaim William Read to be Keeper of the Publick Rolls belonging to the Gov. of Co. of New Castle, Kent & Sussex. Signed: P. Gordon. Affid. signed: John Richardson and Richard Grafton. (K1-398)

454. 9 Oct 1735. George the 2nd King of Great Britain Appoints William Read

as one of His Majesties Justices (duties given). Signed: P. Gordon. Affid. signed: John Richardson and Richard Grafton. (K1-399)

455. Appointment. 30 Oct 1735. John Penn, Thomas Penn & Richard Penn proclaim William Shaw, Esq., Attorney General for the Gov. of Co. of New Castle, Kent & Sussex (duties given). Signed: P. Gordon. Rec: 30 Oct 1735. (K1-400)

456. Oct 1735. Patrick Gordon, Lieut. Gov. appoints William Shaw, Esq. Publick Treasurer and Collector of the Gov. fines (duties given). Signed: P. Gordon. Rec: 31 Oct 1735. (K1-402)

457. Appointment. Oct 1735. The Governor's Warrant for William Read to be Deputy Keeper of the Great Seal for Gov. of Co. of New Castle, Kent & Sussex. Signed: P. Gordon. Affid. Signed: John Richardson, Richard Grafton. (K1-403)

458. Appointment. 5 Nov 1735. Patrick Gordon, Lieut. Gov. appoints William Shaw, Esq. to be Collector of the Duty's on Convicts and for receiving the Entrys of Passengers & Servants imported to New Castle Co. Whereas there is an Act imposing a Duty on persons convicted of heinous crimes and to prevent poor and impotent persons from entering sd County, the Gov. appointed Robert Gordon of Co. of New Castle, George Knowel of Co. of Kent and Simon Kollock of Co. of Sussex, Esq. as Collectors. And whereas sd Robert Gordon is lately deceased, there is a want to fill. Signed: P. Gordon. (K1-403)

459. Deed/mortgage. 17 June 1735. George Yeates of Co. of New Castle, gent., and Mary his wife, for the sum of 165 pounds, sold unto Richard Grafton of sd Co., merchant, a tract of land and marsh where sd Yeates' now dwell. It bounds the land of Thomas Fenton and Mill Creek and contains 700 acres. Terms dictated. Signed: G. Yeates, Mary Yeates. Wit: H. Gonne. Proved by James Armitage. Mary Yeates examined by James Armitage. Rec; 25 Nov 1735. (K1-405)

460. Deed. 15 Nov 1735. Thomas Cartmill of Brandywine Hun. in Co. of New Castle, turner, and Dinah his wife, for the sum of 40 pounds, sold unto John Isaac of same place, yeoman, a tract of land containing 100 acres, situate in the Mannor of Rocklands in sd Hun. & Co. It bounds the lands of Abel ?hileacre, William Loans and Jasper Poulson. Also 10 acres of marsh in Vertree Hook Marsh. This is part of the land that Thomas Cartmill purchased of Martin Cartmill (Book H, pp 110). Sd Martin became seized of sd land by a Deed Poll dated 6 May 1714, from his parents, Nathaniel Cartmill and Dorothy his wife. (Book D, pp 254/5). Signed: Thomas Cartmill, Dinah Cartmill. Wit: Robertson,

Harculah Robertson. Dinah Cartmill examined by James Armitage. Rec: 25 Nov 1725. Will Shaw, rec. David French, pro. (K1-407)

461. Deed. 15 Nov 1735. Thomas Cartmill of Brandywine Hun. in Co. of New Castle, turner, and Dinah his wife, for the sum of 40 pounds, sold unto Jasper Poulson, yeoman, of same place, 100 acres of land, situate in the Mannor of Rocklands in sd Hun. & Co. It bounds Shillpot Creek and lands of William Loans and John Isaac. This is part of the land that Thomas Cartmill purchased of Martin Cartmill (see rec #460). Signed: Thomas Cartmill, Dinah Cartmill. Wit: Robertson, Harculah Robertson. Dinah Cartmill examined by James Armitage. Rec: 27 Nov 1735. Will Shaw, rec. (K1-409)

462. Deed. 14 Nov 1735. William Evans of Pencader Hun. in Co. of New Castle, taylor, for the sum of 40 pounds, sold unto William Lowry of the same place, farmer, a parcel of land containing 150 acres 20 perches, situate in sd Hun. & Co. It bounds the lands of Junior James, Henry Bevans and Thomas Johns. This is part of a larger tract whereon the afsd Henry Bevans formerly dwelt. Signed: William Evans. Wit: James Armitage, Henry Newton. Rec: 28 Nov 1735. (K1-410)

463. Deed. 18 Oct 1735. Susannah Garland, daughter of John Garland, late merchant of Co. of New Castle, dec'd., and Jacobus Williams Neering, sadler, and Barbara his wife, of sd Co., for the sum of 35 pounds, sold unto Stephen Lewis of sd place, farmer and currier, a lott of land and premises, situate in the Town of New Castle. It is bounded by a lott laid out for Hans Coderus Cooper, now belonging to sd Stephen, and a lott late of Anthony Bryant, now in possession of Gideon Griffith. Sd lott was surveyed & laid out for Reyner Vander Coolon in Nov 1683. This lott was purchased by afsd John Garland from Anthony Green, dec'd., late of sd Co. In John Garland's Last Will, he bequeathed half of his estate, real and personal ('except my wearing cloaths'), unto his well beloved wife, Mary Garland, and the other half unto his well beloved daughter, afsd Susannah. Mary Garland then intermarried with afsd Jacobus Williams Neering. Signed: Susannah Garland (mark), Jacobus Williams, Barbara Williams. Wit: John Vanleuvenigh, Robertson, Robt Evans. Barbara Williams examined by James Armitage. Rec: 28 Nov 1735. (K1-412)

464. Deed. 11 Nov 1735. Andrew Justice of Willingtown in Christiana Hun. in Co. of New Castle, yeoman, and Breta his wife, and Thomas Willing of same place, cooper, and Catharine his wife and daughter of afsd Andrew and Breta, for the sum of 30 pounds, sold unto William Shipley of Ridley in Co. of Chester, yeoman, a parcel of land containing 105 acres, situate on the N. side of Christiana Creek. This is part of a larger plantation that John Anderson, late of

sd Hun. & Co. granted unto Samuel Peterson and Lars Corneliuson by indenture dated 10 Oct 1674. Then sd Peterson in his Last Will, dated 20 Nov 1689, devised that his plantation would go to whichever of his sons lived the longest with their mother. His eldest son, Mathias Peterson, confirmed same unto his brother, Peter Peterson, by Deed dated 1 Dec 1702, as the one who stayed longest. In Peter Peterson's Last Will dated 20 Jan 1714, he gave to his eldest son, Peter (after his wife's decease) this plantation. Then the son Peter, and Magdalene his wife did sell sd plantation by Deed dated 8 May 1727, unto afsd Andrew Justis. Signed: Andrew Justice (mark), Breta Justice (mark), Thos. Willing, Catherine Willing (mark). Wit: Wm Read, Joseph Parker. Breta Justice examined by Wm Read. Rec: 29 Nov 1735. (K1-415)

465. Deed. 11 Nov 1735. Andrew Justice of Willington in Christiana Hun. in Co. of New Castle, yeoman, and Breta his wife, and Thomas Willing of same place, cooper, and Catharine his wife and daughter of afsd Andrew and Breta, for the sum of 14 pounds, sold unto William Shipley of Ridley in Co. of Chester, yeoman, an acre of land (part of 105 acres in rec. #464), situate on the N. side of Christiana Creek. Signed: Andrew Justice (mark), Breta Justice (mark), Thos. Willing, Catherine Willing (mark). Wit: Wm Read, Joseph Parker. Breta Justice examined by Wm Read. Rec: 4 Dec 1735. (K1-418)

466. Deed. ? Aug 1735. Andrew Justis of Christiana Hun. in Co. of new Castle, yeoman, and Breta his wife, and Thomas Willing of same place, cooper, and Catharine his wife, for the sum of 104 pounds, sold unto William Shipley of Redley in Co. of Chester in Prov. of Penn., yeoman, a parcel of land (part of 105 acres in rec. #464/5), situate in Willingtown in Christiana Hun. It bounds Parker's lott on Market Street and contains 8 acres 106 perches. Signed: Andrew Justice (mark), Breta Justice (mark), Thos. Willing, Catherine Willing (mark). Wit: Charles Springer, Saml. Kirk. Proved by William Read. Breta Justice and Catherine Willing examined by Charles Springer. Rec: 5 Dec 1735. (K1-422)

467. Receipt. 'George McCall's receipt to George Yeates for the sum of 233 pounds 9 shill and 4 pence in part of a Mortgage Recorded in pages 294 & 295 of this Book as there noted referring ..' Signed: Geo McCall. Test: John Harrison. Affid. signed: John Armor. Wit: Richd. Grafton. Rec: 5 Dec 1735. (K1-425)

468. Deed. 18 Dec 1735. Gideon Griffith of the Town of New Castle and Co., gent., for the sum of 155 pounds, sold unto John Finney of same place, chyrurgeon, the house and lott with appurt. where sd Gideon Griffith now dwells, situate in sd town. It bounds on S. with house & lott of sd Finney, on the W. with Market place, on the N. with house & lott of George Monro with the

120

street leading to the Free Wharf, and to the E. with Water St. Signed: Gideon
Griffith. Wit: David French, Jehu Curtis. Test. David French. Rec: 13 Feb
1735/6. Will. Shaw. (K1-425)

469. Judgement. 18 Sept 1735. Henry Newton, Esq. Sheriff of Co. of New
Castle Send Greetings. Whereas John White and Abraham Taylor (were) lately
in Court and recovered against Samuel James, late of sd Co., yeoman, a debt of
852 pounds and damages. Sheriff ordered to take goods & chattles of sd James.
Taken in execution was a plantation and tract of land containing 200 acres with
dwelling house and outhouses erected on; and also his Forge with all tools and
utensils, a parcel of blacksmith tools, household goods and the eighth part of the
Furnace commonly called Samuel James'. This to the value of 451 pounds 15
shill 6 pence. Exposed to sale at publick vendue but unsold for want of buyers.
Finally sold to afsd John White and Abraham Taylor the the sum of 125 pounds.
Sd property bounds the lands of Thomas Watts, Elisha Thomas, James James
Jun., James James Sen., Thomas James, Thomas John, Hugh Morris and Philip
James. Signed: Henry Newton, Shff. Wit: Philip Van Leuvenigh, H. Gonne.
Rec: 13 Feb 1735/6. (K1-427)

470. Judgement. 18 Dec 1735. John Gooding, Esq. Sheriff of Co. of New Castle
Send Greetings. Whereas Thomas Lawrence (was) lately in Court and recovered
against George Rett of sd Co., yeoman, a debt of 290 pounds and damages.
Sheriff took in execution a messuage and tract of ground situate in the Town of
New Castle. It bounds Beaver St., the Quakers Meeting ground and Otter St. and
contains one acre with improvements. It was sold to William Piper of sd Co. for
the sum of 131 pounds as the highest bidder. Signed: John Gooding, Shff. Wit:
David French, Jehu Curtis. Rec: 13 Feb 1735/6. (K1-429)

471. Deed. 4 Dec 1735. Hugh Watson of Red Lyon Hun. in Co. of New Castle,
planter, and Mary his wife, for the sum of 100 pounds, sold unto John Carman
of Cecil Co. in Prov. of Maryland, merchant, a plantation situate on the west
side of Delaware River & east side of Georges Creek in New Castle Co. This
together with 160 acres of land, (this being the remaining part of a tract called
Lathem that was not conveyed by Benjamin Stout, dec'd., unto Benjamin Stout
Junr. and John Goforth). It bounds land of sd Goforth. But except so much land
that sd Hugh Watson, by Deed already conveyed to Samuel Clements of same
Co., planter, and also by article agreed to covey unto sd Clements the use of
Miln Race & Miln Dam and also 11 acres of land and swamp. Signed: Hugh
Watson, Mary Watson. Wit: John Dunning, H. Gonne. Mary Watson examined
by Wm. Read. Proved by Henry Gonne. Rec: 13 Feb 1735/6. (K1-430)

472. Deed. Feb 1735. Michael Butcher of Red Lyon Hun. in Co. of New Castle,

yeoman, and Maudlin his wife, for the sum of 80 pounds, release unto Hanse Hanse, yeoman, and John Hanse, a minor brother of sd Hanse, her 1/4 share of dec'd brother Peter's Hanse' inheritance. This is whereas their father, Peter Hanse, late of sd place, yeoman dec'd, was seized of sundry parcels of land situate in sd Hun. & Co. In his Last Will, dated 25 April 1729, he devised a Plantation to his son John, and the 150 acres to be equally divided between his other sons, Hans and Peter. Sd Peter to be given the Plantation whereon sd father lived. It was bounded by land of sd John Hanse and Traux. Sd Will gave to his daughter, Maudlin Truax the Plantation purchased of John Boyer with an addition of a small neck bounded with land of Isaac Cannon and John Stout, containing 200 acres total. Also all to share marsh in the Island. Also ordered that if one child dies without issue, that share to be divided with siblings. Then sd son, Peter Hanse died in 1731 without issue. Sd Maudlin Truax, now wife of afsd Michl. Butcher, became entitled to 1/4 part of all bequeathed unto her brother, Peter. Signed: Michel Bucher (mark), Madalen Bucher (mark). Wit: Thos. James, David Thomas. Madalen Bucher examined by Thos. James. Rec: 30 April 1736 by Will Shaw. (K1-432)

473. Judgement. 2 Feb 1735. John Gooding, Esq. Sheriff of Co. of New Castle send Greetings. Whereas John White and Abraham Taylor were lately in Court of Common Pleas, and recovered against Lewis Howell of sd Co., yeoman, (also called Mariner) a debt of 497 pounds and damages. Sheriff seized in execution a house and lott of ground of sd Howell's, situate at Christina Bridge where he then dwelt. And also 27 acres of woodlands and 3 acres of meadow ground. All valued at 150 pounds and was exposed to sale by Publick Vendue. All sd property sold unto afsd John White and Abraham Taylor for the sum of 101 pounds. Sd house & lott bounded by lott of Benjamin Cook, and by house and lott of James James junr. Signed: John Gooding, Sheriff. Wit: H. Gonne, John Legate. Rec: 30 April 1736 by Willm. Shaw. David French, Pro. (K1-434)

474. Deed. 28 Oct 1735. Mordecai Thomas of Brandywine Hun. in Co. of New Castle, labourer, and Jane his wife, for the sum of 19 pounds, sold unto Robert Cloud of Burmingham in Co. of Chester, husbandmand, a piece of land containing 50 acres, bounding the lands of sd Mordecai, Christopher Stedum and Jonathan Kirk. This is part of a larger tract called Leister containing 100 acres that, by virtue of a survey, was laid out unto William Leister. It was situate in the Mannor of Rocklands on the So. side of Skilpott Creek, in Brandywine Hun. Sd William Leister then died intestate, and land descended to his son, Peter Leister. Sd Peter then conveyed same land unto John Fox by indenture dated 10 May 16)6. Sd Fox conveyed same unto William Thomas (father of afsd Mordecai Thomas) by Bill of Sale. Sd Thomas died intestate and sd land now descends to his son, afsd Mordecai. Signed: Mordecai Thomas, Jane Thomas

(mark). Wit: George Brandon, Ralph Withers, Neal Obrian. Jane Thomas examined by Thos. James. Rec: 30 April 1736. (K1-437)

475. Deed. 20 Jan 1735. Robert Cloud of Burmingham in Co. of Chester in Prov. of Penn., husbandman, and Sarah his wife, for the sum of 23 pounds, sold unto William Passmore of Kennet in sd Co. & Prov., a parcel of land situate in Brandywine Hun. in Co. of New Castle, containing 50 acres. (Same land as in rec #474.) Signed: Robert Cloud (mark), Sarah Cloud. Thomas Heat, John Floyd. Sarah Cloud examined by Thos. James. Rec: 30 April 1736. (K1-438)

476. Deed. 30 Feb 1735. John Perry of Pencader Hun. in Co. of New Castle, taylor, and Sarah his wife, for the sum of 129 pounds, sold unto David Jones of same place, yeoman, a tract of land and plantation now in possession of sd Perry's. It bounds the lands of Howell James, James Read, David Evans and John Porter, and contains 209 acres. This is part of a quantity of 30,000 acres of land, commonly called the Welsh Tract that William Penn, by his warrant dated 18th day 8th mo 1701, granted to William Davis and David Evans. Sd Davis and Evans conveyed 209 acres of sd tract unto Thomas Watson, dec'd, by Deed; sd Watson then conveyed same again unto Richard Seren, who died intestate so sd Sarah Seren (alies Perry, party to this) became sole heir. Signed: Jo. Perry, Sarah Perry. Wit: David French, William Shaw. Rec: 30 april 1736. (K1-439)

477. Deed. 14 Feb 1735. John Ogle of White Clay Creek Hun. in Co. of New Castle, farmer, for the sum of 80 pounds, sold unto Benjamin Gibbs and Thomas Ogle of sd Co., farmers, a tract of land containing 200 acres, situate on the So. side of White Clay Creek in sd Hun. & Co. It bounds the land of Broer Senex. This is land that William Markham and John Goodson, by their Patent dated 15th day 4th mo 1688, did grant unto Jonas Arskain. (Except that piece that was sold by sd Arskain unto Thomas Ogle, late of sd creek, by Grant dated 15 Feb 1697. Afterwards sd Ogle, by his Deed of Gift dated 8 Oct 1721, granted unto his son, afsd John Ogle.) Signed: Jno Ogle. Wit: Lewis Howell, Robertson. Rec: 30 April 1736. (K1-441)

478. Deed. 16 Feb 1735. William Patterson of White Clay Creek Hun. in Co. of New Castle, Doctor Administrator to Peter Dollan, late of New Castle Hun. in sd Co., dec'd, and Catherine Dollan, widow of sd Peter, for the sum of 161 pounds, sold unto Alexander Aikien and Agnes his wife of New Castle Hun. in sd Co. a tract containing 143 acres, here described. This is that by indenture dated 10 March 1729/30, John Garretson, farmer, and Jane his wife confirmed unto their daughter, Catharine Garretson (afterwards wife to Peter Dollan), spinster, a parcel of land containing 143 acres. It bounded the lands of Henry Lands (now John Reynolds), Arthur Feraies, Thomas Dakyne (now sd

Reynolds), William Patterson and Thomas Midcif (now William Person's). Whereas sd Peter Dollan died intestate and was considerably in debt, the sd widow refused to take out Letters of Admin. upon which the sd William Patterson and Rees Jones got sd letters granted to them by petitioning the Court to sell Estate of sd Dollan. Signed: W. Patterson, Rees Jones, Cathran Dollan. Wit: Andw. Peterson, Richd. Grafton, H. Gonne. Rec: 30 april 1736. (K1-442)

479. Deed. 17 Feb 1735. Alexander Aikin, weaver, and Agnes his wife, of New Castle Hun. & Co. for the sum of 85 pounds, sold unto John Richardson of Christiana Hun. in sd Co., merchant, one of the Exec. of John Ashton, dec'd, a parcel of land containing 143 acres, situate in sd co. (Same land as described in Rec. #478). Signed: Alexander Eikin (mark), Agnes Eikin. Wit: Andw. Peterson, H. Gonne, Richd. Grafton. Agnes Eikin examined by Richd. Grafton. Rec: 30 April 1736. (K1-444)

480. Deed. 16 Feb 1735. Johanna See, widow & Admin. of Isaac See of St. Georges Hun. in Co. of New Castle, yeoman, dec'd., by virtue of Court Order, for the sum of 125 pounds 11 shilling, sold unto John See, yeoman, a tract of land containing 130 acres, situate in sd Hun & Co., bounding the land of Peter See. Together with 2-1/2 acres of marsh. Sd Isaac See died without leaving a sufficient value of personal estate to cover debts as remained due from him. At the Orphans Court on 1 Oct 1735, John Richardson, Charles Springer, Andrew Peterson, Simon Hadley, James Armitage and Thomas James, Esq., Justices, and William Read, Esq. Register, upon sd widow Johanna See's petition, gave her permission to sell dwelling plantation of Isaac See, (above described 130 acres and marsh). Signed: Johanna See. Wit: John Belueal, John Vance. Rec: 30 April 1736. (K1-446)

481. Deed. 14 Feb 1735. John Gregg of Christiana Hun. in Co. of New Castle, yeoman, and Elizabeth his wife, for the sum of 46 pounds 4 shilling, sold unto Christopher Wilson of the same place, yeoman, a parcel of land containing 66 acres, situate in sd Hun. & Co. It begins at Brandywine Creek and bounds the lands of Joseph Underwood and sd Wilson. This is part of a tract containing 177 acres that John Penn, Thomas Penn & Richard Penn by their Patent dated 4th day instant Feb. did grant unto sd John Gregg (Book A. Vol. 7. pp 423). Signed: John Gregg, Elizabeth Gregg (mark). Wit: Samuel Gregg, Samuel Stewart, Zach Butcher. Elizabeth Gregg examined by Simon Hadly. Rec: 30 april 1736 by Willm. Shaw. David French, pro. (K1-448)

482. Deed. 16 Feb 1735/6. Johanes Jacuqet of Appoquinamink Hun. in Co. of New Castle, yeoman, for the sum of 200 pounds, sold unto Elias Naudain of St. George Hun. in sd Co., mariner, a tract of land and marsh and plantation (now

in actual possession of sd Naudain), situate on Blackbirds Creek in Appoquin. Hun. This is part of a tract called Hartop's Pasture, and contains 229 acres. It bounds the lands of Benjamin Stout, dec'd., and William Harraway. David French appointed to appear in Court to Ack. this Deed. Signed: Johanes Jaquet. Wit: Rd. Cantwell, Jacob Read (mark). Rec: 30 April 1736. (K1-449)

483. Deed. 24 Jan 1735/6. Samuel Cartwright of Appoquinamk Hun. in Co. of New Castle, carpenter, and Margaret his wife, for the sum of 91 pounds 19 shilling, sold unto William Whittet of St. Georges Hun. in sd Co., shopkeeper, a tract of land and plantation (being the dwelling place of sd Cartwright), containing 222 acres. It begins at Appoquinamk Creek and bounds the land of William Williams. Signed: Samll. Cartwright, Mary Cartwright (mark). Wit: Rd. Cantwell, Sapience Harrison (mark). Margaret Cartwright examined by Rd. Cantwell. Rec: 30 April 1736. (K1-451)

484. Deed.16 Feb 1735. Agnes Stout, widow and Relict of Benjamin Stout of Appoquamink Hun. in Co. of New Castle, dec'd, and Jacob Stout, both Execs. of sd Benjamin Stout, for the sum of 110 pounds, sold unto Elias Naudain of St. Georges Hun. in sd Co., mariner, a tract of land and plantation with parcel of marsh adjoining, situate in Appoq. Hun. Property bounds the land of Johanes Jacquet and contains 185 acres. Sd Benjamin Stout in his Last Will, dated 25 April 1732 did bequeath to his son, afsd Jacob Stout, all his Estate, both real & personal. Whereas there was not sufficient value to discharge debts, Jacob Stout on behalf of his mother, petitioned to Orphans Court which gave them an Order to sell dwelling plantation and land (this on 18 Nov 1735 before Charles Springer, Richard Grafton, Simon Hadley and James Armstrong Esq. Justices, and William Read, Esq. Reg.) Advertisements for the sale signed by John Hore, Clk. The property was mentioned in an Indenture of Release made between John, Robert, and Henry Hartop, referring to a division. Signed: Agnes Stout, Jacob Stout. Wit: Edward Hawkins, Ffence Ffame. Rec: 30 April 1736. (K1-453)

485. Deed. 18 Feb 1735/6. Andrew Stalcop of Christiana Hun. in Co. of New Castle, weaver, for the sum of 12 pounds, sold unto Haunse Smith of same place, hatter, a parcel of marsh containing 6-1/2 acres, situate in sd Hun. & Co. Andrew Stalcop empowers his friend, David French, to appear in Court for him. Signed: Andrew Stalcop. Wit: Henry Colesbery, Gisbert Walraven (mark). Rec: 30 April 1736. (K1-455)

486. Deed. 16 Feb 1735. James Merrewether of New Castle town and Co., currier, and Elizabeth his wife, for the sum of 200 pounds, sold unto Sylvanus Hussey of same place, tanner and currier, a lott of ground and premises, situate

in the town of New Castle. This is whereas John Richardson of sd Co. by his Deed dated 31 March 1694, did confirm unto Cornelius Kettle sd lott of ground. It was bounded by Market place, Beaver Street and lott of Richard Griffith. Then sd Kettle by his Deed dated 19 Nov 1724 did confirm sd lott and improvements unto afsd James Merrewether. Signed: James Merrewether, Elise Merrewether. Elizabeth Merrewether examined by Richd. Grafton. Wit: Robertson, Gilbert Deakeyne. Rec: 30 April 1736. (K1-456)

487. Deed. 19 Feb 1735/6. Richard Grafton of New Castle and Co., merchant, and Mary his wife, for the sum of 16 pounds 12 shilling, sold unto William Nivens of Mill Creek Hun. in ye sd Co., yeoman, a lott of ground situate in Willingstown on the No. side of Christiana Creek. It bounds Front St. and the lotts of James Millner and contains one quarter of an acre. Signed: Richd. Grafton, Mary Grafton. Wit: Jnô. Richardson, James Armitage. Rec: 30 April 1736. (K1-458)

488. Deed. 22 Aug 1734. John Lefever of New Castle & Co., weaver, and Susannah his wife, for the sum of 10 pounds 12 shilling, sold unto William Peterson, yeoman, of same place, a lott of ground (part of the lott that sd Lefever now doth dwell), bounding the lott of Widow Williams. Signed: John Lefever, Susannah Lefever (mark). Wit: Moses Degon, Robertson. Susannah Lefever examined by Richd. Grafton. Rec: 30 April 1736. (K1-460)

489. 15 May 1736. "Mr. William Curry, Probr. applying to the Psby of New Castle in Pennsilvania, America, in September 1734, and bringing with him authentick Credentials, was taken on Tryals for the work of the ministry; ....he acquitting himself in all his Tryals to very great satisfaction ... we doe hereby unanimously recomend the above named gent to divine protection where providence may order his Lott as a Sober Christian and well deserving Gentm... his behaviour was very becoming and agreeable ... and now is free of any publick Scandal or Censure known to us... by Joseph Houston P:Clk" (K1-461)

490. Affidavit. 3 June 1736. Robert Gordon and James Houston of New Castle Co., being Sworn.. did declare and say that they saw and heard Mr. Joseph Houston, the subscriber of the within Certificate acknowledge that it was his own hand writing.. Signed: Robt. Gordon, James Houston. Willm. Shaw. John Legate, Dept Prot. certifies that sd William Shaw is one of his Matys Justices of the Peace. (K1-461)

491. Philada. March 1st 1735/6. 'I achnowledge receiving from Mr. George Yeates in New Castle Co. his Bond of this date for 62 pounds 10 shillings payable 11 June next; which Bond is full satisfaction a ballance due to me in

Principal and Interest of a Mortgage on a Plantation in sd Co. which Jasper Yeates, dec'd., left to his son Jasper; who sold the same to sd George Yeates; who mortgages the same to me for 280 pounds 17 shill and a penny ....' Signed: Geo. McCall. Wit: Alexr. Annand, John Harrison. 'Mortgage rec. in page 294:295 this book'. (K1-461)

492. Deed. 12 May 1736. Grace Vance, relict of Owen Carthy of Co. of New Castle, mariner, lately dec'd, and Darby Carthy and Nicholas Vandike, Adm. of the Estate of sd Owen Carthy, for the sum of 194 pounds, sold unto Thomas Bullock of Chester Co., weaver, a plantation and tract of land (late of sd Carthy), situate in Georges Hun. in Co. of New Castle. It bounds the land formerly belonging to William Philips, and contains 210 acres known by the name Philips Point. And also 10 acres of marsh, adjoining the marsh of Garret Dushane. (Adm. received permission of Court to sell property). Signed: Grace Vance (mark), Darby Carthy, Nicholas Vandike. Wit: Rd. Cantwell, Jacob Martin, Alexander Pentland. Examined 10 June 1736 by Willm. Shaw, Rec. (K1-462)

493. Deed. 20 May 1736. Sigfredus Alrichs of New Castle and Co., yeoman, and Mary his wife, for the sum of 11 pounds, sold unto Jacob Grantum of the same place, farmer, a parcel of marsh situate in sd Co. It bounds the land of Peter Alrichs and contains 5 acres. Signed: Sigfredus Alrichs. Wit: Robertson, James Alrichs. Ack: May Term 1736. (K1-463)

494. Deed. 14 May 1736. 'Elizabeth Serey, late of Pencader Hun. in Co. of New Castle, widow and Adm. of Richard Serey, dec'd., for a consideration, have set over unto John Perry, my Son in Law, the Administration of all the Estate of my late Husband, and by the said writing reserved unto myself the Dower of three pounds pr. Annum during the term of my natural life in leiu of my third of a plantation belonging to the Estate. Whereas sd John Perry hath lately granted sd plantation unto David Jones of Pencader Hun., yeoman, under the sd yearly pymt of 3 pounds pr annum to me. I, Elizabeth Serey for the sum of 20 pounds from sd David Jones, quit claim & grant unto him... plantation'. Signed: Elizabeth Serey (mark). (K1-464)

END OF DEED RECORD VOLUME K-1

BEGIN DEED RECORD VOLUME L-1

495. 4 Dec 1673. 'Appeared before me Matthew DeRengh, Clerk of this place New Amstel Harine Janse have abovementioned who has Conveyed like he Conveyeth by these the just half of this Land in this Grant or Deed comprized to the behoof of Hendrick Frause to him and his Heirs forever and Hereditaments with all the Right and Title that he Harine Janse afsd therdo hath for with his own free goods. Thus done without ffraudin prefence of the underwritten' Signed: Harm Jansen. 'Done at New Amstel the 4 December 1673 on the South River in New Netherland. as Witness Joan Bish in prefence of Matth DeRengh'. (L1-0)

496. Affidavit. 23 Feb 1736. Thomas Noxon of New Castle Co. swears that the above is a just and true translation of the assignment endorsed on a patent dated in the year 1667 from Richard Nicholls, Gov. of New York to George Whale and George Moore. Signed: Thos. Noxon. Sworn before Jno. Finney. (L1-0)

497. Patent. 1 Jan 1667. Richard Nicolls, Esq. Prin. Comm. from His Majesty in New England Gov. under James Duke of York and Albany and all forces employed to the Dutch Nation and Lands and Plantations.. (etc) grants unto George Hale and George Moore a parcel of land called Minquaes Plantation, situate in Christene Kill at Delaware, containing 200 acres. It bounds the plantations of Andries Benns and Andries Andries. Signed: Richard Nicholls. Recorded by Matthias Nicholls, Sec. (L1-1)

498. Patent signed over. August 1673. George Hale and George Moore sign over (rec. #467) Patent to Herman Johnson. Signed: Geo. Hale, Geo. Moore. Memorandum: 2 Dec 1679 Herman Janson made over a plantation to William Rainbow and parcel of land (part of Patent land) with half of all marshes. Signed: Eph. Herman. (Passage in Dutch follows, probably the original document that was traslated) (L1-1)

499. Deed. 22 Feb 1687. John Willingson, successor and Admin. of the Estate of William Rainbow, late of Co. of New Castle, dec'd., for the sum of 70 pounds, grant unto unto Conrade Constantine of sd Co., planter, a tract of land and plantation, situate on the West side of Delaware River & No. side of Christiana Creek. It bounds other land of sd Constantine, and contains 300 acres. Signed: John Willingson (mark). Wit: Thos. Parson, Urian Anderson (mark). Ack: Feb 22 1687 by John White, Clerk. Rec: 23 Feb 1736 by Willm. Shaw. (L1-2)

500. Gift Deed. 3 June 1723. James James of Pencadder Hun. in Co. of New

128

Castle, gent., for the Natural Love and Affection which he hath unto his Son and Heir apparent, Daniel James, and for diverse other reasons of moving, grants unto sd Daniel James a parcel of land situate in sd Hun. & Co. It bounds the lands of James James Junr. and James Armitage and contains 144 acres. Surveyed and laid out from a greater tract on 22 March last for sd James. Signed: James James. Wit: Elisha Thomas, Hanah Armitage, Enoch Morgan, James Armitage, Howell James. Memo: Peaceful possession was given. Also signed: Hugh Morris (mark), Samuel James, James James Junr. (L1-3)

501. James James nominates Thomas James, James Armitage and Simon Hadley as his Attorneys to present Deed in Court. Signed: James James. Wit: Mary Armitage Hannah Armitage. Rec: 23 Feb 1736 by Willm Shaw. David French prot. (L1-4)

502. Deed. 16 Nov 1736. Anthony Dushane, only son and heir of Jerome Dushane, of St. Georges Hun. in Co. of New Castle, yeoman, dec'd., and Jacamyntie his wife, for the sum of 70 pound, sold unto John Daniel Tonay of the Town of St. George in Red Lyon Hun. in sd Co., miller, the following parcels of land. One is a small parcel of marsh containing 39 acres, lying near Dragon Branch, bounding the land of John Gills and land late of Thos. Morgan. Another small parcel of marsh by Dragon Run, containing 3 acres. Also a 2nd small parcel bounding the first mentioned, bounding land of sd Tonay, containing 7 acres 104 perches. Also a 3rd parcel referred by Mathias Hatson Skrick for a Hay Road to afsd marsh. It bounds land lately sold by Gabriel Cox and Magdalen his wife to Jacob VnBebber, dec'd., and land of David Howell and contains 2 acres 20 perches. Anthony Dushane, Jacamyntie Dushane (mark). Wit: Tho. Noxon, Benj. Rowland. Wife examined by Tho. Noxon. Rec: Nov 1736. (L1-4)

503. Deed. 20 Aug 1736. George Hillis of New Castle Hun. & Co., cordwainer, for the sum of 53 pounds, sold unto William Patterson of White Clay Creek Hun. in sd Co., mariner, a parcel of ground situate on the No. side of Christiana Creek. It bounds the lands of Robert Miller, John Ferry and John Harris and contains 2-1/2 acres. Also one other lott situate by Christiana Bridge, bounding lands of sd Ferry and containing half an acre. Signed: George Hillis. Wit: So. Evans, David Williams, Richard Few. Rec: 9 Feb 1736. (L1-7)

504. Deed. 27 Sept 1736. Evan Edmond of Pencader Hun. in Co. of New Castle, yeoman, for the sum of 120 pounds, sold unto Rees Jones of the same place, tanner, 200 acres of land situate in sd Hun. & Co. It bounds the land formerly belonging to Lewis David. This is part of a larger tract sold to afsd Edmont by Howell James by Deed dated 7 Sept 1712. Signed: Evan Edmond. Wit: Hannah

Armitage, Sam. Wild, James Armitage. Rec: Nov Term 1736. (L1-9)

505. Deed. 10 April 1736. 'David Evans of Prov. of No. Carolina, for the sum of 100 pounds, grant unto Soloman Evans of Pencader Hun. in Co. of New Castle, a Plantation tract of land whereon I have lived,' containing 255 acres. Also another tract adjoining it on NE corner, containing 300 acres. Signed: Da. Evans. Wit: Samuel James, John Edwards jun. Thomas Noxon. Rec: Nov Term 1736. (L1-11)

506. Deed. May 1736. William Goforth of Red Lyon Hun. in Co. of New Castle, weaver, and Ann his wife, for the sum of 125 pounds, sold unto Michael Dushene of St. Georges Hun. in sd Co., weaver, a plantation containing 135 acres, situate in sd Hun. & Co. (Except 16 acres cut off north end.) It bounds the lands of sd Goforth and John Gooding, and land formerly of Charles Cox but now of Francis Land. This is part of a larger tract of 1,280 acres that Edmond Andros by his Patent dated 5 Nov 1675, did grant unto Joseph Young, late of sd Co. Sd Young died, leaving issue two sons, Jacob and Joseph Young; who by their Deeds, one dated 10 Nov 1700 and the other dated 21 Aug 1706, did confirm unto Charles Anderson and John Cox all sd tract of land. Sd John Cox by his Last Will dated 3 Dec 1713, bequeathed all his land to be equally divided between his sons, Charles, John and Augustine Cox. Division was made by George Dakeyne on 20 Oct 1720. By a Release dated 1 Nov 1720, sd Charles and Augustine release their shares to their brother John Cox. Sd John Jr., Last Will dated 15 Jan 1731, ordained his beloved wife, Rebecca, and Gabriel Cox as Exec., and ordered them to sell his Plantation. Rebecca then intermarried with Edmond Shaw, yeoman. Sd Exec. by Deed dated 3 Nov 1735, sold 135 acres plantation unto afsd William Goforth. Signed: William Goforth, Ann Goforth (mark). Wit: Jacob VanBebber, Anth. Dushene, John Caldwell. Anne Goforth examined by Thomas James. Rec 8 Feb 1736/7. (L1-12)

507. Deed. 16 Aug 1736. James James junr., of White Clay Creek Hun. in Co. of New Castle, gent., and Francis his wife, for the sum of 55 pounds, sold unto George Hillis of New Castle Hun. & Co., cordwainer, a parcel of ground containing 2-1/2 acres, situate by Christiana Bridge. It bounds the lands of Robert Miller, John Ferry and John Harris. Also another 1/2 acre attached. These 3 acres were sold by John Ogle by Deed dated 17 May 1712 unto Nathaniel Pope, cordwainer, of sd Co. Then from Pope by Deed dated 18 Aug 1726 unto Benjamin Burleigh, and from him unto afsd James James junr. Signed: James James junr., Frances James. Wit: Ben. Cooke, John Herbert. Frances James examined by James Armitage. Rec: 24 Feb 1736. (L1-15)

508. Deed. 24 Sept 1736. Daniel James of Co. of New Castle, yeoman, and

Sarah his wife, for the sum of 200 pounds, sold unto Allen Delap of same Co., gentleman, two tracts of land containing 288 acres. They bound lands of Rees Jones and James Armitage. This is whereas William Penn by his Pattent dated 21 Feb 1703 granted unto James, father of afsd, 1,244 acres of land, situate in Pencader Hun. in sd Co. Then James James conveyed 248 acres of sd land to two of his sons, James James junr. and afsd Daniel James by Deeds dated 3 June 1723. Sd junr. conveyed his part, containing 143 acres 27 perches unto his brother, Daniel. Signed: Signed: Daniel James, Sarah James. Wit: Thomas Allison, Tho. Pagert, James Armitage. Sarah James examined by James Armitage. Rec: 18 Feb 1736. (L1-18)

509. Deed. 15 Dec 1736. Augustine Constantine of Newport Ayre in Christiana Hun. in Co. of New Castle, for the sum of 14 pounds, sold unto Capt. Nathaniel McGee and Thomas McGee, both of Belfast, marriners, a piece of land and premises, situate in Newport Ayre. It begins by Christiana Creek and contains 60 perches. Signed: Augustine Constantine (mark). Wit: John Wilson, James McMullan, David French. Ack: 15 Dec 1736. (L1-20)

510. Deed. 1 Dec 1723. Colonel John French of the Town & Co. of New Castle, for the sum of 250 pounds, sold unto Cornelius Tobey of sd Co., a tract of land commonly called Reneppa Camoocka, containing 400 acres. It is situate on W. side of Delaware River and No. side of Dragon Swamp in sd Co. Signed: John French. Wit: William Battell, Nicholas Mears. Parnellah Gordon, formerly the wife of William Battell, dec'd., and daughter of Colonel John French. Rec: Nov Term 1736. (L1-22)

511. Agreement. 18 Nov 1736. Of Rev. John Eneberg, minister of the Sweeds Church in Christiana Hun. in Co. of New Castle, and of the Testry and the Congregation of sd church for the empowering Trustees and Church Wardens for the Leasing Church Lands (a True Copy). Says that the church is seized of parcels of land containing 500 acres, by Deed dated 18 May 1703 (Book G pp 576). Names persons to be Charles Springer as Trustee for the time being and his successors, and Jacob Stelly and Garret Garretson as Church Wardens now and their successors shall perform this task. Other names to collect rents are Phillip Vandever, Monns Justis, Timothy Stedham, Lucas Stedham, Morton Justis, Henry Colesberry. Vestry Men. Peter Petersonn, Smith William Paulson, William Clenny, Henry Stedham, Joseph Springer, George Read, Jonas Stedham, Charles Springer junior, Charles Cornelinson, Andrew Lina, John Vandever, Justa Justis, John Morton, Andrew Stalcop junior, Israel Peterson, Hance Peterson, Henry VnDever, William Mounce, Zacharias Derrickson, Samuel Peterson, James Anderson, Errick Anderson, Hance Smith, Jasper Clawson, Jacob VnDever, Willaim Tussey, Andrew Cock, Mathias Morton,

Erasmus Stedham, Andrew Hendrickson, Andrew Justison, Andrew
Hendrickson, Paul Justison, Henry Hendrickson, Timothy Lucason Stedham -
Copia Vera as taken from Church Record Book A page 105 this 24th of January
1736/7. Per: Gouldsmith Edward Folwell. Rec: 24 1736 by Willm. Shaw. (L1-
24)

512. Deed. 17 Feb 1735/6. John Justis of Christiana Hun. in Co. of New Castle,
and Bretta his wife, for the sum of 85 pounds, sold unto Samuel Marshell of the
same place, yeoman, a piece of land situate in sd Hun. & Co. It bounds the lands
of Conrade Garretson by Christiana Creek to Kings Road and contains 18 acres
90 perches. Signed: John Justis, Breta Justis (mark). Wit: Augustine Constantine
(mark), Benjamin Paulson (mark). Breta Justis examined by Jehu Curtis. Ack:
Nov Term 1736. (L1-27)

513. Gift Deed. 3 June 1723. James James of Pencader Hun. in Co. of New
Castle, gent., for the Natural Love and affection which he hath unto his Son and
Heir apparent, James James junior, and for divers other good causes, the father
especially moving, hath given unto James James the son, a parcel of land, situate
in sd Hun. It bounds the lands of Rees Jones, James Armitage and contains 143
acres 77 perches. It was surveyed from a larger tract of sd father on 26 March
last. Signed: James James. Wit: Elisha Thomas, James Armitage, Enoch
Morgan, Daniel James, Howell James. Memo of peaceful possession. Wit:
Elisha Thomas, Enoch Morgan, Hugh Morris (mark), Howell James, Samuel
James, Thomas James, Daniel James. Appointed Attorneys were: Thomas
James, James Armitage and Simon Hadley. Wit: Hannah Armitage, Daniel
James. Rec: 25 Feb 1736 by Willm. Shaw. David French, prot. (L1-28)

514. Deed. 12 Nov 1736. Geo. Robinson of Brandywine Hun. in Co. of New
Castle, weaver, and Catharine his wife, in consideration of 5 shillings, grant
unto their son, Valentine Robinson of same place, yeoman, a parcel of land
called Newwark in sd Hun. & Co. It bounds Shilpot Creek and contains 400
acres. Also a tract of marsh containing 40 acres, part of Verdrede Hook. It
bounds lands of Thomas Johns and Henry Hollingsworth. Signed: Geo.
Robinson, Cathrine Robinson (mark). Wit: Adam Buckley, Geo. Robinson junr.
Ack: Nov Term 1736. (L1-30)

515. Deed. 30 Nov 1736. George Robinson of Brandywine Hun. in Co. of New
Castle, weaver, and Catharine his wife, in consideration of the Natural Love
they bear unto their son, Valentine Robinson of same place, yeoman, as well as
50 pounds, grant unto him a tract of land containing 400 acres and 40 acres
marsh. This is whereas William Penn by his Warrant dated 12 March 1682 did
grant unto Valentine Hollingsworth 400 acres of land in the Mannor of

Rockland (surveyed in Sept 1683 and called Newwork). And whereas William Markham, Robert Turner and John Goodson by Patent dated 13 Feb 1693 did grant unto afsd Valentine Hollingsworth a tract of marsh containing 40 acres, situate in Verders Hook Marsh. It bounded marshes of Thomas Johns and Henry Hollingsworth. Then sd Valentine by his Deed Poll dated 16 June 1707 for consideration of 10 pounds yearly paid to sd Valentine during his natural life, granted land and marsh to sd Henry Hollingsworth. Sd Henry became seized of sd property and then dyed, and the whole land & marsh went to Stephen Hollingsworth as his oldest son. Then sd Stephen and Anne his wife by Indenture of Lease and Release dated 30/31 May 1726, did grant same unto afsd George Robinson. Signed: Geo. Robinson, Catharine Robinson (mark). Wit: Adam Buckley, Geo. Robinson junr. Catharine Robinson examined by Adam Buckley. Ack: Nov Term 1736. (L1-31)

516. Deed. 19 Nov 1736. Alexander Berry of Black Birds Creek in Appoquinimink Hun. in Co. of New Castle, weaver, and Mary his wife (of late, Mary Taylor, Widow), for the sum of 25 pounds, sold unto Thomas Noxon of St. Georges Hun. in sd Co., yeoman, a tract of land containing 200 acres, situate on Gillpins Runn. It bounds the land late of Benjamin Allman, dec'd., land of Edmund Hardrics, land near a settlement made by Henry Cowgill and land of John Vardiman's late dwelling place. Signed: Alexander Berry, Mary Berry (mark). Wit: Hans Hanson, John Vance. Mary Berry examined by Hans Hanson. Rec: Nov Term 1736. (L1-34)

517. Deed/mortgage. 29 Aug 1736. Elizabeth Garretson of Appoquinimink Hun. in Co. of New Castle, widow, for the sum of 80 pounds, and also for the Natural Love and affection she beareth her Son-in-law, Richard Colegate, late of the Prov. of Maryland but now of sd Hun. & Co., gent., grants unto him a tract of land and plantation situate in sd Hun. & Co. (part of a tracat called red Clift). It bounds land formerly of John Goulden but now of Paul Alfree's and land of Edmund Garretson, and contains 200 acres of land, marsh and cripple. Terms are yearly payments to the Trustees of the General Loan Office. Signed: Elizabeth Garretson. Wit: Thos. Noxon, John Vanleuvenigh (mark). Proved 15 Dec 1736. (L1-36)

518. Deed. 17 Feb 1730. Thomas Noxon of St. Georges Hun. in Co. of New Castle, gent., and Mary his wife, for the sum of 80 pounds, sold unto John Clark of Red Lyon Hun. in sd Co., yeoman, a messuage plantation and parcel of land containing 200 acres, also 15 acres of marsh. This messuage and land lately belonged to George Hadley, dec'd., who purchased same from Henry Packard. Property now in possession of sd John Clark. It bounds land late of Henry Tilton, dec'd., now of Edmond Shaw, land of Hans Hans and now in tenure of

David Thomas, and land late of Henry Ward, dec'd. The marsh adjoins sd Ward.
Mentions Mary, now wife of sd John Clark, and formerly Widow of afsd
George Hadley. Signed: Tho. Noxon. Wit: Henry Gonne, Sampson Bourn. Rec:
22 Feb 1736. (L1-38)

519. Deed. 27 Jan 1725. James James junr. of New Castle Co., carpenter, for the
sum of 60 pounds, sold unto Daniel James of Pencader Hun. in sd Co., farmer, a
tract of land containing 143 acres, situate in sd Co. This is land that James James
Esq. by his Deed dated 3 June 1723 did convey unto afsd James junr. It bounded
the lands of Samuel James, Rees Jones and sd Daniel James. Signed: James
James junr. Wit: Elisha Thomas, James Armatage, Lewis Howell, Thomas
David (mark), William David. Appointed Attorneys were Thomas James, James
Armitage and Simon Hadley. Rec: 25 Feb 1736. (L1-40)

520. Deed. 3 Nov 1736. Mr. Agustine Constantine of Newport Ayre in
Christiana Hun. in Co. of New Castle, for the sum of 10 pounds, 15 shillings,
sold unto Cap. John Wilson, mariner, of Ayre in North Britain, a lott of land and
premises, situate in Newport Ayre in sd Hun. & Co. It bounds Christiana Creek,
Agustins St. and Water St., and contains 48 perches. Signed: Augustine
Constantine (mark). Wit: John Justis, Geo. Hutchinson, James McMullan. Ack:
15 Dec 1736. (L1-43)

521. Deed. 14 Feb 1736. Thomas Willing of Willingtown in Hun. of Christiana
in Co. of New Castle, cooper, and Catharine his wife, for the sum of 45 pounds,
sold unto Joseph Steel of the Prov. of Maryland, yeoman, and John McArthur of
Prov. of Maryland, weaver, and John Richardson (is Buchanan meant?) of the
Prov. of Penn, yeoman, a part of a 49 acre tract, herein mentioned. It bounds
French St. and 3rd St., and contains 20 perches 9 feet. (John Buchanan
mentioned as purchaser in deed) This is whereas Andrew Justison of
Willingtown, yeoman, was seized of a messuage tract of land containing 105
acres, situate in sd Hun. & Co. And whereas sd Justison and Breta his wife by
Lease & Release did convey 49-50 acres of same unto afsd Thomas Willing.
Signed: Thomas Willing, Catharine Willing (mark). Wit: James Hutchinson,
Saml. Ffandric, Gouldsmith Edward Ffolwell. Memo: Agreed that no advantage
be taken by Survivorship or by Reason of Priority between purchasers. Signed:
Joseph Steel, John McArthur, John Buchanan. Catherine Willing examined by
Jehu Curtis. Rec: 29 March 1737. (L1-45)

522. Release of Dower. 24 Jan 1736. Mary Dushane, widow and Relict of
Valentine Dushane of Co. of New Castle, dec'd., yeoman, who by his Last Will
dated 2 March 1735, did bequeath unto sd Mary Dushane one equal third part of
all his Estate. Now sd Mary, for the Natural Love and Affection which she bears

toward her sons, Valentine and Isaac Dushane, yeomen of sd Co., and for the sum of 5 shillings, releases her Right of Dower unto them. This is one third part of a plantation and tract of land lying on the No. side of Augustine Creek and on the So. side of St. Georges Creek in sd Co. This is part of a larger tract commonly called Groeningen. David French is appointed Attorney. Signed: Mary Dushene. Wit: Nicholas Jaquat, Anthony Dushene. Rec: 29 March 1737. (L1-47)

523. Deed. 13 July 1736. Joseph Way of Willingtown in Christiana Hun. in Co. of New Castle, yeoman, and Sarah his wife, for the sum of 60 pounds, sold unto Thomas Peters of the City of Philadelphia, merchant, a parcel of land and premises lying in sd Town, containing 38 perches. It begins by Christiana Creek and bounds Market St. and Front St. This is part of a larger tract containing 4 acres 35 perches that was purchased by sd Way by conveyance dated 3 July 1732 (Book H pp 23). Signed: Joseph Way, Sarah Way. Wit: Charles Springer, James James junr. Sarah Way examined by Charles Springer. David French is appointed Attorney. Rec: 30 March 1737. (L1-48)

524. Deed. 15 Feb 1736. Augustine Constantine of Newport Ayre in Christiana Hun. in Co. of New Castle, for the sum of 5 shillings, grants unto John Justis of same place, a piece of marsh situate in sd place. It bounds Christiana Creek and contains 5 acres. Signed: Augustine Constantine (mark). Wit: Samuel Marshall, James McMullan. Rec: 30 March 1737. (L1-50)

525. Deed. 26 Dec 1734. Silvanus Hussey of the Town & Co. of New Castle, currier, for the sum of 150 pounds, sold unto Stephen Lewis of same place, tanner, a plantation situate in sd Hun. & Co., commonly known as Jedediah Hussey's Plantation. Sd Jedediah Hussey is afsd Silvanus' father, recently dec'd., who bequeathed same to his son by his Last Will and Testament. Signed: Sylvanus Hussey. Wit: Anne Fitzgerald, Benj. Swett. Rec: 1 April 1737. (L1-52)

526. Deed. 16 Feb 1736. Augustine Constantine of Newport Ayre in Christiana Hun. in Co. of New Castle, for the sum of 10 pounds, sold unto Lewis Howell of White Clay Creek Hun. in sd Co., a piece of land and premises, situate in Newport Ayre. It begins at Christiana Creek and bounds Brittish St. and contains 40 perches. Signed: Augustine Constantine (mark). Wit: Saml. Marshall, Jno. McMullan. Rec: 1 April 1737. (L1-53)

527. Deed/mortgage. 18 Feb 1736. Peter Anderson of Hun. & Co. of New Castle, planter, and Margaret his wife, for the sum of 100 pounds, sold unto John Finney of same place, gent., a messuage plantation and parcel of land called Poplar Neck, situate on the No. side of Red Lyon Creek. Also a parcel of

marsh containing 25 acres, situate on the So. side of sd creek. The land bounds the land formerly of John Williams and contains 220 acres. Terms of payment given. Signed: Peter Anderson, Margaret Anderson (mark). Wit: Henry Gonne, Hans Hanson. Rec: 2 April 1737. (L1-54)

528. Deed. 1736. John Vance of St. Georges Hun. in Co. of New Castle, yeoman, and Hannah his wife, for the sum of 3 pounds 18 shilling, grant unto Abraham Goulden of same place, yeoman, a parcel of land situate on Snowdens' Branch, near to the fence of sd Goulden's dwelling plantation (part of a tract called Rowles Sepulehre). It bounds the land with the dwelling house of John Houston, and contains 3 acres 63 perches. Signed: John Vance, Hannah Vance (mark). Wit: John Cooper, Thos. Noxon. Hannah Vance examined by Thos. Noxon. Rec: 2 April 1737. (L1-56)

529. Deed. 16 Feb 1736. David McComb of Hun. & Co. of New Castle, yeoman, and Agnes his wife, for the sum of 101 pounds, sold unto John Stoops of the same place, cordwainer, a parcel of land containing 80 acres, and a parcel of swamp containing 10 acres 70 perches, situate in sd Hun. & Co. This is part of the land that John Hussey, late of same place, yeoman, dec'd., was seized of. He made his Last Will dated 28 Aug 1729 and bequeathed unto his son, Nathan Hussey, 80 acres (part of the land sd John Hussey owned and dwelled on). Also to sd Nathan was given 20 acres of marsh adjoining the land formerly belonging to Christopher Hussey, dec'd. Land bounds dec'd. Vopher Hussey's land. Sd Nathan Hussey and Anne his wife by Deed dated 12 May 1735, confirmed same unto afsd David McComb (Lib K. pp 338). Signed: Signed: David McComb, Agnes McComb (mark). Wit: John Williams, H. Gonne. Agnes McComb examined by Thomas James. Rec: 4 April 1737. (L1-58)

530. Deed. 1 Feb 1736. Jacob Smith of the Parish of Trevel in Prince William Co. in Colony of Virginia, planter, only son and heir of Nicholas Smith, late of Blackbirds Creek in Co. of New Castle, dec'd., for the sum of 40 pounds, sold unto Sapiens Harrison of Appoquinimink Hun. in Sd Co., yeoman, a tract of land with a plantation thereon which Thomas Jackson, dec'd, formerly dwell, situate on the head of sd Creek. This property was surveyed to sd father, Nicholas Smith, by virtue of a Warrant dated 25 June 1705. It bounds the land late of William Horn and land called Russell's Meadow, and contains 201-1/4 acres. Signed: Jacob Smith (mark). Wit: Fra. Awbrey, John Melton, Thom Elliott (mark). Rec: 5 April 1737. Will. Shaw, rec., David French, prot. (L1-61)

531. Deed. 30 April 1736. John Vance of St. Georges Hun. in Co. of New Castle, farmer, and Hannah his wife, for the Natural Love and Affection which he bear his father, Samuel Vance of sd Co., joyner, and for the sum of 5

shillings, grant unto him a parcel of land containing one acre, situate in sd Hun. & Co. Signed: John Vance, Hannah Vance (mark). Wit: Charles Robinson, John Hore. Hannah Vance examined by Thos. Noxon. Rec: 7 April 1737. (L1-63)

532. Deed. 24 Dec 1736. John Neal of Brandywine Hun. in Co. of New Castle, yeoman, and Margery his wife, for the sum of 270 pounds, sold unto William Derrickson of sd Co., a plantation and track of land commonly called Vun Dru Hook, situate in sd Hun. & Co.. It bounds the Delaware River, and land of John Bird and contains 150 acres 60 perches. Also one equal half part of all the marsh belonging to sd plantation. Mentions a mortgage made out to David French and Andrew Peterson, Trustees of the Loan Office, for the sum of 50 pounds. John Richardson is appointed Attorney. Signed: John Neal, Margery Neal (mark). Wit: John Richardson, Thos. Allmond, Zacharias Derrickson. Margery Neal examined by sd Richardson. Rec: 8 April 1737. (L1-65)

533. Deed. Feb 1736. Thomas Willing of Willingstown in Co. of New Castle, cooper, and Catherine his wife, for the sum of 45 pounds, sold unto James Chalmers of sd Co., gent., a piece of ground situate in sd town. It bounds the land of William Shipley by Christiana Creek and French St. Also all the Bank and Water fronting sd Lott as far as the channel of sd creek. Signed: Thomas Willing, Catherine Willing (mark). Wit: John Curtis, Thos. Maxwell. Catherine Willing examined by John Curtis. Rec: 9 April 1737. (L1-67)

534. Deed. 6 Nov 1735. Andrew Justis of Christiana Hun. in Co. of New Castle, planter, and Breta his wife, and Thomas Willing of same place, cooper, and Catherine his wife and daughter of sd Andrew and Bretta, for the sum of 15 pounds, grant unto Thomas Downing of Christiana Ferry in sd Co., innholder, a lott of land and premises, situate in Willingtown on No. side of Christiana Creek in sd Co. It bounds Market and 3rd Sts. Henry Gonne appointed Attorney. Signed: Thos. Willing, Catherine Willing (mark), Andrew Justis (mark), Breta Justis (mark). Wit: Samuel Faudrie, Alex. Stoop, Jaimmous John Hanna. The wives examined by John Curtis. Rec: 11 April 1737. (L1-69)

535. Deed. 16 Feb 1736/7. Augustine Constantine of Newport Ayre in Christiana Hun. in Co. of New Castle, for the sum of 10 pounds, sold unto James McMechan of Mill Creek Hun. in sd Co., miller, a lott of land containing 58 perches, situate in Christiana Hun. in sd Co. It bounds Christiana Creek and Brittish St., Water St. and lott of Capt. Nathaniel McGee. Signed: Augustine Constantine (mark). Wit: Samuel Marshall, Jas. McMullary. Rec: 11 Apr. 1737. (L1-71)

536. Deed. 1736. Thomas Janvier of the town of New Castle, cooper, and

Susannah his wife, for the sum of 16 pounds 10 shillings, sold unto Sigfredus Alrichs, yeoman, of same place, a parcel of marsh containing 2 acres 8 perches, situate on the Delaware River, at the lower end of sd town. This is land that William Penn by his Patent dated 1st day 6th mo 1718 did grant unto Thomas Janvier, gent., dec'd. Sd Janvier made his Last Will, dated 7 March 1728, and bequeathed sd marsh unto afsd Thomas Janvier, to be divided between him and John Land, also dec'd. (Originally set out as 2 acres but resurveyed to be 2 acres 8 perches). Sd Land released his portion to sd Janvier. Signed: Thomas Janvier, Susannah Janvier. Wit: George Fling, John Janvier. Rec: 12 April 1737. (L1-73)

537. Deed. 16 Feb 1736/7. Thomas John of Pencader Hun. in Co. of New Castle, gent., and Susanna his wife, for considerations, sold unto John Devor of the Township of Lancashire in Co. of Lancanshire, and George Moore, late of Ireland, now in Pencader Hun., yeoman, a tract of land containing 553 acres 68 perches, situate in New Castle Co. (Surveyed 30 Oct 1736.) This is part of a larger tract of 1,156 acres which sd Thomas John purchased by Deed, dated 15 Oct 1701, from William Davis and David Evance. It was surveyed by Warrant dated 18th day, same month. Signed: Thomas John, Susanah John (mark). Wit: Thomas James, George Reynolds, John Evans. Susannah John examined by Thomas James. Rec: 12 April 1737. (L1-75)

538. Deed. 10 Feb 1736/7. Thomas Willing of Willingtown in Christiana Hun. in Co. of New Castle, cooper, and Catherine his wife, for the sum of 22 pounds, sold unto William Shipley, gent., Thomas West, yeoman, Joseph Way, yeoman, and Joshua Way, all of Willingstown, a parcel of land containing 2 acres, situate in same place. It bounds Queen St., High St., and land of sd Shipley. This is whereas John Anderson by virtue of a Patent from James the second, King of Great Britain, dated on or before 1624, became seized of a plantation and tract of land situate in sd Hun. Sd Anderson by his Deed dated 10 Oct 1674 did grant sd land unto Samuel Peterson. Sd Peterson by his Last Will dated 20th day 9th mo 1689 did devise sd lands unto him of his sons who should live longest with their Mother. Son Peter Peterson became thus possessed of sd lands which Mathias Peterson, his eldest brother, granted to him by terms of Will, deed dated 4 Dec 1702. Sd Peter made his Last Will dated 29 Jan 1714 and devised sd land unto his son, Peter. Then son Peter, and Magdalene his wife, by Deed dated 8 May 1727, conveyed 105 acres of sd land to Andrew Justison (Book H, pp 199/200). Then Hans Peterson (son and heir of sd Peter), and Catharine his wife by indenture dated 29 Oct 1734, releases sd 105 acres to sd Justison. Then sd Justison and Breta his wife by Release dated 16/17 Sept 1736 did convey 49 acres of same unto afsd Thomas Willing. Signed: Thos. Willing, Catharine Willing (mark). Wit: William Nicholson, Samuel Fandrie, Gouldsmith Edward Folwell. Catharine Willing examined by Jehu Curtis. Wit: H. Gonne, Elizabeth

Gonne. Rec: 13 April 1737. (L1-76)

539. Deed. 15 Feb 1736/7. Augustine Constantine of Newport Ayre in
Christiana Hun. in Co. of New Castle, for the sum of 7 pounds, sold unto
Thomas Gray of Mill Creek Hun. in sd Co., merchant, a lott of land containing
42 perches, situate in Newport Ayre. It bounds Jonas Runs on Water St., and
Christiana Creek. Signed: Augustine Constantine (mark). Wit: Robt.
McCrackin, John Justis, James McMullan. Rec; 14 April 1737. (L1-79)

540. Deed. 20 Oct 1736. Thomas Willing of Willington in Christiana Hun. in
Co. of New Castle, cooper, and Catherine his wife, for the sum of 14 pounds,
sold unto Alexander Hooge of same place, carpenter, a lott of land in
Willington. This is part of a plantation and tract of land that Andrew Justison,
yeoman, was seized of by conveyance dated 8 May 1727 (Book N pp 199/200).
Then sd Justison and Breta his wife by their deed dated 26 Sept 1731, and also
by their Lease & Release dated 16 Sept 1736, sold a quantity of sd plantation
unto afsd Thomas Willing. Signed: Thos. Willing, Catharine Willing (mark).
Wit: James Speary, Gouldsmith Edward Folwell. Catharine Willing examined
by Jehu Curtis. Rec: 14 April 1737. (L1-80)

541. Deed. 5 Jan 1736. Charles Empson of Willing Town in Christiana Hun. in
Co. of New Castle, marriner, and Mary his wife, for the sum of 100 pounds,
sold unto James Hutchison of Willington, marriner, a lott of land situate in same
place, containing 16 perches. It bounds Front St. and lott of Joseph Way, Water
St. & Market St. to low water mark in Christiana Creek. This is part of a lott
containing 45 perches that became sd Empson's by conveyance dated 3 July
1732 (Book R pp 233/4). Signed: Charles Empson, Mary Empson (mark). Wit:
Adam Buckley, Gouldsmith Edwd. Folwell. Mary Empson examined by Adam
Buckley. Rec: 15 April 1737. (L1-82)

542. Appointment. 23 Oct 1737. 'George the second.... To David French of Co.
of New Castle .. you are assigned to be one of our Justices of the Court of
Common Pleas to be held for sd Co. Wit: James Logan Esq. with consent of
Andrew Hamilton, Speaker of the House of Representatives, John Richardson of
New Castle Co., Mark Manlove of Kent Co., William Till of Sussex Co.'
Signed: James Logan. Rec: 8 June 1737 by Willm. Shaw. (L1-84)

543. Judgement. 19 May 1737. Henry Newton, Esq. Shff of Co. of New Castle
Send Greetings. Whereas Andrew Hamilton of the City of Philadelphia, gent.,
was lately in Court before Justices and recovered against Gideon Griffith,
Admin. of All that were of Patrick Reilly, late of sd Co., Surgeon, dec'd., (not
admin. by Margaret Reilly, Exec. of the Last Will of sd Reilly) a debt of 80

pounds and damages. Sheriff seized goods and chattles of sd Reilly. Seized was a tenement and bank lott of ground, situate on SE side of Water St. in the Town of New Castle, opposite to the dwelling house of George Monroe. It was appraised by sd Monroe and John Williams and valued at 40 pounds. It was exposed to sale and sold for the sum of 63 pounds unto sd George Monroe as the highest bidder. Signed: Henry Newton, Shff. Wit: Samuel Ques, John Herbert. Rec: 6 June 1737. (L1-85)

544. Deed/mortgage. 25 March 1737. Broer Synnexon of Christiana Hun. in Co. of New Castle, yeoman, and Bridget his wife, for the sum of 5 shillings, grant unto Joseph Robinson of Brandywine Hun. in sd Co., yeoman, a parcel of land situate in Christiana Hun. It bounds the lands of John Richardson and contains 55 acres. Terms for one year from now. Signed: Bn. Sinaxin, Bridget Sinaxin. Wit: John Richardson, Anna Richardson, Mary Richardson. Rec: 8 June 1737. (L1-86)

545. Deed. 26 March 1737. Broer Synnexon of Christiana Hun. in Co. of New Castle, yeoman, and Bridget his wife, for the sum of 50 pounds, sold unto Joseph Robinson, a parcel of land containing 55 acres, situate in sd Hun. & Co. This is part of a larger tract of land and marsh that Francis Lovelace, by Patent, granted unto Andrew Anderson, Seneca Broer and Waldraven Johnson. Sd Anderson died and his third share was divided amongst his children, who were minors under age 21. County Court ordered that Broer Synnaxon (who married the Widow of sd Anderson, and was the Grandfather of afsd Broer) should hold third part of sd tract for breeding up and educating the sd minors, and to pay to each of them at 21 years, 500 gilders. Whereupon James Claypoole and Robert Turner, Comm. of William Penn, by their Patent dated 7 June 1686, did grant sd third part of sd tract & marsh (found to be 425 acres) unto sd Broer Synnaxon. Whereas Junan Anderson (one of the sons of sd Anderson) by his Release dated 19 Sept 1687 did release his share unto his grandfather. Then Peter Anderson (another son) released also his share unto his grandfather in 1696. Then Christian Jurianson by Release dated 13 April 1685 and Errick Anderson by Release of 26 April 1692 unto sd Broer. Then sd grandfather by his Deed dated 10 July 1703, granted a moiety of sd 425 acres unto his son, James Synnexon. By his Last Will dated 25 Nov 1708, devised the other half with messuage and plantation unto Sophia, his wife, during her life but then to go to sd son James. Then Sophia died and James died leaving 3 children, the afsd Broer (party to this), John and James to share. Then sons John & James did release unto afsd Broer, by date instant March. Signed: Bru. Sinnexon, Bridget Sinnexon. Wit: John Richardson, Anna Richardson, Mary Richardson. Rec: 10 June 1737. (L1-87)

546. Deed. 19 May 1737. Margaret Williamson of the Town & Co. of New Castle, Widow Executrix of the Last Will of Alexander Davis, late of same place, innholder, dec'd., send Greetings. Whereas afsd Williamson, in her own right, was seized of a lott of ground in sd place. It bounded lott formerly of Sylvester Garland but now of John French, Esq., dec'd., and lands of Nicholas Meers, Samuel Griffith, dec'd., and Thomas Smith. Then sd Margaret Williamson by her Indenture dated 24 Feb 1726, did sell a part of sd property unto afsd Alexander Davis. It was 23 feet on Market Street and same width down to the marsh of sd Meers. Then Davis erected on sd lott a small brick dwelling house and in 1734 made his Last Will and made sd Williamson his Exec., who was ordered by the Court to sell property to pay debts of sd Davis. She sold it to Henry Gonne, gent. as the highest bidder for 100 pounds 5 shilling. Signed: Marg. Williamson. Wit: Saml. Eves, John McGhee. Rec: 11 June 1737. (L1-91)

547. Deed. 19 May 1737. Henry Gonne of New Castle and Co., gent., and Elizabeth his wife, for the sum of 100 pounds 5 shilling, sold unto Margaret Williamson of the same place, Widow, a messuage and lott of ground situate in the Town of New Castle. It bounds the large brick house formerly of Sylvester Garland dec'd., afterwards of John French dec'd. Signed: H. Gonne, Elizabeth Gonne. Wit: Saml. Eves, John McGhee. Elizabeth Gonne examined by Richd. Cantwell. Rec: 14 June 1737. (L1-93)

548. Deed. 18 May 1737. Thomas Smith of the Town & Co. of New Castle, merchant, for the sum of 350 pounds, sold unto Margaret Williamson of the same place, Widow, a messuage and lott of ground, situate in sd Town & Co. It bounds the lott laid out for Giles Barret, now in tenure of Daniel Mercier, and lott belonging to Hermanus Alrichs. It is 54 feet on Market place or Wood St., and on Minquaes St. is 60 feet. Signed: Thomas Smith. Wit: John McGhee, H. Gonne. Rec: 15 June 1737. (L1-94)

549. Deed. 19 May 1737. Simon Parsons and William Parsons of New Castle Hun. & Co., planters, only children of William Parsons, dec'd., for the sum of 24 pounds 12 shilling, discharge unto James Crawford of White Clay Creek Hun. in sd Co., weaver, a parcel of land called Foxborough, containing 100 acres, situate in White Clay Creek Hun.. This is whereas afsd William Parsons, in his lifetime on 17 Oct 1733, by an instrument in writting, did agree with afsd James Crawford for the sum of 20 pounds, payable on 1 April last, together with interest, to grant unto sd Crawford the sd 100 acres. Signed: Simon Parsons, Will. Parsons. Wit: H. Gonne, Elizabeth Gonne. Rec: 15 June 1737. (L1-96)

550. Deed. 21 March 1736. Sapience Harrison of Appoquimink Hun. in Co. of

New Castle, yeoman, and Catharine his wife, for the sum of 60 pounds, sold
unto William Wittel of St. Georges Hun. in sd Co., shopkeeper, a tract of land
containing 201 acres and plantation, situate in Appoquimink Hun. on a branch
of Blackbirds Creek in the forest. (This is the plantation whereon Thomas
Jackson, dec'd., formerly dwelt.) It bounds the land formerly of John Cowgill,
dec'd., land called Russell's Meadow, and land formerly of William Hernes.
Signed: Sapience Harrison (mark), Catherine Harrison (mark). Wit: John Scott,
Edward Hawkins. Catherine Harrison examined by Thos. Noxon. Rec: 16 June
1737. (L1-98)

551. Deed. 18 May 1737. John Ogle of White Clay Creek Hun. in Co. of New
Castle, planter, for the sum of 331 pounds, sold unto James McMechan of Miln
Creek Hun. in sd Co., a tract of land containing 200 acres, situate on the south
side of White Clay Creek, in sd Hun. & Co. This is land that afsd John Ogle
acquired from Thomas Ogle, planter, dec'd., by deed dated 8 Oct 1721. Signed:
John Ogle. Wit: David French, Francis Graham. Rec: 16 June 1737. (L1-100)

552. Deed. 19 May 1737. Thomas Ogle and Benjamin Gibbs of the Co. of New
Castle, yeomen, for the sum of 80 pounds, sold unto James McMechan, of sd
Co., a tract of land and premises, situate on the south side of White Clay Hun. in
sd Co. It bounds the creek and contains 200 acres. Signed: Thomas Ogle,
Benjamin Gibbs. Wit: David French, John Hore. Rec: 17 June 1737. (L1-102)

553. Judgement. 10 May 1737. Henry Newton, Esq. Sheriff of Co. of New
Castle, send Greetings. Whereas Thomas Gray was lately in Court before
Justices to recover against James Hamilton of sd Co., tanner, a debt of 28
pounds and damages. Sheriff ordered to seize goods & chattles of sd Hamilton.
Taken in execution was a parcel of land valued and appraised by James Jordan
and Nathaniel Wainsford, for the sum of 40 pounds. Sd Sheriff sold same for the
sum of 50 pounds by sd Thomas Gray as highest bidder. It bounds the lands of
Duncan Drummond, John Preston and Morton Justis, and contains 67 acres.
Signed: Henry Newton. Wit: John Legate, Abel Armstrong. Rec: 17 June 1737.
(L1-104)

554. Deed. 25 April 1737. 'John Price of Township of Nottingham in Chester
Co., blacksmith, son and heir of David Price of Pencader Hun. in Co. of New
Castle, send Greetings. Know ye that for good causes and other considerations
me moving, and for the sum of 84 pounds, grants unto my Mother, Mary Price,
Admin. of my sd deceased father, all my claim on a tract of land of 500 acres.
This is part of a larger tract of 1,050 acres that was formerly purchased by my
Grandfather, David Price which is since improved, located in Pencader Hun,
called David Price's Land.' Sd grandfather received this land by Patent granted

from William Penn, dated 22 Feb 1703, and bequeathed same to his son, David
Price Jun. by his Last Will and Testament. Signed: John Price. Wit: Nathan.
Williams, John Watson, Thos. Evans. Rec: 17 June 1737. (L1-105)

555. Deed. 17 May 1737. Mr. Samuel Marshall of Newport Ayre in Christiana
Hun. in Co. of New Castle, and Sarah his wife, for the sum of 7 pounds, sold
unto John Twiggs of Mill Creek Hun. in sd Co., yeoman, a lott of land and
premises containing 25 perches, situate in Newport Ayre. Signed: Saml.
Marshall, Sarah Marshall. Wit: Robet. Nealy, James McMullan. Sarah Marshall
examined by Jehu Curtis. Rec: 20 June 1737. (L1-107)

556. Deed. 17 May 1737. John Ball Sen. of Miln Creek Hun. in Co. of New
Castle, blacksmith, and Mary his wife, for the sum of 20 pounds, grant unto
John Ball Junr. of sd Co., a parcel of land containing 202 acres. It is situate on
the west side of Delaware River and a branch of White Clay Creek, called Miln
Creek, between the land of William Ball and Joseph Barns. It also bounds lands
of the Governors Widow Thomas and Benjamin Poulson. Signed: John Ball.
Wit: Robt. Robertson, Hereulah Robertson. Rec: 20 June 1737. (L1-109)

557. Deed. 14 Feb 1736/7. John Justis of Newport Ayre in Christiana Hun. in
Co. of New Castle, and Britta his wife, for the sum of 6 pounds, sold unto
Thomas Anderson, smith, of Mill Creek Hun. in sd Co., a lott of land and
premises containing 32 perches, situate in Newport Ayre. It bounds Market St.
and John's St.. Signed: John Justis, Britta Justis (mark). Wit: Mathias Morton,
Ja. McMullan. Rec: 21 June 1737. (L1-110)

558. Deed. 16 May 1737. Peter Parker of St. Georges Hun. in Co. of New
Castle, yeoman, and Mary his wife, for the sum of 100 pounds, sold unto
Thomas Hyatt of same place, yeoman, a tract of land containing 100 acres,
situate in sd Hun. & Co. It bounds the land of John Greenwater and Scott's
Runn. This is whereas Amos Nicholas, late of afsd place, yeoman, dec'd.,
received a warrant from William Penn dated 17th of 4 mo. 1684 for 300 acres of
land with an addition for 200 acres in sd Co. Then Henry Hollingsworth
surveyed unto him a quantity of 525 acres (by survey dated 6th of 6 mo 1684).
Then sd Nicholas by his indenture dated 9 Oct 1716 did sell 100 acres of sd land
to afsd Peter Parker. Signed: Peter Parker (mark), Mary Parker. Wit: Thos.
Noxon, Susanna Dushane. Mary Parker examined by sd Noxon. Rec: 21 June
1737. (L1-112)

559. Deed. 28 Feb 1736. John Justis of Newport Ayre in Co. of New Castle,
yeoman, and Britta his wife, for the sum of 10 pounds sold unto Thomas Gray
and Patrick McKenzie, gent., of sd Co., a lott of ground and premises containing

36 perches, situate in Newport Ayre. It begins at Marshall St. to Christiana Creek and down creek to Rainbow Runn. Signed: John Justis, Britta Justis (mark). Wit: Hans Rudolph, Jas. McMullan, David Lewis. Rec: 22 June 1737. (L1-114)

560. Deed. 13 April 1737. Mr. Samuel Marshal of Newport Ayre in Christiana Hun. in Co. of New Castle, and Sarah his wife, for the sum of 8 pounds, sold unto Alexander Frazier of Kent Township in Chester Co. in Prov. of Penn., a lott of ground and premises containing 64 perches, situate in Newport Ayre. It bounds John's St. and Ayre St. Signed: Saml. Marshall, Sarah Marshall. Wit: Thomas Bracken, Jas. McMullan. Sarah Marshall examined by Jehu Curtis. Rec: 22 June 1737. (L1-115)

561. Deed. 16 Feb 1736/7. Mr. Samuel Marshall of Newport Ayre in Christiana Hun. in Co. of New Castle, and Sarah his wife, for the sum of 7 pounds, sold unto Isaac Vernon of West Bradford in Chester Co. in Prov. of Penn., a lott of land and premises containing 20 perches, situate in Newport Ayre. It bounds Marshall's St. and Market St.. Signed: Saml. Marshall, Sarah Marshall. Wit: John Justis, Jas. McMullan. Sarah Marshall examined by Jehu Curtis. (L1-117)

562. Deed. 18 May 1737. Jasper Walraven of Christiana Hun. in Co. of New Castle, yeoman, and Anne his wife, for the sum of 46 pounds 7 shillings, sold unto Joseph Robinson of Brandywine Hun. in sd Co., farmer, a parcel of grounds containing 7 acres 140 perches, situate in Christiana Hun. It bounds Christiana Creek. Also a parcel of marsh containing 10 acres, situate in same place, bounding Double Gutt on sd creek. Signed: Jasper Wallraven (mark), Anne Wallraven (mark). Wit: David French, James Chalmers, Thomas Gray. Anne Wallraven examined by John Finney. Rec: 24 June 1737. (L1-118)

563. Judgement. 19 May 1737. Henry Newton, Sheriff of Co. of New Castle send Greetings. Whereas William Patterson of sd Co., yeoman, lately in Court before Justices recovered against Nicholas Hayman of sd Co. a debt of 111 pounds and damages. Sheriff ordered to seize lands and tenements of sd Hayman. Seized and taken in execution was the plantation whereon sd Hayman dwelt, containing 150 acres of land together with houses and wharves and other improvments. Afsd sheriff for the sum of 170 pounds sold property unto John Read, merchant of sd Co. as the highest bidder at the publick Auction. Property bounds the land claimed by Abraham Buckley, but of late found to be vacant land, and land late of James Waters and Jeremiah Heruan, land near Paul Garretson's old house, and land late of Col. John French. Within these bounds equal 100 acres 68 perches. The Creek Land is 49 acres 2 perches. Also a parcel of land with a landing thereon bounding Eagle Runn and John Lewden's marsh.

144

Signed: Henry Newton, Shff. Wit: David French, Lewis Howell. Rec: 24 June
1737. (L1-120)

564. Deed. 17 May 1737. Leonard Humphrys of St.Georges Hun. in Co. of New
Castle, sadler, and Mary his wife, for the sum of 66 pounds, sold unto Edward
Baxter of sd place, yeoman, a tract of land and premises containing 66 acres,
situate in sd Hun. & Co. It lies on the No. side of a branch out of Doctor's
Swamp and bounds land late of John Hales, dec'd., and land belonging to the
children of Richard Humphry, dec'd.. Signed: Leonard Humphrys, Mary
Humphrys (mark). Wit: Tho. Noxon, Adam Buckley. Mary Humphrys
examined by Tho. Noxon. Rec: 1 July 1737. (L1-123)

565. Deed. 19 April 1737. Edward Dulse of Appoquinimink in Co. of New
Castle, yeoman, for the sum of 30 pounds, sold unto Edward FitzRandolph of sd
Co., blacksmith, a tract of land and premises containing 146 acres, situate on the
So. side of Blackbird Creek in sd Co. It bounds the land of Daniel Large by
Landom Run to Blackbird Bridge. This is land that afsd Edward Dulse obtained
by an indenture dated 30 July 1729 from Samuel Pound of sd Co. Signed:
Edward Dwools. Wit: Jehu Curtis, Edward Richardson. Affidavit of sale signed
by Mary Dulse (mark), wife of sd Edward. She was examined by Jehu Curtis.
Rec: 1 July 1737. (L1-125)

566. Deed. 18 Dec 1736. Andrew Justison of Willingtown in Christiana Hun. in
Co. of New Castle, yeoman, and Brita his wife, for the sum of 106 pounds 15
shilling 4 pence, sold unto Thomas West of sd place, yeoman, a parcel of land
containing 3 acres 128 perches, situate in same place. This bounds the land of
William Levis and Front St. Also another lott in same place, bounding the lott of
Dr. Millner on Christiana Creek. This is part of the tract whereas John Anderson
by a Patent from James the Second dated about 1674 became seized of. Then sd
Anderson by deed dated 10 Oct 1674 granted sd land unto Samuel Patterson and
Lars Cornelison who afterwards divided it. Sd Patterson in his Last Will, dated
20 Nov 1689, devised that of his sons that lived longest with his mother would
receive his dwelling house and plantation. After which Matthias Patterson,
eldest son of sd Samuel by his instrument of writing dated 1 Dec 1702 did
confirm sd property over to his brother Peter Patterson, who stayed. Sd Peter
made his Last Will dated 29 Jan 1714/5 and divised the plantation to his eldest
son Peter, after his wife's decease. Afterwards son Peter and his wife Magdalene
by their deed dated 8 May 1727 granted 105 acres of sd land unto afsd Andrew
Justison. Afterwards Hanse Petterson, son of first mentioned Peter, and
Catharine his wife by Deed dated 29 Oct 1734 did release sd 105 acres unto sd
Justison. Signed: Andrew Justison (mark), Breta Justison (mark). Wit: Charles
Springer, Wm. Shipley, Wm. Levis, Gouldsmith Edw. Folwell, Joseph Way.

David French appointed Attorney. Breta Justison examined by Charles Springer. Rec: 2 July 1737. (L1-128)

567. Deed. 18 May 1737. Mr. Samuel Marshall of Newport Ayre in Christiana Hun. in Co. of New Castle, and Sarah his wife, for the sum of 5 pounds sold unto Abraham Marshall of West Bradford in Chester Co. in Prov. of Penn., a lott of land or premises containing 32 perches, situate in Newport Ayre. It bounds James St., Ayre St. and Marshall St. Signed: Saml. Marshall, Sarah Marshall. Wit: Robert Neely, Jas. McMullan. Sarah Marshall examined by Jehu Curtis. Rec: 4 July 1737. (L1-130)

568. Deed. 5 Feb 1736/7. John Justis of Newport Ayre in Christiana Hun. in Co. of New Castle, and Britta his wife, for the sum of 7 pounds, sold unto John Ashmead junr. of Germantown in Philada. Co. in Prov. of Penn., smith, a lott of land and premises containing 30 perches, situate in Newport Ayre. It bounds Marshall St. and Market St. Signed: John Justis, Britta Justis (mark). Wit: Saml. Marshall, Jas. McMullan. Rec: 4 July 1737. (L1-132)

569. Deed. 18 May 1737. John Justis of Newport Ayre in Christiana Hun. in Co. of New Castle, for the sum of 12 pounds, sold unto Morton Justis of Mill Creek Hun. in sd Co. a lott of land containing 64 perches, situate in Newport Ayre. It bounds James St. and Market St.. Signed: John Justis. Wit: John Ashmead junr., Jas. McMullan. Rec: 5 July 1737. (L1-134)

570. Deed. 9 Dec 1736/7. Rees Jones of Co. of New Castle, tanner, and Rachel his wife, for the sum of 77 pounds, sold unto Samuel Kerr of same place, farmer, a parcel of land and plantation containing 200 acres of land, situate part in Pencadder Hun. and part in White Clay Creek Hun. in sd Co. Signed: Rees Jones, Rachel Jones. Wit: William Eynon, James Armitage. Rachel Jones examined by James Armitage. Rec: 6 July 1737. (L1-135)

571. Deed. 14 May 1737. John Jones of the City of Phila. in Co. & Prov. of Penn., yeoman, for the sum of 3 pounds, grant unto Joseph Brown of the Co. of New Castle, yeoman, a tract of land and plantation now in the full and peaceable possession of sd Joseph Brown. It is situate by Christeen Creek in Pencadder Hun. in New Castle Co. This plantation was formerly of Phillip James and mortgaged by him to afsd John Jones. It contains 200 acres. Signed: John Jones. Wit: Jas. Carter, James Steel. Rec: 7 July 1737. (L1-136)

572. Deed. 24 Feb 1726. Edward Dewoolf of Appoquinimink Hun. in Co. of New Castle, yeoman, for the sum of 46 pounds, sold unto James Griffing of same place, yeoman, a plantation with improvements where Daniel Rees now

lives. It was bought by sd Dewoolf of William Sherrard and formerly did belong to Edward Burrows. And also another tract containing 200 acres adjoining that was lately taken up by sd Dewoolf by a Warrant. This was surveyed by Thomas Noxon and is situate below Blackbird Creek on SE side of Kings Road in sd Hun. & Co. It was surveyed for sd Burrows by virtue of a Warrant dated 25 March 1715. Also another small tract of land adjoyning which bounds the lands of James Alfrees, William Holliday and Edward Richardson. Total of 285 acres. Signed: Edward Dwoolf. Wit: Jehu Curtis, Edward Fitzrandolph. Affidavit of Mary Dewoolf, wife of sd Edward, sign: Mary Dewoolf (mark). Mary Dewoolf examined by Jehu Curtis. Rec: 8 July 1737. (L1-137)

573. Deed. 17 May 1737. Richard Hall junior, and his wife Margaret Hall of Mill Creek Hun. in Co. of New Castle, yeoman, for the sum of 7 pounds, sold unto Edward Fitzrandolph of Appoquinimink Hun. in sd Co., blacksmith, a plantation with improvements where Edward Dulse did lately live, situate on the So. side of Blackbirds Creek. It bounds the land of Daniel Lange and contains 146 acres. Signed: Richard Hall junr. (mark), Marg. Hall (mark). Wit: Francis Graham, Jas. Armitage. Margaret Hall examined by James Armitage. Rec: 8 July 1737. (L1-139)

574. Deed. 18 May 1737. Allis Milles, Executor of Estate of David Milles, Edward Milles, John David and Jean David of Co. of New Castle, for the sum of 40 pounds, sold unto Hugh McMuldraugh, yeoman, of sd Co., a messuage and tract of land containing 50 acres, situate in sd Co. on the south side of Christiana Creek above the bridge. This is part of a Patent, dated 13 Sept 1692, granted to John Ellis and Israel Harrison for 445 acres. Then 50 acres of it was sold by sd Ellis to Thomas Meadcalf; then by sd Meadcalf unto David Milles, dec'd., in 1710/11. Signed: Alice Mills (mark), Edward Miles, John David, Jean David. Wit: Jane David examined by Thos. James. Rec: 9 July 1737. (L1-140)

575. Deed. 18 May 1737. Hugh McMuldraugh of Co. of New Castle, for the sum of 30 pounds, sold unto Agness McMechan, widow of sd Co., a dwelling house and a tract of land containing 50 acres, situate in sd Co. on the south side of Christiana Creek above the bridge. This is land recently purchased from Allis Milles, Executor of Estate of David Milles, Edward Milles, John David and Jean David of sd Co. Signed: Hugh McMuldraugh (mark). Wit: James McMechen, Francis Graham, Arthur Faries. Rec: 9 July 1737. (L1-142)

576. Deed. 18 May 1737. Samuel Marshall of Newport Ayre in Christiana Hun. & Co. of New Castle, storekeeper, for the Good Will and Regard he beareth William Shaw of the Town & Co. of New Castle, gent., and for 10 shillings, grants unto sd Shaw a lott of ground and premises containing 15-3/4 perches,

situate in Newport Ayre. It bounds Hutchinson's Runn, Water St. and James St.. Sarah, wife of sd Marshall releases her dower rights (examined by Jehu Curtis). Signed: Saml. Marshall, Sarah Marshall. Wit: John Ashmead junr., H. Gonne. Rec: 9 July 1737. (L1-143)

577. Deed. 17 Aug 1737. Augustine Constantine of Newport Ayre in Co. of New Castle, for the sum of 10 pounds, sold unto William Patterson of White Clay Creek Hun. in sd Co., a lott of land and premises containing 50 perches, situate in Newport Ayre. It bounds the land of Capt. John Wilson by Christiana Creek to Water St.. Signed: Augustine Constantine (mark). Wit: James Steel, James McMullan. Rec: 26 Aug 1737. (L1-145)

578. Deed. 4 Aug 1737. Simon Parsons of New Castle Hun. & Co., Exec. of the Last Will and Testament of William Parsons, his late father dec'd., for the sum of 30 pounds, sold unto William Patterson of White Clay Creek Hun. in sd Co., a tract of land and premises containing 30 acres, situate near the main road leading from Christiana Bridge to Nottingham in sd Co. It bounds the lands of Doctor Jones, Andrew Murphews, Robert Black's late dwelling house, James Craford and John Read. This is part of a tract of 300 acres that was surveyed for afsd William Parsons by order dated 1 June 1720 to George Dakeyne, surveyor. This is whereas James Steel of Phila. by his Warrant dated 24th 3rd Mo 1720, directed to sd Dakeyne, to lay out for sd Parsons a piece of vacant land near Christiana where Nathaniel Pope and John Ogle made a small improvement thereon. Signed: Simon Parsons. Wit: John McCleuachan, John Barry, Reyn. Howell. Jas McMullan, Nicholas Hayman. Rec: 26 Aug 1737. (L1-146)

579. Deed. 15 March 1736. Ralph Winterton of New Castle Co., farmer, and Mary his wife, for the sum of 21 pounds, sold unto William Paterson of Christiana, marriner, a piece of land containing 50 acres, being in White Clay Creek Hun. in sd Co. It is bounds with land late of Col. John French, dec'd., with land late of Morgan Morgan, land late of Jeremiah Sherman, land late of afsd William Paterson, and land late of John Emley now in possession of William Cox. Signed: Ralph Winterton, Mary Winterton (mark). Wit: Hurbert Vanbebber, Rt. Robertson, Parnellah Gordon. Mary Winterton examined by Jehu Curtis. Rec: 27 Aug. 1737. (L1-148)

580. Deed. 15 Aug 1737 Simon Parsons, Exec. of tho Last Will of William Parsons, late of New Castle Hun. & Co., farmer, for the sum of 20 pounds, sold unto Reynold Howell of White Clay Creek Hun. in sd Co., farmer, a tract of land containing 100 acres (now in the possession of Andrew Murphew) situate near the main road leading from Christiana Bridge to Nottingham in sd Co. It bounds the lands of William Paterson, James Craford and Thomas Gray. This is

148

part of a tract of 300 acres that was surveyed for afsd William Parsons by order dated 24th 3rd Mo 1720, from James Steel of Phila. to George Dakeyne, surveyor to lay out for sd Parsons 200 acres or more. Signed: Simon Parsons. Wit: Philip James, Robert Mc Clenachan. Affidavit signed: Wm. Patterson. Wit: John Read, Giles Hayman (mark), Peter Hayman (mark). Rec: 27th Aug 1737. (L1-149)

581. Deed. 26 Oct 1736. Sylvanus Hussey of Town & Co. of New Castle, tanner, for the sum of 100 pounds, sold unto Stephen Lewis of same place, tanner, a lott of ground and premises situate in sd town. This is land that John Richardson by instrument of writting dated 1 March 1694, sold unto Cornelius Kettle. It was bounded by Market place, Beaver St. and lott of Richard Griffith. Then sd Kettle by his Deed dated 19 Nov 1724 did grant same with improvements unto James Merreweather, tanner and currier, of same place. Then sd Merreweather and his wife Elizabeth, by their Deed dated 16 Feb 1735, sold same unto afsd Sylvanus Hussey. Signed: Sylvanus Hussey. Wit: Gilbert Dakeyne, Rob. Robertson. Rec: 27 Aug 1737. (L1-151)

582. Article of Agreement. 3 March 1736/7. Anthony Dushene of St. Georges Hun. in Co. of New Castle, yeoman, grants unto John Anderson of same place, yeoman, all his Title to 100 acres of land situate in Maryland near the head of Elk River adjoyning to John Kincey Mill. Also a piece of marsh that sd Dushene bought of Henry Runals and Bartholomew Josuson. Agree that sd Anthony Dushene to sign over afsd land unto Urias Anderson and Peter Parker and sign over to sd Anderson all his Right and Title to same. Signed: Anthony Dushene, John Anderson (mark). Wit: John Rougier, Chas. Robinson. Rec: 29 Aug 1737. (L1-153)

583. Deed. 16 Aug 1737. Elizabeth Anderson, widow and Exec. of John Anderson, late of St. Georges Hun. in Co. of New Castle, yeoman dec'd., in performance of the Agreement between sd John Anderson and Anthony Dushene, late of Elk River but now of sd Hun. & Co., yeoman, grants unto him a parcel of land containing 66 acres, bounding sd Dushen's plantation. This is whereas sd John Anderson in his lifetime was seized of a tract of land and plantation situate on Scotts Run near St. Georges Creek in sd Hun. & Co. where he dwell. Sd Anderson made his Last Will dated 26 Feb 1734/5, and bequeathed unto his sons, Jacob and John Anderson, 'and if it be a Male Child whom my wife now goeth with', all his dwelling plantation and marsh to be divided between. He named his wife sole Executrix. Then after sd Anderson made out his Last Will, he did enter into Articles of Agreement with afsd Anthony Dushene, for exchanging part of the above mentioned property for a tract of land and plantation whereon sd Dushene formerly dwelt. It was situate near the

head of Elk River in Cecil Co. in Prov. of Maryland wherein sd Anderson doth covenant under the penalty of 200 pounds. Signed: Elizabeth Anderson (mark). Wit: Thomas True, Thomas Noxon. Rec: 30 Aug 1737. (L1-154)

584. Deed. 10 May 1736. John Neal and Margery his wife of Co. of New Castle, for the sum of 45 pounds, sold unto John Burns of Brandywine Hun. in sd Co., farmer, a tract of land and premises situate in the Manner of Rocks Land in sd Co., on the north side of Brandywine Creek. It bounds the land of Cornelius Empson and contains 56 acres. This was surveyed by George Dakeyne on 20 April 1719 by virtue of a Warrant granted unto Hance Petterson by William Markham and John Goodson, Comm. of Property and directed unto James Bradshaw to survey unto sd Petterson 300 acres. This land purchased from the Indians. Warrant dated 1 Aug 1689. Sd Petterson Senr. sold sd 56 acres unto Timothy Stedham on 23 April 1720; sd Stedham sold same unto afsd John Neal. Signed: John Neal, Margery Neal (mark). Wit: Jacob Welldin, John Godfrey. Margery Neal examined by Adam Buckley. Rec: 31 Aug 1737. (L1-156)

585. Deed. 16 Aug 1737. Jacob Martin of Appoquinimink Hun. in Co. of New Castle, yeoman, for the sum of 130 pounds, sold unto William Whittet of St. Georges Hun. in sd Co., shopkeeper, a tract of land and plantation containing 100 acres, situate in Appoq. Hun. on Appoq. Creek. It bounds the land of Rebecca Dyre and is part of a tract of 400 acres lately belonging to Adam Peterson, cooper. Signed: Jacob Martin. Wit: Jno. Richardson, Thos. Noxon. Rec: 31 Aug 1737. (L1-158)

586. Deed. 4 March 1736. Joseph Way of Willing Town in Christiana Hun. in Co. of New Castle, yeoman, and Sarah his wife, for the sum of 55 pounds, sold unto Simon Edgell of the City of Philadelphia, merchant, a lott of land containing 1/4 acre, situate in sd town. It bounds the lott of William Nivins, Front St., Market St. to the low water mark of Christiana Creek. This is part of a larger tract belonging to sd Way. Signed: Joseph Way, Sarah Way. Wit: David Bush, Thos. Willing, Gouldsmith Edw. Follwell. Sarah Way examined by Charles Springer. Rec: 5 Sept 1737. (L1-159)

587. Deed. 11 April 1737. Thomas Willing of Willingtown in Hun. of Christiana in Co. of New Castle, cooper, and Catherine his wife, for the sum of 100 pounds, sold unto Simon Edgell of same place, merchant, a lott of land containing 1 acres 31 perches (part of a 49 acre tract), situate in sd Hun. & Co. This is whereas John Anderson in 1674, by virtue of a Patent from James the Second, became seized of a plantation or tract of land situate on Christiana Creek in sd Hun. & Co. Then sd Anderson on 10th da 8th mo 1674, did convey sd land unto Samuel Patterson and Lars Cornelison, who divided it between

themselves. Sd Patterson made his Last Will dated 20 Nov 1689 and devised
that of his sons that lived longest with his mother would receive his dwelling
house and plantation. After which Matthias Patterson, eldest son of sd Samuel
by his instrument of writing dated 1 Dec 1702 did confirm sd property over to
his brother Peter Patterson, who stayed. Sd Peter made his Last Will dated 29
Jan 1714/5 and divised the plantation to his eldest son Peter, after his wife's
decease. Afterwards son Peter and his wife Magdalene by their deed dated 8
May 1727 granted 105 acres of sd land unto Andrew Justison. Afterwards Hans
Petterson, son of first mentioned Peter, and Catharine his wife by Deed dated 29
Oct 1734 did release sd 105 acres unto sd Andrew Justison. Then sd Justison
and Bretta his wife by their Lease and Release dated 16/17 Sept 1736, conveyed
49 acres of sd land unto afsd Willing. Signed: Thos. Willing, Catherine Willing
(mark). Wit: Samuel Scott, David Bush, Gouldsmith Edward Folwell. Catherine
Willing examined by Charles Springer. Rec: 13 Sep 1737. (L1-161)

588. Deed. 17 Aug 1737. Gabriel Cox of Red Lyon Hun. in Co. of New Castle,
innholder, and Magdalen his wife, for the sum of 30 pounds, sold unto John
McCoole of St. Georges Hun. in sd Co., yeoman, a tenement with divers lotts of
land and marshes adjoining, situate in the Town of St. Georges in Red Lyon
Hun. It bounds the lott belonging to the estate of Jacob VnBebber, dec'd., and a
Run on St. Georges Creek to the Mill Race. It contains 4 acres, excepting a
small parcel by sd Race that had been granted by sd Magdalen to Samuel
Sorenny, and by him sold to Jacob VnBebber, who at present possesses it.
Signed: Gabriel Cox (mark) Magdalene Cox. Wit: Thos. Noxon, John See.
Magdalene Cox examined by James Armitage. Rec: 13 Sept 1737. (L1-163)

589. Deed. 15 Aug 1737. Augustine Constantine of Newport Ayre in Co. of
New Castle, for the sum of 6 pounds 10 shilling, sold unto Thomas Gray of Mill
Creek Hun. in sd Co. a piece of land and premises situate in Newport Ayre. It
bounds Market St. and a small Run and contains 50-4/10 perches. Signed:
Augustine Constantine (mark). Wit: Swithin Justis, Jas. McMullan. Rec: 14 Sept
1737. (L1-165)

590. Deed. 5 Dec 1736. John Wilson, mariner, of Ayre in North Britain, for the
sum of 6 pounds, sold unto Mrs Margett Bell of Co. of New Castle, a lott of land
and premises situate in Newport Ayre in Christiana Hun. in sd Co. It bounds
Water and Agustines Sts. and contains 26 perches. Signed: Jno. Wilson. Wit:
Jos. Weldon, Hance Rudolph, Saml. Marshall. Rec: 14 Sept 1737. (L1-166)

591. Deed. 28 July 1737. Harcules Reall, late of Philadelphia, cooper, for the
sum of 30 pounds, sold unto Andrew Peterson of New Castle Co., gentleman, all
the lands, tenements and appurt. together with all houses, outhouses, barns,

stables, orchards, gardens, common pasture whatever to be found in any part of sd Co. formerly left and bequeathed to his Mother Ellenor by her Father, Adam Peterson, by his Last Will and Testament dated 6 Dec 1702. Sd Elenor was vested of Estate by inheritance, then as a Widow and Relique of Harcules Reall, dec'd., by whom she had one child and dyed intested, the full estate descended to him, and being now of the age of 22 years fully possessed estate of his grandfather. Signed: Harcules Reall. Wit: Rd. Cantwell. J. Tuite. Rec: 15 Sept 1737. (L1-167)

592. Deed. 16 Aug 1737. John Justis and Christian his wife, and Augustine Constantine, all of Newport Ayre in Christiana Hun. in Co. of New Castle, for the sum of 7 pounds, sold unto Thomas Morgan of the Town and Co. of Chester, a lott of land and premises situate in Newport Ayre. It bounds Market and Marshall Sts., and contains 40-1/2 perches. Signed: John Justis, Christiana Justis (mark), Augustine Constantine (mark). Wit: Justa Justis, Jas. McMullan. Christian Justis examined by Thos. James. Rec: 15 Sept 1737. (L1-169)

593. Deed. 16 Aug 1737. Elizabeth Vandike, one of Daughters of Andrew Vandike, late of St. Georges Hun. in Co. of New Castle, yeoman dec'd., for the sum of 40 pounds, and for the love and affection she bears her brother, John Vandike, one of Sons of sd Andrew Vandike, she releases unto him her share of their father's inheritance. This is whereas, in his lifetime, sd Vandike was possessed of a plantation and tract of land containing 160 acres, situate on the north side of Drawyers Creek in sd Hun. & Co. It was bounded by sd creek, and the lands of Thomas Hyatt, Abraham Gooding and Garret Dushane. In his Last Will dated 20 May 1730, he bequeathed sd plantation to be equally divided amongst his sons, afsd John, Abrm, Andrew and Jacob, and his daughters Mary and afsd Elizabeth, and the child his wife was then bigg with. Signed: Elizabeth Vandike. Wit: Elizabeth Anderson (mark), Thos Noxon. Rec: 16 Sept. 1737. (L1-170)

594. Deed. 6 Aug 1737. John Justis of Newport Ayre in Christiana Hun. in Co. of New Castle, and Christian his wife, for the sum of 6 pounds, grant unto Swithen Justis of Mill Creek Hun. in sd Co., a lott of land and premises situate in Newport Ayre. It bounds James and Justis Sts., and contains 32 perches. Signed: John Justis, Christiana Justis (mark). Wit: Justa Justis, Jas. McMullan. Christiana Justis examined by Thos James. Rec: 16 Sept 1737. (L1 171)

595. Deed. 13 Aug 1737. John Justis of Newport Ayre in Christiana Hun. in Co. of New Castle, and Christian his wife, for the sum of 6 pounds, sold unto Benjamin Paulson of the same place, a lott of land containing 32 perches situate in Newport Ayre. It bounds Justis St., and the lott of Morton Justis. Signed: John

152

Justis, Christiana Justis (mark). Wit: James Steel, Jas. McMullan. Christian Justis examined by Thos. James. Rec: 15 Sept 1737. (L1-172)

596. Deed. 15 Aug 1737. Gisbord Walraven of Middle Burrough in Christiana Hun. in Co. of New Castle, and Ann his wife, for the sum of 8 pounds, sold unto Joseph Springer of the same place, yeoman, a piece of land situate in same place. It bounds Front and Beaver Sts. and contains 32 perches. Also a piece of marsh which bounds marshes of Joseph Robinson and Monnce Justis, and contains 4-1/2 acres. This is whereas Francis Lovelace in 1669 granted unto Andries Anderson, Syneck Broer and Walraven Jansen a parcel of land lying on the north side of Christiana Kill, containing 450 acres. In 1684/5 came an Order to divide same by Thomas Peirson, Surveyor. Then Gisbord Walraven and his brother, Jonas Walraven, by article of Agreement dated 19 April 1708, divided their third of the original tract. Then on 29 April 1735, the sons of sd Gisbord and Jonas, afsd Gisbord and Walraven, signed Releases to each other. Signed: Gisbord Walraven (mark), Anna Walraven (mark). Wit: Justa Justis, Jas. McMullan. Rec: 17 Sept 1737. (L1-174)

597. Deed. 10 Aug 1737. John Justis of Newport Ayre in Christiana Hun. in Co. of New Castle, and Christian his wife, for the sum of 6 pounds, sold unto Justah Justis of sd Hun. & Co., a lott of land situate in Newport Ayre. It bounds Justis and James Sts. and contains 32 perches. Signed: John Justis, Christiana Justis (mark). Wit: Swithen Justis, Jas. McMullan. Christian Justis examined by Thos. James. Rec: 17 Sept 1737. (L1-175)

598. Deed. 15 Aug 1737. Gisbord Walraven of Middle Burrough in Christiana Hun. in Co. of New Castle, and Ann his wife, for the sum of 10 pounds, sold unto Mounce Justis of sd Hun. & Co. a lott of land situate in Middle Burrough. It bounds Front and Muberry Sts. and contains 32 perches. This is whereas Francis Lovelace in 1669 granted unto Andries Anderson, Syneck Broer and Walraven Jansen a parcel of land lying on the north side of Christiana Kill, containing 450 acres. In 1684/5 came an Order to divide same by Thomas Peirson, Surveyor. Then Gisbord Walraven and his brother, Jonas Walraven, by article of Agreement dated 19 April 1708, divided their third of the original tract. Then on 29 April 1735, the sons of sd Gisbord and Jonas, afsd Gisbord and Walraven, signed Releases to each other. Signed: Gisbord Walraven (mark), Anna Walraven (mark). Wit: Henry Colesbury, Ja. McMullan. Rec: 19 Sept 1737. (L1-177)

599. Deed. 17 Aug 1737. Nicholas Jaquet of Hun. and Co. of New Castle, planter, for the sum of 55 pounds, grants unto Richard Bermingham of the Town of New Castle in sd Co., sadler, all the lands and marshes which owners

herein described claimed. This is whereas Henry Newton, Sheriff of sd Co. by virtue of a Writ from Court of Common Pleas at the Suit of Robert Bolton against afsd Richard Bermingham, by his Deed Poll dated 20 March 1734, did grant unto afsd Nicholas Jaquet a tract of land Plantation, situate in sd Co. One part situate near the Horse Neck on the Delaware River. It contained on the river side 150 perches and reached to land formerly belonging to Arent Jansen. The other part adjoyns the other and Ferkins Creek, and joins land late of Nicholas Lockyes. Total contains 400 acres. And whereas owners of land called Crane Hook do claim property in afsd tract of land. Signed: Nicholas Jaquat. Wit: John VnGezell, H. Gonne. Rec: 20 Sept 1737. (L1-178)

600. Deed. 20 May 1735. Benjamin Devan and Thomas Turner, both of Co. of New Castle, farmers, for the love and good will they bear toward Anthony Jaquat, and for the sum of 5 pounds, grant unto him a piece of ground opposite to the house of Sifg. Alrichs on the Road going to Maryland. This is part of a larger tract belonging formerly to Major John Donaldson and bequeathed to his daughter Katherine. Sd Katherine and Michael Vaughton her husband to Henry Oblenus and from sd Oblenus to afsd Benjamin Devan and Thomas Turner. Signed: Benjamin Devan (mark), Thomas Tourner. Wit: G. Yeates, Andrew Gravenrat, Joseph Miller. Rec: 20 Sept 1737. (L1-180)

601. Deed. 18 Aug 1737. George Williamson of Kent Co. in Prov. of Maryland, weaver, for the sum of 25 pounds current money of Maryland, sold unto John Farmer of the same Co. & Prov., planter, a parcel of land lying in New Castle Co. in Prov. of Penn. It was taken up by John Williamson (father of afsd George) by a certificate dated 29 Aug 1721. It bounds the lands of John Cowgill and Mathew Corbett, and contains 184 acres. Signed: George Williamson. Wit: Richard Philips, John See. Rec: 21 Sept 1737. (L1-180)

602. Bond. Mary Gartside, Dorothy Gartside and Betty Gartside, all of Manchester in Co. of Lancaster, spinsters, are all firmly bound unto Barbara Gartside of Salford in sd Co., spinster, in 400 pounds of lawful money of Great Britain, to be paid to sd Barbara, her Attny or Assns. We bind ourself the 7th day of June 1736. The condition of this obligation is such that if all or any one of afsd Mary, Dorothy and Betty, or one of their heirs do pay unto sd Barbara the full sum of 200 pounds with interest on the sale of the Estate which will raise clear of all deductions the sum of 1,600 pounds. Signed: Mary Gartside, Dorothy Gartside, Betty Gartside. Wit: Ellen Moody, Wm. Vinley. (L1-181)

603. Deed. 1 Feb 1710. Urian Anderson of St. Georges Hun. in Co. of New Castle, yeoman, for the sum of 50 pounds, sold unto John Morgan and Evan Morgan, both of the Welsh Tract Hun. in sd Co. yeoman, a parcel of land

containing 125 acres, lying on the south side of Dragons Swamp in sd Co. It bounds the lands of Joseph Hanson and John Darby. Signed: Urian Anderson (mark). Wit: John Reece, Wm Williams. Memo: 8 Feb 1710 quiet possession was delivered to sd Morgans. Wit: Jno Reece, Peter Watkins. Rec: 24 Oct 1737. (L1-182)

604. Deed. 6 July 1711. John Morgan of Welch Tract Hun. in Co. of New Castle, yeoman, and Evan Morgan of same place, yeoman, for the sum of 50 pounds, sold unto Thomas Morgan of same place, blacksmith, a parcel of land containing 125 acres, situate on the south side of Dragon Swamp. It bounds the house late of Joseph Hanson and land of John Darby. Signed: John Morgan (mark), Evan Morgan. Wit: Morgan Herbert, Wm. Kemp, John Reece. Memo: Quiet possession delivered. Wit: John Reece, Morgan Herbert, William Kemp. Rec: 25 Oct 1737. (L1-183)

605. Affidavit. 19 Nov 1737. John Rougier and Charles Robinson, being sworn on the Holy Evangelists of Almighty God, dispose and say that they saw Anthony Dushane and John Anderson sign, seal and as their act and deed deliver the within written Article of Agreement, dated 3 March 1736/7. Signed: John Rougier, Chas. Robinson. Wit: Andrew Peterson, Jehu Curtis. Rec: 22 Nov 1727. (L1-185)

606. Declaration. 14 Oct 1736. George Phenny, Esq. Surveyor Gen. of His Majesties Customs in the So. District on the Continent of America, send Greetings. Know ye that by virtue of Powers given me, I hereby appoint John How, gentleman, to be searcher of all Rates Duties within the Creeks, Harbours, Coasts and Rivers from Cape Henlopen to Christine Creek by several Acts of Parliment. He hath power to enter any ship or vessel or shophouse or anyplace whatever to make diligent Search into any trunck chest pack or other parcel... for collecting the said duties. Signed: G. Phenny. (L1-185)

607. Deed. 30 Sept 1737. Richard Grafton of the Town and Co. of New Castle, merchant, and Margaret Williamson of the same place, Widow, Exec. of the Last Will of Thomas Smith, late of sd town, merchant dec'd., for the sum of 30 pounds, grant unto John VnLeuvenigh as highest bidder, the first lott herein described. This is whereas Andrew Wooten, late of sd town, blacksmith, dec'd., by his indenture dated 3 March 1728 (Lib.I, pp 79), did confirm unto Thomas Smith a lott of ground situate in sd Town and Co. It bounded Beaver, Otter and Hart Sts., and the lott late of John Powell. Also another piece of a lott late of Richard Reynolds, now in the tenure of afsd VnLeuvenigh. And whereas Edward Nelson, late of sd town, yeoman, and Mary his wife by Indenture of Mortgage dated 20 Oct 1730 (Lib.I. pp 368), did confirm unto sd Smith a

155

messuage and lott. It bounded lott of sd Smith, now in possession of sd
VnLeuvenigh, and lott late of William Cox, now in tenure of sd Smith. And
whereas sd Smith made his Last Will dated 4 May last past, in which he said he
was indebted to several persons and he empowered his Exec. to convey his real
estate in order to raise money to pay his debts. Signed: Richard Grafton, Mary
Willamson, Wit: James Wood, H. Gonne. Rec: 9 Dec 1737. (L1-185)

608. Deed. 17 Nov 1737. Richard Grafton of the Town and Co. of New Castle,
merchant, surviving Exec. of the Last Will of Thomas Smith, late of same place,
merchant dec'd., for the sum of 200 pounds, sold unto Thomas Thompson three
lotts of land with messuages and tenements thereon, herein described. This is
whereas William Read, dec'd late sheriff of sd Co., by his Deed Poll dated 19
May 1730 did confirm unto afsd Thomas Smith a messuage and lott of ground,
situate in sd Town. It bounded Market place and lott late of Anthony Green,
since of Margaret Williamson, dec'd., commonly called Orange Tree, and marsh
in possession of Nicholas Meers, and lott lately belonging to James Claypoole,
dec'd., afterwards to Josiah Rolfe. Whereas sd Williamson by her Deed Poll
dated 9 Oct year afsd, granted unto sd Smith her lott of ground. Sd Smith built a
brick tenement thereon. Whereas Sarah Rolfe, widow of sd Josiah Rolfe, dec'd.,
and Josiah Rolfe his son, by their Lease & Release dated 25 Nov 1732, granted
unto sd Smith a messuage and lott whereon an old brewhouse stood. It bounded
the house and lott of Samuel Griffith, dec'd., and house and lott of Francis
Janvier, marsh late of Samuel Lowman, dec'd., now in possession of Nicholas
Meers. Whereas sd Smith's Last Will devised his Exec's to sell his real estate to
pay his debts. Signed: Richard Grafton. Wit: John Richardson, Henry Gonne.
Rec: 13 Dec 1737. (L1-188)

609. Deed. 18 Nov 1737. Peter Sigfridus Alrichs of Co. of New Castle, house
carpenter, only son and sole heir of Sigfridus Alrichs, late of sd Co. dec'd., for
the sum of 45 pounds, grant unto Peter Alrichs of Georges Hun. in sd Co., two
parcels of land and marsh (now in his possession). These are a moiety of land
called Greoninger, situate on the NE side of St. Augustines Creek in sd Co.
They bound land formerly Anne Hales, now John Ashton's, and sd creek, and
contains 280 acres. This land was granted by Abigail Alrichs, spinster, by her
Lease and Release dated 7/8 April 1729 unto afsd Peter Alrichs (Lib I, pp190).
Signed: Peter Sigfridus Alrichs. Wit: Thos. Thompson, John Richardson. Rec:
14 Dec 1737. (L1-190)

610. Deed. 13 Aug 1737. Peter Sigfridus Alrichs of Co. of New Castle, house
carpenter, only son and sole heir of Sigfridus Alrichs, late of sd Co. dec'd., and
Grandson of Peter Alrichs, late of sd Co., for the sum of 50 pounds, grant unto
Peter Alrichs, a parcel of land (now in his possession), situate in New Castle

Hun. & Co. It bounds the lands of Christopher Eaton and Sigfridus Alrichs (brother to afsd Peter) and contains 340 acres. This is three equal fourth parts of a tract Willed by afsd grandfather unto his son, Jacobus Alrichs, father of sd Peter and last named Sigfridus Alrichs. Benjamin Swett, tanner, is appointed Attorney. Signed: Peter Sigfridus Alrichs. Rec: 16 Dec 1737. (L1-192)

611. Deed/mortgage. 13 Nov 1737. Thomas Berry of Christiana Hun. in Co. of New Castle, cordwainer, and Jean his wife, for the sum of 20 pounds, sold unto Joseph Barker of Mill Creek Hun. in sd Co., yeoman, a tract of land containing 74 acres, situate in Christiana Hun. It bounds the lands of Lucy Tomlinson, Andrew Cock, Erick Anderson and Robert Pearce, and is part of a tract called Adam Garden. Terms of mortgage to Trustees of Loan Office. Signed: Thomas Berry, Jean Berry (mark). Wit: Timothy Cummins (mark), Arch. Baird. (Noted: "2 June 1747, mortgage is discharged. Signed: Rich. McWilliams"). Rec: 16 Dec 1737. (L1-194)

612. Deed. 11 June 1737. John Read of Dorsett Co. in Prov. of Maryland, planter, eldest son and heir of James Read, late of New Castle Co., yeoman, dec'd., for a sum of money and other good causes of him moving, convey unto Elias Bonnine, farmer, son and heir of Elias Bonnine, his right to a plantation and tract of land situate on Appoquimony Creek in Appoquinimink Hun. It bounds the land of John Bradborne and Abraham Cofines. This property was bought of Job and Honsecoyne by afsd James Read, who dyed intestate and left four children. Afsd John Read sold his Right of sd property to his brother, James Read, who sold the sd property to afsd Elias Bonnine. William Shaw or David French to be Attorney as the Act and Deed of sd Read. Signed: John Read. Wit: James Brown, Jacob Read (mark). Rec: 17 Dec 1737. (L1-196)

613. Deed. 16 Nov 1737. Jacob Read of New Castle Co. in Terr. of Penn., carpenter, one of the sons of James Read, yeoman, dec'd., for a sum of money and other good causes of him moving, convey unto Elias Bonnine, farmer, son and heir of Elias Bonnine, his right to a plantation and tract of land situate on Appoquimony Creek in Appoquinimink Hun. (see rec #612). Signed: Jacob Read (mark). Wit: Rd. Cantwell, Gart. Dushene. Rec: 19 Dec 1737. (L1-197)

614. Deed. 17 Nov 1737. Azarias Miles of Red Lyon Hun. in Co. of New Castle, yeoman, for the sum of 60 pounds, confirm unto Isaac Cannon of same place, shallopman, all interest sd Miles has in a tract of land and plantation containing 118 acres, (formerly belonging to his father, Charles Miles, dec'd.), situate in sd Hun. & Co., now in actual possession of sd Cannon. Signed: Azarias Miles (mark). Wit: David Thomas, Thos. Noxon. Rec: 20 Dec 1737. (L1-198)

615. Release. 18 Nov 1737. Whereas Azarias Miles and Hannah his wife did sell unto David Thomas a plantation and tract of land. And whereas sd Thomas by his indenture bearing even date did agree with afsd Miles that on payment of the sum of 29 pounds 10 shillings to sd Thomas that he would acquit his Right and Title to sd plantation and the Indenture of Sale would be void as if the same had never been made. And whereas afsd Miles by his indenture dated 17 Nov did convey to Isaac Cannon of Red Lyon Hun. all his Right and Title to sd property. Now Know Ye that for the sum of 29 pound 10 shillings, sd Thomas releases Interest. Signed: David Thomas. Wit: Azarias Miles (mark), Hannah Miles (mark). Rec: 20 Dec 1737. (L1-199)

616. Deed. 8 Nov 1737. Philip James of Co. of New Castle, yeoman, and Elizabeth his wife, for the sum of 130 pounds, sold unto Samuel Allen of sd place, farmer, a tract of land formerly (of) Simon Thomas, and a second tract formerly (of) Benjamin Gibbs of 100 acres. They are joined into one tract and are situate on the north side of Christiana Creek. These were sold to afsd James by Deed dated 15 May 1736. It bounds the lands of sd Gibbs and John Robison, and contain 210 acres. Signed: Philip James, Elizabeth James (mark). Wit: Alice Miles (mark), James Armitage. Elizabeth James examined by James Armitage. Rec: 21 Dec 1737. (L1-200)

617. Deed. 15 Nov 1737. Peter Mercellet of St. Georges Hun. in Co. of New Castle, blacksmith, and Mary his wife, for the sum of 90 pounds, sold unto William Meriss, late of Prov. of Penn. but now of sd Hun. & Co., blacksmith, a parcel of land with tenement thereon containing 45 acres, situate on the So. side of Scotts Runn. in sd Hun. & Co. It bounds the lands of William Bennet and Charles Robinson, land leading from the fulling mill toward Reeden Island, and a parcel of land belonging to sd mill, late of Valentine Dushene, dec'd. This land was granted to sd Mercellet by Warrant dated 9 Dec 1736, and surveyed. Signed: Peter Mercellet (mark), Mary Mercellet (mark). Wit: Thos. Noxon, Jacob Marsilliot. Mary Marcellet examined by Thos. Noxon. Rec: 22 Dec. 1737. (L1-201)

618. Deed. 11 Nov 1737. John Hailey, son to Daniel Haily, dec's., James Towland and Sarah his wife, daughter to same, Edward Towland and Elener his wife, daughter to same, Patrick Towland and Margaret his wife, daughter to same, John Borros and Mary his wife, daughter to same, all of Co. of Newcastle, labourers, for the sum of 50 pounds, sold unto John Towland, weaver of sd Co., 100 acres of land situate in sd Co. This is part of two tracts formerly belonging to William Carden, dec'd., that was originally taken up by John Webster by virtue of a Warrant from James Bradshaw and purchased by sd father, Daniel Haily from sd Carden by Deed (Liber H pp210). Signed: Marg. Towland

(mark), John Borros, Mary Towland (mark), Edw. Towland (mark), Elenor
Towland (mark), Patrick Towland (mark), John Hailey (mark), Jas Towland
(mark), Sarah Towland (mark). Wit: Andrew Peterson, Michl Brown. Women
examined by Andw. Peterson. Rec: 23 Dec 1737. (L1-203)

619. Deed. 15 May 1736. Benjamin Gibbs of Co. of New Castle, farmer, and
Esther his wife, for the sum of 67 pounds sold unto Philip James of sd Co.,
yeoman, a tract of land containing 100 acres. It begins by the Welsh Road and
bounds the land of Simon Thomas. This is whereas John Robinson, late of
Christiana Creek in sd Co., by virtue of a Warrant dated 4 March 1716, was
possessed of a tract of land containing 100 acres, situate on sd Creek. Sd
Robinson by his Deed dated 30 Aug 1717, sold same land to William Parsons,
weaver of sd Co. Then sd Parsons by indenture dated 11 Sept 1719 did sell same
unto William Battel, gent. dec'd. Whereas sd land was lacking 14 acres and sd
Battel wanted to make good the lack, he allowed 14 acres of his own land next
adjoyning to make up 100 acres. Then sd Battel and Parnellah his wife sold sd
land unto afsd Benjamin Gibbs by Deed dated 7 Nov 1732. Signed: Benj. Gibbs,
Esther Gibbs. Wit: James Read, John Harris. Esther Gibbs examined by James
Armitage. Rec: 24 Dec. 1737. (L1-205)

620. Deed. 19 Nov 1737. John Connolly of the Town & Co. of New Castle,
wheelwright, and Esther his wife (lately called Esther Glen, widow), for the sum
of 150 pounds, sold unto Thomas Reynolds of sd Co., farmer, a piece of ground
situate in sd Town. (Part of a front lott whereon John VanGezell now dwelleth).
It bounds Market place, a lott late of George Hogg, and a lott sd VanGezell
released to John McGhee, taylor of sd town. Sd land was surveyed by John
Hore. Signed: John Connlly, Esther Connlly (mark). Wit: Rd. Cantwell, Thos.
James. Esther Connolly examined by sd Cantwell and sd James. Rec: 10 Jan
1737. (L1-207)

621. Deed. 1 Jan 1714. William Penn of London in Kingdom of Great Britain,
eldest son of William Penn Esq. of the first part, Griffith Owen, Practioner in
Physick, James Logan, Gent., and Robert Asheton, Gent., all of City of
Philadelphia of second part, and Daniel Worsley of the Co. of Chester, yeoman,
of the third part. Whereas sd Penn the father, by a patent under the hands of
Edward Shippen, Griffith Owen, Thomas Story and James Logan, did grant unto
his afsd son, William Penn junr., a tract of land on the So. side of Brandywine
Creek (part in Chester Co. & part in New Castle Co.), containing 1,4500 acres.
(Patent dated 24 May 1706. Patent Book A, vol 3, pp279). Then Penn junr
appointed afsd Owen, Logan and Asheton his Attny to sell sd land. Now for the
sum of 50 pounds, sd Attny's sell unto afsd Daniel Worsley a parcel of land
containing 250 acres, situate in Co. of New Castle. It bounds the lands of

Abraham Marshall, Simon Hadly and William Routhledge. Signed: Griffith
Owen, James Logan, Robt. Asheton. Wit: Simon Hadly, Gayen Miller. John
French was appointed Attny. of Attny's. Rec: 23 Jan 1737. (L1-209)

622. Power of Attny. 1 Dec 1737, Charles Edgar of the City of Philadelphia,
mariner, have ordained in my place my trusty and loving friend, Richard Nixon,
and my beloved wife, Rebecca Edgar, my lawful Attorneys for me in my name.
Signed: Charles Edgar. Wit: John Hopkins, James Morris. (L1-211)

623. Affidavit. 19 Dec 1737. James Morris, one of the people called Quakers,
appeared before one of His Majesties Justices for the City & Co. of
Philadelphia, and upon his solemn affirmation did declare that he was present
and did see Charles Edgar deliver his Power of Attny. Signed: Saml. Hassell.
Rec: 28 March 1738. Willm. Shaw. (L1-212)

624. Deed. 8 Feb 1737. Richard Davis of Appoquinimink Hun. in Co. of New
Castle, yeoman, and Rachel his wife, for the sum of 73 pounds, sold unto
Abraham Goulden of sd place, yeoman, a tract of land and premises containing
66-2/3 acres, situate in sd Hun. and Co. It bounds the dwelling plantation of afsd
Abraham Goulden and land said to be Albert VanSants and land allotted to Peter
Davis. This is whereas Richard Davis, late of sd place, dec'd., in his lifetime
was seized of a tract of 200 acres of land with plantation thereon, on a branch of
Augustine Creek called Strawberry Hill. In his Last Will dated 9 Ap 1719, he
gave sd land to his sons to be divided. Signed: Richard Davis (mark), Rachel
Davis (mark). Wit: John Vance, Jacob Gooding, Thomas Noxon. Rachel
examined by Thos. Noxon. Rec: 3 April 1738. (L1-212)

625. Deed. Nov 1737. Mathew Walton of Appoquinimink Hun. in Co. of New
Castle, yeoman, youngest son of Mathew Walton, late of same place, dec'd., for
the sum of 5 pounds, and for the natural love which he beareth his brother, quit
claims unto Abraham Walton, yeoman of same place, eldest son of sd Walton
dec'd., his claim to two tracts of land and marsh. One tract contains the old
Mansion House. This is land that their father in his lifetime was seized of. One
tract was the late dwelling plantation of sd Walton and is bounded by the
Delaware River, land late of John Marsh, dec'd., land of John Brown and land of
Jno. Egbertson, and contains 400 acres with some marshes. The other tract is
situate on a branch of Duck Creek and bounds land of John Owen (formerly
George Cummins), land of Samuel Fitzrandolph (formerly Thomas Wards), land
lately surveyed for Alexander Dean, and land late of Peter Staats, dec'd. This
contains 208 acres. In sd Walton's Last Will dated 28 March 1712, he
bequeathed all his lands to be divided equally between his two afsd sons.
Signed: Mathew Walton. Wit: Sampson Bourn, Anthony Dowdall. Rec: 4 April

160

1738. (L1-214)

626. Deed. Nov 1737. Abraham Walton, eldest son of Mathew Walton, late of Appoquinimink Hun. in Co. of New Castle, dec'd. yeoman, for the sum of 5 pounds, and also for the natural affection for his brother, Matthew Walton (youngest son of sd Walton, dec'd.), releases his half share of two tracts of land bequeathed to him. This is whereas sd Walton in his lifetime was seized of two tracts of land situate near the Thorough Fare of Duck Creek. One was bounded with marshes on Delaware Bay, land late of John Marsh dec'd., now of Patrick Kelley and John Marsh's son, land of John Owen and land of John Egbertson. It contains 400 acres and was the dwelling plantation of sd Walton. The other bounded land of John Owens (formerly George Cummins), land of Samuel Fitzrandolph (formerly Thomas Ward), land lately surveyed for Alexander Dean and land late of Peter Staats, dec'd., containing 208 acres. Signed: Abraham Walton (mark). Wit: Sampson Bourn, Anthony Dowdall. Rec: 5 April 1738. (L1-216)

627. Deed. 8 Feb 1737. Peter Davis of St. Georges Hun. in Co. of New Castle, and Hanah his wife, and Richard Davis of sd place, yeoman, and Rachel his wife, for the sum of 86 pounds 18 shillings, sold unto Abraham Golden of sd place, yeoman, a tract of land containing 79 acres, situate in sd Hun. & Co.. This is land that sd Peter and Richard Davis, by virtue of a Warrant dated 24 Oct last had surveyed unto them. It bounds the dwelling plantation of sd Golden, land of Thomas Hyat, supposed land of Albert VanSant and land of sd Richard Davis. Signed: Peter Davis, Hannah Davis, Richard Davis (mark), Rachel Davis (mark). Wit: John Vance, Jacob Gooding, Thos. Noxon. Hannah and Rachel examined by Tho. Noxon. Rec: 5 April 1738. (L1-218)

628. Deed. 27 Dec 1735. Joseph Way of Willingstown in Christiana Hun. in Co. of New Castle, yeoman, and Sarah his wife, for the sum of 20 pounds, sold unto Joshua Way of Springfield in Co. of Chester, carpenter, a parcel of land containing 41 perches, situate in sd town. It bounds lands of Robt Read and sd Joseph Way. This is part of a tract containing 4 acres 35 perches that sd Way purchased of Andrew Justis of sd Hun., yeoman, and Bridget his wife by indenture dated 3 July 1732 (book H, pp 232). Signed: Joseph Way, Sarah Way. David French is appointed Attny. Wit: Charles Springer, James James jun. Rec: 6 April 1738. (L1-220)

629. Deed. 18 Feb 1737. Thomas Noxon of St. Georges Hun. in Co. of New Castle, yeoman, and Mary his wife, for the sum of 50 pounds, sold unto Charles Robinson of same place, cordwainer, a parcel of land, being one third part of a tract now in possession of John Demarest, dec'd., situate in Appoquinimink

Hun. in sd Co. It bounds the land of Richard Cantwell and land formerly belonging to John Williams, dec'd., land of John Anderson (late of sd Williams), and contains 104 acres 55 perches of land and sixth part of all marsh. Also, sd Thomas Noxon for the sum of 115 pounds, grants unto sd Charles Robinson all his interest to the other two thirds of tract formerly belonging to sd Demarest. It bounds the land of sd Cantwell, land of Adam Peterson, and contains 208 acres 110 perches. Signed: Tho. Noxon, Mary Noxon. Wit: Jacob Gooding, Ant. Dushane. Mary Noxon examined by Richard Cantwell. Rec: 7 April 1738. (L1-221)

630. Deed. 23 Feb 1737. Thomas Reynolds, farmer of New Castle Co., for the sum of 205 pounds, sold to John Connolly of Town & sd Co., wheelwright, a piece of ground lying in town of New Castle, part of the front lott whereon John Vangezel now dwelleth. This was heretofore conveyed by sd Vangezel unto Esther Glen, widow. It bounds the lott of George Hogg and lott sd Vangezel released to John McGhee, taylor. Signed: Thomas Reynolds, Margt. Reynolds (mark). Wit: John Dunning, Peter Anderson, Rd. Cantwell. Margaret Reynolds examined by sd Cantewll and Thos. James. Rec: 8 Aprill 1738. (L1-224)

631. Deed. 23 Feb 1737. Christian Land, Samuel Land, John Land and Thomas Land, Exers. of the Last Will of Francis Land, late of New Castle Co., yeoman dec'd., for the sum of 83 pounds 10 shilling 9 pence, sold unto William Whittel of Georges Hun. in sd Co., mariner, a plantation and tract of land containing 150 acres. This is part of a tract called Red Cliff, and bounds land conveyed to John Goulden on Appoquinimink Creek. This is property that sd Francis Land purchased of Edmund Garretson of Appoquinimink Hun., yeoman, and Elizabeth his wife, by indenture dated 20 Aug 1731. Signed: John Land, Thos. Land, Christian Land, Saml. Land. Wit: Josiah Lewden, Js. Ruaird. Rec: 10 April 1738. (L1-226)

632. Deed. 19 Feb 1737. Edmund Garretson of Appoquinimink Hun. in Co. of New Castle, farmer, and Elizabeth his wife, for the sum of 5 shillings, release unto William Whittet of sd Co., merchant, a parcel of land situate on Appoquin. Creek. It bounds tract sold to John Goulden and contains 150 acres (except one acre, part of the premises next adjoyning to the Mill Damm of Thomas Noxon, Esq. sold to sd Noxon by sd Garretson). Signed: Edmd. Gerretson, Elizabeth Gerretson. Wit: Jos. Rolfe, John Rudick. Rec: 11 April 1838. (L1-227)

633. Deed. 20 Feb 1737. Edmund Garretson of Appoquinimnk Hun. in Co. of New Castle, and Elizabeth his wife, for the sum of 184 pounds, grant unto William Whittel, merchant of sd place, a parcel of land situate on appoquinimink Creek. (same property as Rec.632). Signed: Edmd. Gerritson,

Elizabeth Gerritson. Wit: Jos. Rolfe, John Ridick. Elizabeth examined by Rd Cantwell. Rec: 11 April 1738. (L1-228)

634. Deed. 22 June 1737. Henry Chadeayne of the town of New Rochell in Co. of West Chester in Prov. of New York, shipwright, and Blanche his wife, for the sum of 125 pounds, sold unto James Gano of Appoquinimink Hun. in Co. of New Castle, waterman, a tract of land and plantation, situate in sd Hun. on Duck Creek. It bounds the dwelling plantation of sd Gano, and land late of John Chadeayne, dec'd., and contains 125 acares. John Dony of Co. of Kent, jun, and Richard Grafton of Co. of New Castle appointed Attorneys. Signed: Henry Chadeayne, Blanche Chadeayne. Wit: James Steel jun., James Whitehead. (L1-231)

635. Affidavit. 9 Dec 1737. James Whitehead and James Steel jun. appeared before Andrew Hamilton, Esq., Recorder of City of Philadelphia, and swore they saw Henry Chadeayne and Blanche Chadeayne sign afsd written instrument. Signed: A. Hamilton, Ack: David French. Rec: 12 April 1738. Will Shaw. (L1-232)

636. Deed. 9 Feb 1737. Nicholas Belveal of St. Georges Hun. in Co. of New Castle, weaver, and Susanna his wife, for the sum of 60 pounds, sold to Anthony Dushene of sd place, shopkeeper, one of the sons of Garret Dushene, yeoman, a tract of land with premises, containing 50-1/2 acres, situate in sd Hun. & Co. This is a third of a tract that Philip Belveal of sd place, yeoman dec'd., was seized of. He dyed intestate leaving 3 sons, John, afsd Nicholas and Philip Belveal, and sd land was divided between them. Signed: Nicholas Belveal, Susana Belveal (mark). Wit: Tho Noxon, John Belveal. Susanna examined by sd Noxon. Rec: 13 April 1738. (L1-233)

637. Deed. 23 Feb 1737. Jacob Gooding of Town of St. Georges in Co. of New Castle, shopkeeper, and Hester his wife, for the sum of 118 pounds, sold to John McCoole, yeoman, of same place, seven lotts of land and marsh, situate on the west side of Delaware River near Reeden Island. The first, called Home Lott, bounds the land of Isaac Gooding and contains 17-1/4 acres. The second bounds lands of John Hanson jun., John Hanson sen. and land late of Peter Strycker, and contains 34 acres. The third bounds lands of both sd Hanson's and sd Gooding and contains 150 acres. Next bounds land late of John Burgees and contains 8 acres of marsh. Next two contains 8 acres of marsh each. Next contains 20 acres of marsh. Signed: Jacob Gooding, Esther Gooding. Wit: Tho Noxon, Wm Williams. Hester examined by sd Noxon. Rec: 14 April 1738. (L1-234)

638. Deed. 30 Jan 1737. John Ogle of White Clay Creek Hun. in Co. of New

Castle, planter, for the sum of 40 pounds, sold to George Dakeyne of Pencader Hun. in sd Co., planter, a tract of land and premises in Pencader Hun. containing 266 acres. This is part of 30,000 acres, now called Welsh Tract, that was laid out by Warrant for William Davies, David Evans and others. Then sd Davies by his Deed did confirm unto John Morgan, late of Pencader Hun, dec'd., 1,000 acres of sd land, situate about the branches of Red Lyon Runn. Then sd Morgan by his Deed dated 14 Jan 1725/6 (Liber H. Pp.37), did grant unto Hugh Morice of Pencader Hun., yeoman, 266 acres of his land. It bounded the lands of Simon James, Nicolas Meers, Watkins Morgan and land late of Henry Bevan, now of sd George Dakeyne. Then sd Morice and Margaret his wife by their Deed dated 22 Aug 1733 (Liber K. Pp.162), did confirm same unto afsd John Ogle. Signed: John Ogle. Wit: William Griffith junr., Alax Creager, Henry Gonne. Rec: 14 April 1738. (L1-237)

639. Deed. 23 Feb 1737. William Meriss of St.Georges Hun. in Co. of New Castle, blacksmith, and Mary his wife, for the sum of 38 pounds, sold to John McCoole of same place, yeoman, a messuage and small plantation, situate on So. side of Scotts Run in sd Hun. & Co. It bounds the lands of William Bennet and Charles Robinson, and contains 45 acres of land. Signed: William Meriss, Mary Meriss (mark). Wit: Jacob Gooding, Tho. Noxon. Mary Meriss examined by sd Noxon. Rec: 15 April 1738. (L1-239)

640. Deed. 27 Jan 1737/8. Martha McComb, Widow and Admin. of John McComb, late of Mill Creek Hun. in Co. of New Castle, dec'd., for the sum of 83 pounds, sold unto William Nivins of same place, a messuage plantation tract of land containing 100 acres 6 perches, situate in Latitia Penn's Mannor, adjoyning to London Tract. This is land that sd McComb became seized of by Deed dated 12 May 1735 (Lib K. pp351). And whereas sd McComb's personal estate not enough to cover debts, the Orphans Court ordered property sold at publick Vendue. Signed: Martha McComb (mark). Wit: James Kerr, James Barly. Rec: 15 April 1738. (L1-241)

641. Deed/mortgage. 23 Feb 1737. Between John McCoole of St.Georges Hun. in Co. of New Castle, yeoman, and Jacob Gooding of Town of St.Georges in sd Co., shopkeeper. This is whereas sd Jacob Gooding and Hester his wife by their indenture bearing even date for consideration of 118 pounds, confirm unto sd McCoole seven lotts of land and marsh, part of Reeden Island between Augustine Creek and Delaware River. The first three lots contain 201-1/4 acres of land and the other four lotts contain 44 acres of marsh. Terms are 6 pounds on 23 Feb next, 6 pounds on 23 Feb 1739, and residue of 106 pounds on 23 Feb 1740. Signed: John McCoole. Wit: Tho Noxon, Wm Williams. Rec: 17 April 1738. (L1-242)

642. Deed. 20 Sept 1737. William Shipley of Willingtown in Christiana Hun. in Co. of New Castle, gent, and Elizabeth his wife, for the sum of 40 pounds, sold unto Joshua Way of same place, joyner, a tract of land containing 8-1/2 acres, situate in sd Hun. & Co. This is whereas by a Patent from Francis Lovelace dated before 1674, John Anderson Stalcop became seized of a tract of land containing 800 acres. Then Stalcop by Deed dated 16 April 1675 did sell one moiety of sd land to Samuel Peterson and Lars Cornelison, who made a division. Then by agreement between Christiana (widow of sd Stalcop) and Andrew Stalcop (son) and Charles Pickering (assignee of sd Cornelison & Peterson), there was surveyed 211 acres (dated 26 March 1686). Then by sd Peterson's Last Will, dated 28 Nov 1689, he devised sd land to whichever of his sons lived longest with their mother. Mathias Peterson, oldest son, devised sd land to Peter Peterson, who gave same to his son Peter in his Last Will (dated 29 Jan 1714/5). Then sd Peter and Magdalene his wife by indenture dated 8 May 1727, sold 105 acres unto Andrew Justison (Book H pp 199/200). Afterwards Hanse Peterson (another son) and Catharine his wife by indenture dated 29 Oct 1734 did release sd 105 acres unto sd Justison. Whereas sd Justison and Breta his wife and Thos Willing (son in law to Andrew Justison and Catharine his wife), by their indenture dated 9 Aug 1735 did grant unto afsd William Shiply a part of sd land containing 8-1/2 acres. Signed: William Shipley, Elizabeth Shipley. Wit: John Richardson, Thos West. Rec: 18 April 1738. (L1-243)

643. Deed. 22 Feb 1737/8. John Justis of Newport Ayre in Christiana Hun. in Co. of New Castle, and Christian his wife, for the sum of 14 pounds sold to James Steel and Moses Steel, both of White Clay Creek Hun. in sd Co., a lott of land and premises situate in Newport Ayre. It bounds the land of Mr. Thomas Gray and contains 42 perches. Signed: John Justis, Christian Justis (mark). Wit: William McCrea, Jas. McMullan. Christiana Justis examined by Jehu Curtis. Rec: 20 April 1738. (L1-245)

644. Deed. 30 Dec 1737. Augustine Constantine of Newport Ayre in Xiana Hun. in Co. of New Castle, for the sum of 4 pounds, release unto Israel Robinson of sd Hun. & Co., a lott of land or premises situate in Newport Ayre. It bounds the lott of Thos Gray on Market St. and lott of Thos Morgan and contains 32 perches. Signed: Augustine Constantine (mark). Wit: Saml. Marshall, Jas. McMullan. Rec: 21 April 1738. (L1-246)

645. Deed. 12 Nov 1736. Mr. Samuel Marshall of Newport Ayre in Christiana Hun. in Co. of New Castle, and Sarah his wife, for the sum of 8 pounds, sold unto Mr. George Hutchison of Ayre in North Britain, mariner, a lott of land premises containing 35 perches, situate in Newport Ayre. It bounds the lands of sd Marshall and Conrade Garretson by Christiana Creek. Signed: Samuel

Marshall, Sarah Marshall. Wit: Jno Wilson, John York, Jas. McMullan. Sarah Marshall examined by Jno Richardson. Rec: 21 April 1738. (L1-247)

646. Deed. 12 Nov 1736. Mr. Samuel Marshall of Newport Ayre in Christiana Hun. in Co. of New Castle, and Sarah his wife, for the sum of 9 pounds, sold unto Mr. George Hutchison of Ayre in North Britain, mariner, a lott of land containing 1/4 acre, situate in Newport Ayre. It bounds James and Front Sts. and the lott of John McCammonds. Signed: Saml. Marshall, Sarah Marshall. Wit: Jno Wilson, John York, Jas McMullan. Sarah Marshall examined by Jno Richardson. Rec: 22 April 1738. (L1-249)

647. Deed. 24 Feb 1737. Samuel Mains of White Clay Creek Hun. in Co. of New Castle, yeoman, and Grizel his wife, for the sum of 146 pounds, sold unto Thomas Tagart, late of the Island of Jamaica but now of sd Co., gent., a tract of land containing 139 acres, situate in sd Hun. & Co. It bounds White Clay Creek and the land of Reynold Howell. This is the residue of a larger tract, commonly called Oakburn, containing 200 acres that was purchased by sd Mains from Roger Shennan, taylor of sd Co. Sd Mains sold part of this land to William Howard. Signed: Samuel Means, Grizel Means (mark). Wit: James Armitage, H. Gonne. Grizel Means examined by sd Armitage. Rec: 22 April 1738. (L1-250)

648. Deed. 2 April 1711. Urian Anderson of St.Georges Hun. in Co. of New Castle, yeoman, for the sum of 20 pounds sold unto Floren Sorency of the Welsh Tract Hun. in sd Co., merch., a parcel of land situate on the So. side of St. Georges Creek. It begins at the path from sd Anderson's house leading to the bridge, up sd creek and contains 50 acres. Signed: Urian Anderson (mark). Wit: Joseph Neale, John Reece. Memo: 11 April 1712 sd land delivered by Turf and Twigg in presence of Fra. Jones, Alin Clark, Joseph Neale, Josp Spregg (mark). Rec: 27 April 1738. (L1-252)

649. Deed. 20 April 1711. Joseph Neal of St. Georges Creek in Co. of New Castle, yeoman, for the sum of 6 pounds sold unto Floren Sorency of the Welsh Tract Hun. in sd Co., merchant, a parcel of land and premises situate on the No. side of St. Georges Creek. It begins by bridge and bounds the fence of sd Neal and land of James Anderson. Signed: Joseph Neale. Wit: Thos Evan, Henry David, Jno Reece. (L1-254)

650. Deed. 28 Jan 1735/6. John Neal and Margery his wife of Co. of New Castle in Brandywine Hun., husbandman, for the sum of 120 pounds sold unto Thomas Allmond, yeoman of sd Hun. & Co., a tract of land in sd Hun. unto the River Delaware. It bounds the land of sd Neal and contains 117 acres of land and 10 acres of marsh in Verdue Hook. The land is in the Patent of the Inhabitants of

166

Verdrie de hook and Peter Andrus Halliman and Siger Duke, alias Sick, sold the same unto Hance Petterson Smith sen. in 1685. Then sd Hance sold same unto Charles Springer and other Church Wardens of Christiana Congregation in 1699. In 1702 sd tract was sold unto James Clemson, who sold the same again in 17?? unto William Tussen and the heirs of sd Tussen, namely Stephen Tussen, Thomas Clark and his wife, who sold sd tract unto afsd John Neal. Signed: John Neal, Margery Neal (mark). Wit: John Wilson, Thos. Clark (mark). Adam Buckley appointed Attny. Rec: 28 April 1738. (ll-255)

651. Deed. 15 Nov 1737. Jane Guest, Widow, and Nathaniel Wainsford of Mill Creek Hun. in Co. of New Castle, for the sum of 25 pounds sold unto William Sutton of same place, 7 acres of land (which was) specify'd in a Deed touching a Marriage Settlement intended to be had between William Guest of West Bromwitch in sd Co. and the sd Jane Guest his Relict and Widdow, which was afterwards solomized. Sd deed dated 5 Sept 1717 (page 140 in Record Office). Land surveyed 12 June 1719 by George Dakeyne, surveyor. Signed: Ann Guest (mark), Nath. Wainsford. (both names Ann & Jane used) Wit: Simon Hadly, Edward Robinson. Rec: 15 May 1738. (L1-257)

652. Appointment. 3 Aug 1736. John Estaugh of Haddonfield in Co. of Gloucester and West Div. of Prov. of New Jersey, gent., send Greeting. Whereas Samuel Bonham of London in England, merchant, by Letter of Attny dated 7 Nov 1735 did appoint me, John Estaugh, his Attny with power to sell/demand payment (etc) in Pensilvania Land Company. By virtue of this power, sd Estaugh appoints William Rawle of the City & Co. of Phila., merchant, as his lawful Attorney with same power. Signed: John Estaugh. Wit: William Cooper, Benj. Rawle. (L1-258)

653. Affidavit. 13 March 1737. Prov. of New Jersey. John Estaugh came before John Kay, one of the Justices of Court of Common Pleas and acknowledges signing Power of Attny. Signed: John Kay. Witness: Clement Plumsted, Esq. Mayor of City of Phila. one of the Justices of the Peace and William Cooper of sd City, shopkeeper declared they witnessed the signing. Signed: Clem Plumsted, Mayor. Rec: 15 May 1738. (L1-259)

654. Judgement. 24 Feb 1737. Henry Newton, Esq. Sheriff of Co. of New Castle send Greetings. Whereas Daniel Oburn lately in Court before Justices and did recover agst John Price and Mary Price, Admin. of All which were of David Price, late of sd Co., yeoman dec'd., as a debt of 55 pounds and damages. Taken in Execution of the lands & tenements of sd Price was a piece of land situate in Pencader Hun. in sd Co. It contained 184 acres to the value of 55 pounds. Sd land was sold unto Daniel Oburn, the Plff., for the sum of 63 pounds one shill 6

pence. Signed: Henry Newton, Shff. Wit: Sigf. Alrichs, David McMullen, John See. Rec: 25 May 1738. (L1-259)

655. Deed. 16 Feb 1737/8. James Laughlin of Mill Creek Hun. in Co. of New Castle, cordwainer, and Mary his wife, for the sum of 50 pounds sold unto Robert Kirkwood of sd Hun. & Co., wheelwright, a plantation or tract of land containing 94 acres, situate in same place. It bounds the lands of George Ball, William Laughlin and Widow Robinson. Signed: James Laughlin, Mary Laughlin (mark). Wit: Saml. Corry, Jas. McMeechen. Mary Laughlin examined by Simon Hadly. Rec: 26 May 1738. (L1-260)

656. Deed. 10 Dec 1737. Samuel Marshall of Newport Ayre in Christiana Hun. in Co. of New Castle, and Sarah his wife, for the sum of 20 pounds sold unto Neil McNeil of Audely in the Shire of Argyle in North Britain, gentleman, and George Stewart, mariner, two lotts of land situate in Newport Ayre. The first lott bounds John St. by Christiana Creek and contains 18-1/2 perches. The second lott bounds the lott of John McCommonds on James St. and contains 32 perches. Signed: Saml. Marchall, Sarah Marshall. Wit: Nic. Land, Jas. McMullan, George Hutchison. Sarah Marshall examined by Jno Richardson. Rec: 27 May 1738. (L1-161)

657. Deed. 20 Feb 1737/8. Samuel Marshall of Newport Ayre in Co. of New Castle, and Sarah his wife, for the sum of 6 pounds sold unto James Hays of the same place, weaver, a lott of land and premises containing 32 perches, situate in Newport Ayre. It bounds the lott of James McMullan on James St. and lott of Abun? Marshall. Signed: Saml. Marshall, Sarah Marshall. Wit: William Sutton, Jas. McMullan. Sarah Marshall examined by John Richardson. Rec: 27 May 1738. (L1-263)

658. Deed. 2 Sept 1737. Samuel Marshall of Newport Ayre in Co. of New Castle, and Sarah his wife, for the sum of 18 pounds sold unto William Sutton of Mill Creek Hun. in sd Co. a lott of land and premises, situate in Newport Ayre. It bounds James & Front Sts. and Christiana Creek and contains 53 perches. Signed: Saml Marshall, Sarah Marshall. Wit: Alexd Land, Jas. McMullan. Sarah Marshall examined by Jno Richardson. Rec: 29 May 1738. (L1-264)

659. Deed. 16 Nov 1737. Mr Samuel Marshall of Newport Ayre in Christiana Hun. in Co. of New Castle, and Sarah his wife, for the sum of 6 pounds, sold unto William Pasmore of Kent Township in Chester Co., a lott of land and premises containing 36 perches, situate in Newport Ayre. It bounds the lotts of John Heald and Conrad Garretson, and Johns & Front Sts. Signed: Saml

168

Marshall, Sarah Marshall. Wit: Nic Land, Jac. McMullan. Sarah Marshall examined by Jno Richardson. Rec: 29 May 1738. (L1-265)

660. Deed. 7 Feb 1737/8. Samuel Marshall of Newport Ayre in Christiana Hun. in Co. of New Castle, and Sarah his wife, for the sum of 26 pounds sold unto John Heald of Kennet Township of Chester Co., three lotts of land situate in Newport Ayre. The first bounds Market, Johns, Ayre and Marys Strs., and lotts of Alex Frazien and Conrade Garretson, and contains 1-1/4 acre of land. The second bounds Ayre & Johns Sts. and lott of sd Garretson, and contains 1/2 acre. The third bounds lott of William Shaw, Hut Hensonns Runn and James St., and contains 11 perches. Signed: Saml Marshall, Sarah Marshall. Wit: Jas McMullan, Jno Richardson. Sarah Marshall examined by Jno Richardson. Rec: 30 May 1738. (L1-267)

661. Deed. 23 Feb 1737/8. Augustine Constantine of Newport Ayre in Co. of New Castle, for the sum of 3 pounds sold unto George Lawson in the branches of Elk River, Cecil Co., Maryland, merchant, a lott of land and premises containing 42 perches, situate in Newport Ayre. It bounds Ayre & Wallnut Sts. and Rainbow Runn. Signed: Augustine Constantine (mark). Wit: Jehu Curtis, Jas. McMullan. 'Rec'd of Lewis Howell three pounds in full in behalf of within named George Lawson'. Rec: 1 June 1738. (L1-268)

662. Appointment. 28 March 1737. John Penn, Thomas Penn and Richard Penn to George Thomas, Esq. Whereas the late King Charles by his Patent granted unto William Penn, Esq., father of afsd John, Thomas and Richard Penn, the Prov. of Pennsylvania with Powers. Now know that by virtue of Letters, Patents, Deeds (etc) we nominate and appoint you, George Thomas, Esq. to be Lieutenant Governor of Provinces and Counties. Duties and Authorities described in full. Signed: John Penn, Thomas Penn, Richard Penn. Rec: 9 June 1738 by Willm Shaw. (L1-270)

663. Approval of the Appointment of George Thomas by the Penns. "At the Court at St. James 15th day of February 1737. Present The Kings Most Excellent Majesty: Lord Chancellor, Lord President, Lord Privy Seal, Lord Chamberlain, Duke of Rutland, Duke of Argyle, Duke of Montaga, Earl of Essex, Earl of Selkirk, Earl Waldegrave, Earl frtz Walkr, Viscount Torrington, ? Comholler. Recorded 7 June 1738 by Willm Shaw. (L1-271)

664. Deed. 15 Jeb 1737. John Justis of Newport Ayre in Christiana Hun. in Co. of New Castle and Christian his wife, for the sum of 8 pounds sold unto William Sample of Chester Co. in Prov. of Penn., a lott of land and premises containing 32 perches, situate in Newport Ayre. It bounds James and Justis Sts. and the

lotts of sd Justis, James McMullan and John White. Signed: John Justis, Christiana Justis (mark). Wit: Joseph Rinken, Jas. McMullan. Christiana Justis examined by Jehu Curtis. Rec: 12 June 1738. (L1-272)

665. Deed. 15 Dec 1737. William Thomas of Mill Creek Hun. in Co. of New Castle, yeoman, and Katherine his wife, for the sum of 100 pounds sold unto Archibald McDonald of same place, yeoman, a plantation and tract of land situate in sd Hun. and Co. It bounds the land of Evan Rees and contains 150 acres. This land was laid out by a Warrant from James Logan of Phila. Gent. unto sd Thomas. Signed: William Thomas (mark), Katherine Thomas (mark). Wit: Simon Hadly, Joseph Hadly. Katherine Thomas examined by Simon Hadly. Rec: 13 June 1738. (L1-273)

666. Deed. 4 March 1734. Stephen Tussey, yeoman, and Thomas Clarke, weaver, and Catherine Clark his wife, all of Brandywine Hun. in Co. of New Castle, send Greetings. Know that sd Stephen Tussey for the sum of 60 pounds from John Neal, yeoman, of same place; and Know that sd Thomas Clarke and Catherine his wife for the sum of 11 pounds from sd Neal, and for other diverse reasons us thereunto moving, grant unto sd John Neal a parcel of land and premises lying at Vardredee Hook on the west side of Delaware River. It is bounded by land of sd Neal, formerly Jacob Clemanson, and land belonging to the family of Mountons, and contains 100 acres. This tract of land and premises was sold to William Tussey, father of afsd Stephen Tussey and Catharine Clark by James Clempson of Chester Co. by Deed dated 14 March 1709/10. It was purchased by sd Clempson by Deed from Charles Springer and Lucas Stedham in 1702. Signed: Stephen Tussey (mark), Thomas Clark (mark), Catherine Clark (mark). Wit: Thomas Allmond, Thomas Byrd (mark). Rec: 15 June 1738. (L1-274)

667. Agreement. 23 June 1737. George Yeates, Daniel Turner, James Bryan and Robert Bryan, all of New Castle Hun. & Co., farmers being owners of a marsh lying near River Delaware. They all agree to a Bank or Dyke of 9 feet wide and 3 feet deep to be put around sd marsh and agree to repair it. Signed: G. Yeates, Daniel Tourneur, James Bryan, Robert Bryan. Rec: 13 June 1738. (L1-275)

END

171

INDEX

171

INDEX

...COMHOLLER, 168
...DMARSH, ?arth, 51
...HILEACRE, Abel, 117
...ONNE, H., 27
...ORCE, Joshua, 47
...RED, Benj., 52
ADAMS, Alexander/Alex., 4, 6, 26, 86, 109: James, 26
AIKIEN, Agnes, 122, 123; Alexander, 122, 123
ALBERTSON, Dirick, 93
ALCONAT, Gill, 31
ALFREE, Paul, 132
ALFREES, James, 146
ALLEN, Agnes, 76; John/Jon., 76, 77; Samuel, 157; William, 81, 104
ALLET, Ann, 21; Thomas/Thos., 21, 68
ALLFACE, Paul, 69
ALLFREE, John, 113; Paul, 113
ALLIN, John, 25
ALLISON, Thomas, 130
ALLMAN, Benjamin, 132
ALLMOND, Thomas/Thos., 136, 165, 169; William, 65, 78
ALLRICH, Abigail, 73
ALLRICKS, Sigfredus, 29
ALRECK, Fredase, 45
ALRICH, Fredrick, 44; Peter, 115; Sigf./Sigfs., 78
ALRICHS, Abigail/Abigal, 43, 44, 48, 155; Harms., 93, 96, 99; Hermanus, 75, 140; Jacobus, 2, 38, 39, 93, 156; James, 126; Mary, 126; Peter, 2, 38, 39, 79, 90, 93, 126, 155; Peter Sigfridus, 155, 156; Sigfredus/Sigfredous, 39, 126, 136, 155, 156; Sigfridus/Sigf., 38, 56, 153, 167; Wessell, 47, 93; Widow, 39

ALRICK, 47
ALRICKS, Abigail/Abigal, 35, 59; Hermanas/Herm., 16, 35, 53, 54, 59; Mary, 35, 54, 59; Peter, 35, 59, 62; Wessell, 33, 35
ANDERS?, Justa, 40
ANDERSON, Andrew, 15, 74, 139; Andries, 152; Anne, 54, 82; Charles, 86, 98, 129; Elizabeth, 148, 149, 151; Erick/Errick, 14, 130, 139, 156; Hilleka, 89; Jacob, 148; James, 12, 52, 54, 71, 73, 77, 82, 88, 90, 97, 130, 165; John, 4, 5, 28, 54, 109, 110, 114, 118, 137, 144, 148, 150, 154, 161; Jonas, 28, 45, 46, 54; Junan, 139; Justa, 9, 46; Justin, 7; Margaret, 134, 135; Mouns, 46, 54; Peter, 2, 12, 38, 79, 86, 91, 134, 135, 139, 161; Roelof, 89; Thomas, 142; Urian, 46, 54, 127, 153, 154, 165; Urias, 148; William, 49, 107
ANDRIES, Andries, 127; Justa, 40
ANDRIESON, Justs, 63
ANDROS/ANDREOS, E./Edmond/Edmund, 7, 8, 35, 59, 62, 63, 67, 70, 74, 86, 87, 98, 102, 112, 129
ANGEW, James, 105; Margaret/Margrit, 105
ANNAND, Alexr., 126
ARMATAGE, James, 53
ARMITAGE, Hanah/Hannah, 92, 97, 128, 129, 131; James, 15, 54, 62, 64, 65, 71, 76, 77, 89, 90, 92, 94, 95, 96, 97, 99, 100, 103, 106, 110, 113, 115, 117, 118, 123, 124, 125, 128, 129, 130, 131, 133, 145, 146, 150, 157, 158, 165; Mary, 128
ARMOR, John, 119

172

ARMSTRONG, Abel, 93, 141;
Edward, 67; William, 110
ARSKAIN, Jonas, 122
ASHETON, Robert, 158, 159
ASHMEAD, John junr., 145, 147
ASHTON, 73; John, 6, 78, 93, 109,
123, 155; Ralph, 22
ASKEW, James/Jas., 60
ASKUES, John, 63
ASLTONS, Jno., 54
ATKINSON, James, 109; Samson, 52
ATTWOOD, William, 113
AUBERY/AUBREY, Latitia, 15, 55,
65, 68, 79, 80; William/Wm., 15,
55, 65, 68, 79, 80
AWBREY, Fra., 135
AYNODS, Rd., 75
BABB, Thomas, 35
BAFFELL/BAFFOLL, W., 12;
William, 12
BAIRD, Arch.,156
BAKER, Joshia, 103
BAKLEY, Sam, 61
BALDWIN, John, 97
BALL, George, 167; John, 40, 106,
107; John Junr., 142; John Sen.,
107, 142; Mary, 142; William,
106, 107, 142
BARBER, John, 102
BARD, Peter, 102, 104
BARKER, Daniel, 31, 34, 65;
Elizabeth, 31, 65; Joseph, 156
BARLY, James, 163
BARNS, Joseph, 107, 142
BARR, Thomas, 64, 105
BARREFO, Giles, 17
BARRET/BARRETT, Giles/Gilles, 3,
24, 28, 44, 45, 47, 140
BARRY, John, 147; Richard, 97
BASSET/BASSETT, Jane, 73, 88;
Thomas/Thos., 73, 88
BATTEL, Parnella/Parnellah, 158;

William/Wm., 2, 158
BATTELE, Captain William, 28
BATTELL, Parmehah/Pernallah, 84;
Parnela/Parnell, 75, 104;
Parnella/Parnellah, 2, 60, 61, 76,
112, 130; W., 2, 22, 31, 34, 36,
39, 41, 43, 44, 45, 61, 62, 76, 79;
William/Wm., 21, 22, 23, 38, 39,
45, 60, 62, 75, 78, 84, 95, 104,
112, 130
BAXTER, Edward, 144
BEARD, John, 31, 34, 65;
Rebeca/Rebecca, 34, 65
BEBBER, Jacob, 44, 45, 53, 54, 59;
Mary, 54
BECKE, Wm., 79
BECKS, Wm., 43
BEDFORD, Gunning, 70, 84; Mary,
84; William, 51
BEEKE, Wm., 113
BELL, James, 40; Jeremiah, 4;
Margett, 150; Thomas, 56, 57, 59,
101, 103
BELVEAL, John, 123; Nicholas,
162; Philip, 162; Susanna/Susana,
162
BENNET, William, 55, 157, 163
BENNS, Andries, 127
BERGE/BERGES, John, 19, 25, 116
BERMINGHAM, Richard/Richd., 84,
85, 152, 153
BERRY, Alexander, 132; Jean, 156;
Mary, 132; Thomas/Thos., 88,
110, 156
BEST, Edward, 89; Humphrey, 31
BESWICK/BESWICKE, James, 56,
57, 59, 101, 103
BEVAN/BEVANS, David, 53;
Henry, 92, 118, 163
BEVEN, David, 44, 58; Henry, 44,
58
BIARD, John, 34

BICKLEY/BICKLY, Abm., 26;
Abraham, 26; Sam, 76
BIKERSTAFF, Elizabeth, 11
BIORK, Reverend Ericus, 12
BIRD, John, 108, 109, 136; Margaret,
109
BISH, Joan, 127
BISHOP, John, 93
BITLER, Margaret, 36
BLACK, James, 99; Robert, 147
BLACKBORN, Richard, 108
BLACKWELL, Elizabeth, 35; Hugh,
35
BLAKE, Ann/Anna, 11, 12, 21, 23,
24, 47, 48; Edward, 11, 12, 14,
21, 23, 24, 25, 33, 35, 43, 45, 47,
48, 57, 59, 107; Sarah, 48
BLANSON, Picffer, 11
BLOOK, Albert, 8
BOE, Robert, 13, 15, 16
BOGGS, James/Jas., 67, 71, 82, 106
BOLTON, John, 68; Robert, 153
BONHAM, Samuel, 166
BONINE/BONNINE, Elias, 101,
103, 156
BOORAM, Hendrick, 46
BORKOLLS, Mathias, 87
BORROS, John, 157, 158; Mary, 157
BOURN, 33, 35, 37, 48, 51, 60, 61,
67, 68, 78, 79; S., 70, 85;
Sam./Saml, 107, 109; Sampson,
85, 133, 159, 160; T., 56
BOWEN, Thos., 75
BOX, Phillis, 31; Robert, 31, 50
BOYER, John, 72, 121
BRACHAN, Hannah, 64;
William/Wm., 64
BRACKEN, Thomas/Thos., 13, 16,
143; William/Wm., 15
BRACKIN, John, 14; Thomas/Thos.,
31, 50; William/Wm., 105
BRACKING, Thomas, 50

BRADBORNE, John, 156
BRADLEY, Daneil, 16; Francis, 13,
14, 16, 68; Rebeca/Rebecca, 13,
14, 16
BRADSHAW, James, 30, 149, 157
BRANDON, George, 122
BRANK, Ann/Anne, 15, 16, 74;
Peter, 15, 16, 74, 82, 83
BRASELTON, John, 4
BREWER, Senche, 7; Seneca, 7, 9;
Sinxon, 7
BREWSTER, John, 11, 32
BRIAN, Andrew, 68
BRIGGS, James, 30, 61; Margery, 61
BRISTOW, Ann, 63; John, 63
BRITTEN, John,46
BROER, Seneca, 139; Syneck, 152
BROOKS, Ann, 67; Patrick, 31
BROOMFIELD, Patrick, 111
BROWN, Jacob, 159; James, 156;
John, 159; Joseph, 69, 113, 145;
Michl., 158
BRYAN, James, 169; John, 47, 100;
Nathaniel, 100; Robert, 169
BRYANS, Charles, 81
BRYANT, Anthony, 118
BRYON, James, 100
BUCHANAN, John, 133
BUCHER, Madalen, 121; Michel,
121
BUCKLEY/BUCKLY, Abraham,
143; Adam, 35, 114, 131, 132,
138, 144, 149, 166; John, 35
BULLOCK, Thomas, 126
BUNTING, Job, 3
BURCH, D., 9
BURGESS, John, 162
BURLEIGH, Benjamin/Benj., 6, 12,
31, 101, 129
BURMINGHAM, John, 20
BURNS, John, 149
BURROWS, Edward, 146

CLEMENS, Hendrick, 62
CLEMENT/CLEMENTS, Isabella,
53; Jacob, 53; Samuel, 77, 93, 98,
114, 120
CLEMONTSON, Jacob, 108
CLEMPSON, James, 169
CLEMSON, James, 166
CLEMT, Samuel, 66
CLENNY, William, 130
CLENSAY, William, 110
CLOUD, Jeremiah, 35; Robert, 121,
122; Sarah, 122
COCK/COCKS, Andrew, 88, 106,
110, 130, 156; Johannes, 110;
John Anderson, 107; Justas, 107;
William, 27
COFINES, Abraham, 156
COLEGATE, Richard - Rich. -
Richd., 106, 113, 132
COLESBERRY/COLESBERY,
Henry, 124, 130
COLESBURY, Henry, 152
COLLINS, Timothy,67
COLVILL, Thos., 41
CONN, John, 76
CONNE, W., 13
CONNOLLY, Esther, 158; John, 158,
161
CONSTANTINE, Augustine, 105,
106, 130, 131, 133, 134, 136, 138,
147, 150, 151, 164, 168;
Conrad/Conrade, 5, 70, 127
CONWAY, Enoch, 77
COOBER, Wm., 59
COOK/COOKE, Benjamin/Ben.,
114, 121, 129; Joseph, 40; Neal,
54, 65; Neil, 28; William, 61
COOLS, Johnen, 28
COOPER, Charity, 35; Elizabeth, 35;
Hans Coderus, 118; John, 34, 35,
135; Mary, 34, 35; Oliver, 34;
Rebecca, 35; William, 34, 35, 37,

166, 180
CORBET/CORBETT, Daniel, 70,
109; Jane, 73, 88; Mary, 73, 88;
Mathew, 73, 88, 153
CORBIT/CORBITT, James, 73; Jane,
73; Mary, 73
CORK, Elizabeth, 86; Valentine, 86
CORNELINSON, Charles, 130
CORNELISON/CORNELIUSON,
Lars, 110, 114, 119, 144, 149, 164
CORNELIUS, Stephen, 27, 28, 107;
Willemein, 28
CORNELYON, Andrew, 8
CORNWALL/CORNWELL, Enoch,
53, 54, 86
CORRY, Saml., 167
COULBRTSON, Andrew, 115
COURTNEY, Robert, 17
COURTONY, John, 30
COUTS, James, 37
COWGILL, Henry, 132; John, 46,
141, 153
COWGILS, John, 3
COWLEY, John, 22
COX, Amy, 96, 97; Andrew, 106;
Augustine, 24, 50, 67, 98, 129;
Charles/Charlie, 24, 50, 67, 98,
129; Gabriel, 97, 98, 128, 129,
150; Hannah, 108; John, 24, 50,
67, 77, 86, 98, 129; John jr., 129;
Magdalen, 128, 150; Rebecca, 98,
129; William, 58, 65, 95, 96, 97,
98, 147, 155
COZGON, P., 5; Patrick, 5
CRAFORD, James, 99, 147
CRAIG, Elizabeth, 98, 99, 100;
James, 100, John, 98, 99, 100
CRAIGHEAD, Thomas, 36
CRAWFORD, James, 14, 140; John,
54, 65
CREAGER, Alax, 163
CREAGHEAD, Margt., 71; Thomas,

GOMES, Jacob, 112
GONNE, ?, 37; Elizabeth, 84, 137,
138, 140; H., 50, 51, 56, 58, 60,
61, 68, 72, 84, 85, 102, 109, 113,
116, 120, 121, 123, 135, 137, 140,
147, 153, 155, 156; Henry, 84, 85,
113, 120, 133, 135, 136, 140, 155,
163; J., 16, 21
GOODARD, William, 113
GOODIEN, Henry, 35
GOODING, Abraham/Abram., 6, 11,
73, 74, 77, 82, 89, 109, 151;
Esther, 162; Hester, 162, 163;
Isaac, 19, 25, 73, 116, 162; Isaac
(sen), 73; Isaiah, 52; Jacob, 1, 19,
25, 67, 73, 89, 109, 115, 116, 159,
160, 161, 162, 163; John, 1, 3, 19,
20, 26, 50, 53, 54, 57, 59, 67, 80,
88, 94, 95, 115, 120, 121, 129
GOODSON, John, 31, 34, 65, 81,
122, 132, 149
GORDON, ?., 53; J. jun., 57; P., 10,
24, 75, 116, 117; Parnellah, 130,
147; Patrick, 10, 49, 117; R./Rd.,
56, 85, 92; Robert/Robt., 2, 10,
15, 22, 42, 49, 55, 57, 67, 78, 84,
88, 93, 94, 106, 117, 125;
William, 15, 25, 26
GORSUCH, Charles/Chas., 14, 17;
John, 14, 17
GOULDEN, Abraham/Abrm., 4, 82,
87, 88, 91, 135, 159; Daniel, 24;
John, 69, 70, 102, 132;
William/Wm., 69, 70; Abraham,
86; Ann, 86; John, 161
GRAFTON, Mary, 103, 104, 125;
Reid, 20; Richard/Rich., 15, 24,
36, 55, 56, 57, 60, 61, 63, 64, 68,
84, 85, 87, 89, 102, 103, 115, 116,
117, 119, 123, 124, 125, 154, 155;
Richd., 104
GRAHAM, Francis, 91, 106, 109,

110, 141, 146; George, 78; Hugh,
22; William/Wm., 19, 111
GRANT, John, 109; William/Wm., 9,
73
GRANTHAM, John, 79
GRANTOM/GRANUM, Jacob, 126;
John, 1, 79
GRAVE, Samuel, 55
GRAVENRACT, Isaack, 70
GRAVENRAT, Andrew, 153
GRAVES, Thos., 60
GRAY, Thomas/Thos., 78, 88, 94,
95, 138, 141, 142, 143, 147, 150,
164
GREEN, Anthony, 51, 118, 155;
Edward, 19, 80; Henry, 32, 68, 79
GREENWATER, Elizabeth, 29;
John, 29, 30, 142
GREER, Joseph, 105
GREGG, Elizabeth, 48, 123;
George/Geo., 14, 24, 49; John, 48,
55, 123; Magery/Margery, 55;
Samuel, 123; Sarah, 24; William,
48, 55
GRIFFING, James, 145
GRIFFITH, Gideon, 22, 60, 61, 64,
68, 84, 85, 94, 100, 104, 105, 113,
115, 118, 119, 120, 138; Isaac, 31;
Margaret/Margt., 60, 61, 68, 69;
Mary, 23; Richard, 125, 148;
Samuel, 23, 55, 56, 140, 155;
Thomas, 23, 34, 45, 51; William,
97; William junr., 163
GRIFITH, Samuel, 11, 51; Thomas,
108
GRIGG/GRIGGS, Elizabeth, 81;
John, 81; William, 32
GROME, Thomas, 112
GRUBB, John, 100
GUEST, Ann, 166; Jane, 166; John,
58, 71, 74, 80, 109;
Susanna/Susannah, 74, 80;

107, 140, 147, 148;
William/Will./Wm., 3, 6, 17, 21,
23, 28, 41, 43, 47, 78, 140, 147,
158
PASEMORE/PASMORE,
Elizabeth/Eliz., 104; John, 104;
William, 80, 167
PASSMORE, William, 122
PATERSON, Mary, 29;
William/Wm., 39, 47, 102, 147
PATTERSON, Jane, 42; Magdalene,
144, 149; Mary, 29, 37, 43, 87;
Matthias, 144, 149; Nathal., 87;
Peter, 144, 149; Samuel/Saml.,
42, 76, 144, 149; W., 123;
William/Wm., 26, 29, 37, 41, 42,
43, 78, 80, 87, 93, 122, 123, 128,
143, 147, 148
PATTISON, Elizabeth, 87; Mary, 87,
88; William, 19, 25, 87, 116
PATTY, George, 65, 91
PAULSON, Benjamin, 131, 151;
Smith William, 130
PEARCE, Robert, 156
PEARSE, Robert, 106
PEARSON, D., 75; James, 68; Sarah,
75; Thomas, 50
PECKER, Henry, 50
PEEL/PEELE, John, 73, 88, 115
PEIRCE, Henry, 41; Henry jun., 41
PEIRSON, Thomas, 152
PENN, Gov., 46, 91; John, 81, 94,
103, 116, 117, 123, 168; Latitia,
48, 55, 65, 97, 107, 163; Richard,
81, 103, 116, 117, 123, 168;
Springer, 10; Springet/Springett,
24, 49, Thomas/Thos., 81, 94,
103, 116, 117, 123, 168;
William/Wm., 9, 10, 12, 15, 24,
26, 27, 32, 33, 34, 35, 41, 49, 53,
55, 65, 72, 74, 79, 80, 81, 87, 88,
97, 101, 109, 114, 122, 130, 131,

137, 139, 142, 158, 168
PENNINGTON, Edward, 48, 55
PENTLAND, Alexander, 126
PERRY, Jo., 122; John, 122, 126;
Samuel, 59; Sarah, 122
PERSON, William, 123
PERTSON, Robt., 96
PETER/PETERS, John, 75; Thomas,
134
PETERSON, Adam, 89, 149, 151,
161; Andrew/Andw./And., 1, 13,
17, 18, 21, 27, 31, 50, 67, 68, 69,
73, 82, 86, 87, 89, 93, 94, 102,
123, 136, 150, 154, 158, 162;
Andria, 61; Catharine, 137, 164;
Cornelius, 49, 50; Ellenor, 151;
George, 49, 50;
Hance/Hans/Hanse, 108, 130,
137, 164; Israel, 130; John, 53,
54, 115; Magdalan/Magdalene,
110, 114, 119, 137, 164; Mary,
89; Mathias, 12, 110, 114, 119,
137, 164; Peter, 110, 114, 119,
137, 164; Samuel, 110, 114, 119,
130, 137, 164; William/Wm., 50,
125
PETERSONN, Peter, 130
PETTERSON, Andrew, 3; Catharine,
144, 150; Hance/Hanse, 144, 149,
150; Senr., 149
PHENNY, G., 85, 154; George, 85,
154
PHILIPS, John, 4, 79; Richard, 153;
William, 5, 6, 126
PHILLIPS, James, 60
PHILLPOT/PHILPOT, Edward/Edw,
28, 29, 30
PHIPPS, Eleanor Elinor Elioner, 18,
20, 52, 108; Isaac/Isaak, 18; Isaia,
20; Isaiah/Izaiah, 20, 52, 108
PICKERING, Charles, 164
PIERCE, Robert, 110

Benjamin/Benj., 73, 88; Edward,
144, 146; James, 27; John/Jno., 4,
5, 11, 12, 13, 16, 19, 21, 36, 45,
50, 55, 56, 57, 61, 62, 78, 79, 89,
92, 105, 106, 115, 116, 117, 123,
125, 133, 136, 138, 139, 148, 149,
155, 164, 165, 167; Mary, 73, 88,
139; Robt., 45
RIDICK/RIDDICK, John, 102, 162
RINKEN, Joseph, 169
RITE, John, 12
ROAD/ROADS, Joseph, 2, 79
ROBERTS, Edward, 67
ROBERTSON, 2, 3, 4, 31, 34, 45, 72,
84, 93, 96, 97, 98, 106, 107, 117,
118, 122, 125, 126; Derrick, 46;
Harculah/Hereulah, 142;
Hernelea/Harnulah, 78, 118;
Mandrick, 46; Robert/Robt., 11,
14, 16, 18, 21, 23, 24, 56, 78, 142,
147, 148; Anne/Ann, 9, 10;
Catharine, 131, 132;
Charles/Chas., 6, 30, 48, 83, 103,
109, 136, 148, 154, 157, 160, 163;
David, 111; Edward/Edw., 5, 23,
166; Geo. junr., 131, 132;
George/Geo., 10, 12, 13, 67, 92,
111, 131, 132; Israel, 164;
James/Jas., 13, 60, 76; John, 10,
111, 158; Joseph, 10, 48, 64, 105,
111, 139, 143, 152; Mary, 30;
Phebe, 111; Pricilla/Prizcilla, 51,
111; Richard, 107; Valentine, 92,
131; Widow, 167
ROBISON, John, 157; Joseph, 52
ROBSON, Robert, 55
RODDEY, William, 38
RODDYE, Wm./Will., 27, 28
RODGERS, Samuel, 53;
Thomas/Thos., 52, 53
ROGEIRS, Jacob Sen., 52; Johanna,
52

ROGERS, Jacob, 11, 32, 80; Johana,
11, 32; Richard, 87, 96
ROGIERS, Jacob, 51, 52
ROLFE, Jos., 161, 162; Josiah, 21,
155; Sarah, 155
ROSES, Paul, 23
ROSS, Ann Catharine, 43; Catharine,
43, 69; David, 61; George/Geo.,
43, 69, 84, 85; John, 51; Revrd.
George, 69
ROTHWELL, Thos., 62
ROUGIER, John, 148, 154
ROUTHLEDGE, William, 159
ROWLAND, Benj., 128; John, 12
ROWLES, Walter, 26
RUAIRD, Js., 161
RUDICK, John, 161
RUDOLPH, Hance, 150; Hans, 143
RUMSEY, Richard, 57
RUNALS, Henry, 148
RUNS, Jonas, 138
RUSSELL, John, 23, 84, 112;
Sapiens, 46
RUTH, Samuel, 71, 80, 106, 109
RYCKER/RYKEER, Jacob, 111
RYKE, Jacob, 112; Sytie, 112
SAILE, Joseph, 15
SAMPLE, William, 168
SANDERSON, Richard/Rd., 94, 114
SANDS, John, 86, 88
SANTFORD, Abraham/Abrah., 77
SAROUX, Peter, 6
SASMORE, John, 81
SAVAGE, John, 63
SAWYER, Thomas/Thos., 31, 34, 65,
82, 83
SCAGG, Richard, 54
SCHARE, Johanis, 74; Martin, 74;
Mary, 74
SCOGGINS, Jonas, 14
SCOT/SCOTT, John, 73, 102, 103,
141; Samuel, 83, 150

www.ingramcontent.com/pod-product-compliance
Lightning Source LLC
Chambersburg PA
CBHW070914270326
41927CB00011B/2563